MULTICULTURAL MANAGEMENT 2000

THE **MCD** SERIES
MANAGING CULTURAL DIFFERENCES

Series Editors: Philip R. Harris, Ph.D., and Robert T. Moran, Ph.D.

Developing the Global Organization: Strategies for Human Resource Professionals
Robert T. Moran, Philip R. Harris, and William G. Stripp

Dynamics of Successful International Business Negotiations
Robert T. Moran and William G. Stripp

International Business Case Studies for the Multicultural Marketplace
Robert T. Moran, David O. Braaten, and John E. Walsh
(Instructor's Guide also available for qualified instructors)

Managing Cultural Differences, Fourth Edition
Philip R. Harris and Robert T. Moran
(Instructor's Guide also available for qualified instructors)

Multicultural Management 2000: Essential Cultural Insights for Global Business Success
Farid Elashmawi and Philip R. Harris

Transcultural Leadership: Empowering the Diverse Workforce
George F. Simons, Carmen Vázquez, and Philip R. Harris

MULTICULTURAL

ESSENTIAL CULTURAL INSIGHTS FOR GLOBAL BUSINESS SUCCESS

MANAGEMENT 2000

FARID ELASHMAWI, PH.D. • PHILIP R. HARRIS, PH.D.

Gulf Publishing Company
Houston, Texas

THE MCD SERIES
MANAGING CULTURAL DIFFERENCES

Multicultural Management 2000

This is a revised edition. The first edition was published under the title *Multicultural Management.* Copyright © 1993 by Gulf Publishing Company.

Gulf Publishing Company
Book Division
P.O. Box 2608 □ Houston, Texas 77252-2608

10 9 8 7 6 5 4 3 2 1

Library of Congress Cataloging-in-Publication Data

Elashmawi, Farid.
    Multicultural management 2000: essential cultural insights for global business success / Farid Elashmawi, Philip R. Harris.
        p.   cm.—(The MCD series, managing cultural differences)
    Rev. ed. of: Multicultural management. c1993.
    Includes bibliographical references and index.
    ISBN 0-88415-625-7
    1. International business enterprises—Management.
    2. International business enterprises—Management—Cross-cultural studies. 3. Intercultural communication. I. Harris, Philip R. (Philip Robert), 1926–   . II. Elashmawi, Farid. Multicultural management.   III. Title.   IV. Series: Managing cultural differences series.
    HD62.4.E427   1998
    658.3′008—dc21   97-53251
                                                                 CIP

Contents

Acknowledgments

We are grateful to our clients, all of whom directly or indirectly contributed to the contents of this work. We are particularly appreciative of the insightful comments provided by the participatory managers in our management training seminars at Apple Computer, Advanced Micro Devices, Sony Corporation, Fujitsu Limited, Nissan Motor, China Steel, Petronas of Malaysia, Motorola Corporation, Indosat, PT Telkom, and many others, who gave us true insight into their cultures. Special thanks go to Bill Wiggenhorn of Motorola University, for his thoughtful foreword.

We would particularly like to acknowledge the tolerance and support of our families, Mrs. Fatma Elashmawi and sons Amre and Esam, and Dr. Dorothy Harris, while this manuscript was being prepared.

In the preparation of this new edition, *Multicultural Management 2000,* we acknowledge the valuable assistance of our editor at Gulf Publishing Co., Kristine A. Fahrenholz. To others who enabled us to share our thoughts by helping with the manuscript, we thank Sally McAuliffe; and to Karen Kline-Simon, Brian Agustin, Brad Agustin, Ken Yamamoto, Steven M. Scully, and Matt Berto.

Also, we owe a special debt for the encouragement of Gulf Publishing Company's former editor-in-chief, William J. Lowe. Finally, we recognize you, our readers, whose positive reception and feedback prompted us to revise and update this volume.

Series Preface

To thrive and, in many cases, to survive into the 21st Century, it is necessary for organizations to globalize in strategy, structure, and people. Companies have realized that developing strategies or managing people as if the internal and external environments of the organization had not changed is a major mistake. "Bashing" others rather than taking the inward journey and becoming a revolutionary learning organization is dysfunctional and counterproductive to corporate survival. As expected, many organizations in various countries have taken the inward journey and are effectively managing this challenge. Some are not.

The books in the *Managing Cultural Differences Series* are intended to stimulate and support the effort of globalization in all of its dimensions. The books have been widely accepted in academic circles and by practicing internationalists.

As series editors, we are pleased that Gulf Publishing Company has risen to the challenge of addressing questions of people, cultures, organizations, and strategy in a rapidly changing, highly interdependent community.

Philip R. Harris, Ph.D.
Robert T. Moran, Ph.D.

Foreword

Multicultural Management 2000 provides an excellent overview of the challenges we face today in the demanding arena of global business interactions. The book is a value-added primer for readers who need an orientation to varied business cultures. It allows readers to achieve a higher level of awareness of the requirements posed by different cultural situations.

The detailed list of the characteristics of the successful multicultural manager is especially interesting. The authors stress that cultural diversity includes territorial, corporate, and gender issues. The scenarios where Arabs, Asians, and Americans experience conflict reveal the explicit need for increased cultural understanding and sensitivity. The authors insightfully describe and demonstrate cultural differences in nonverbal communication, language use, as well as space and time orientation.

Managers working in multinational corporations will find valuable the portion of the book describing how a country's cultural values affect corporate cultural values.

Effective business communications are critical to the growth of every organization and are often difficult even in a local business unit. The authors provide good examples of how business introductions, telephone calls, presentations, and written communication can lead to an operation's success or failure.

Of special significance to those of us managing Motorola University are the contrasts in training, motivation, and performance appraisals in diverse cultures. The authors' discussion of group composition, time, preparation, training materials, and knowledge tests is of great value to the reader with responsibilities in human resources.

This book is filled with a great deal of new information. It is ideal for individuals and organizations who are seeking high performance in today's and tomorrow's competitive global marketplace.

A. William Wiggenhorn
President, Motorola University
Corporate Vice-President for Training and Education,
Motorola Corporation

Introduction

The success of our original publication has led to this new edition, which not only revises and updates the material, but provides additional case studies and information to each chapter. Among the numerous cultures found in the human family, we have chosen three cultural groupings to guide readers toward valuing and managing cultural diversity. These macrocultures have been targeted to offer cultural contrasts and specifics about Arabs, Americans, and Asians. In addition, we have added an Appendix which profiles some characteristics of culture in Hispanic or Latin America.

Since it was impossible for us to cover all the diverse cultures of humankind, we thought the ones selected would demonstrate the challenges and complexities of multicultural interactions everywhere. With the growth of the global marketplace and information highway, cultural sensitivity is essential. By using your imagination, you can transfer our message and examples to many other cultures not included in this text.

The Epilogue summarizes the themes of this book, while the Bibliography expands the references, which you may wish to consult to supplement the content of *Multicultural Management 2000*. We hope the scope and depth of this book, as well as its practical business applications, will enrich our readers' understanding of cultural differences and synergy. We hope the insights you receive from this volume will help you to be more skillful and successful for global business exchanges of the 21st Century.

Multicultural Management 2000 is presented in eight chapters and two appendices. In each, we have tried to stimulate the reader's thinking by presenting several specific cross-cultural business situations. These situations are followed by cultural contrasts among the three cultures highlighted, and descriptions of how they would respond to specific situations. Most of the chapters are supplemented by tables that give the reader a deeper understanding of the cultural differences.

The opening chapter provides a rationale for multicultural management. It poses three arenas for practicing cross-cultural skills:

the domestic work environment, the integration of organizational cultures, and the international marketplace.

Chapter 2 explores business challenges encountered in global management, particularly personal introductions, telephone conversations, meetings and presentations, and training and motivation.

Chapter 3 offers a discussion of our cultural dimensions and values, and their priorities across several cultures. These priorities were compiled after extensive interviews and research in several of the world's cultures. Images of culture, nonverbal communication, and use of time and space across cultures are presented.

Chapter 4 explores contrasts in corporate cultures of several multinational, multicultural organizations, and how their cultural business values differ and reflect the country's values. In Chapter 5, we present specific skills for the global manager, for effective conduct of multicultural business communications.

Chapter 6 focuses on human resource management, and includes how to conduct training, motivation, and performance reviews across cultures, especially in joint ventures.

Chapter 7 is dedicated to developing skills for successful intercultural negotiations and how establishing rapport, persuasion, and closing the sale varies across cultures.

Finally, in Chapter 8, we present guidelines for globalization strategy and technology transfer management.

Appendix A offers supplementary material on the cultures and peoples of Hispanic origin, whether in North, Central, or South America. To facilitate doing business with Latinos, this profile focuses especially on Mexico and Argentina. Appendix B examines Russian/American space programs.

We hope that the scope and richness of the book, as well as the depth of its specific practical business situations, will help you develop an understanding of the world's many cultural differences, and will enable you to compete more successfully in the emerging global, multicultural world.

Praise for the previous edition

". . . a concise guide . . . Chock full of examples and checklists . . . would fit easily into any business or management course. . . ."

The Japan Times

"Insightful, powerful, and practical . . . a 'must read' guide . . . an invaluable reference. . . ."

Canadian Manager

"Business leaders, executives, diplomats, students, technical and marketing personnel . . . will find the book a welcome repertoire."

Malaysian Business

"It should greatly assist those who seek to become successful global managers coping with obstacles caused by cultural differences. Very impressed . . . Powerful."

Takashi Tozuka
General Manager
Matsushita Education Center

"This book is invaluable if you plan to compete in the global marketplace or work with people from diverse backgrounds. *Multicultural Management* will assist from the first meeting through final negotiations, to continuous successful business relationships with coworkers and customers alike."

Helena Hannonen
Human Resources Consultant
FMC Corporation

"Filled with new information. Ideal for individuals and organizations seeking high performance in today's and tomorrow's competitive global marketplace."

A. William Wiggenhorn
Corporate Vice President for Training and Education
Motorola Corporation

"A much needed work. Contains much valuable information to assist managers and students in understanding the complexities of cultural differences."

Gary G. Williams
Dean
McClaren School of Business
University of San Francisco

"Should be required reading for any student of international relations and business, as well as for executives new to transnational business management."

Humphrey P. Polanen
Manager
International Business Development
Tandem Computers, Inc.

THE **M❋❋SERIES**
MANAGING CULTURAL DIFFERENCES

CHAPTER 1

Multicultural Management Insights

An Overview

Management today is increasingly multicultural. This has come to pass in the last quarter of the 20th century, as national populations have become more informed, heterogeneous, and less isolated. With continued movement toward a global marketplace, growing transborder exchanges are leading to trade agreements and economic unions. Thanks to stunning technological advances in communications and transportation, the world's cultures are increasingly starting to interact with one another. In the 1990s, we are also witnessing a counterphenomenon—breakdowns of large, traditional political entities, such as the former U.S.S.R. and Eastern bloc countries. There, smaller republics and ethnic groups are demanding more independence, while moving toward democratic free enterprise and away from socialistic systems that feature centralized planning and control. The challenge is whether locals will be driven out by destructive ethnic rivalries, or realize the advantages of cultural and economic synergy with their neighbors.

Because of the significant social and political changes that are currently under way, there is real opportunity for world traders and entrepreneurs, free of ideologies, to engage in peaceful commerce for the benefit of humankind. The globalization of the mass media has shown many people the possibilities available within modern society, and has made them desire improvements in their quality of life. Such market needs can only be met on a global scale when a new class of managers and professionals come prepared with multicultural skills. Such cultural competencies are critical as we transition into the 21st century.

Diversity in the Multicultural Workforce

The domestic work environment in most countries is becoming more complex. Most national workforces are experiencing a population growth among traditional minorities, who also seek to move beyond entry-level jobs. Improved access to education and training for people in such microcultures fuels their vocational ambitions. Enlightened legislation, whether called "equal employment opportunity" or "affirmative action," is designed to ensure fairness in the workplace. Gender barriers are also slowly being eliminated, and many women are now in supervisory, management, and other executive positions.

In the United States this multicultural resurgence is evident with the increase in Asian, Latino, and Afro-American populations, new immigrants from many different countries, and millions of illegal aliens. In Canada, French-speaking and Inuit minorities have become more assertive in seeking their job rights; expanding immigrant populations from Central Europe and the Far East have joined in their demands. Across the Atlantic, workforces have become more diverse as border crossings have become easier, while labor shortages have forced some countries to import "guest workers" from a variety of places. France not only has a large North African minority population, but economic refugees from numerous impoverished lands to the south have immigrated there as well. Germany struggles to cope with previous guest workers from Italy, Turkey, India, and Pakistan, along with new onslaughts of job seekers from former East Germany and Europe. The United Kingdom tries to cope with a multicultural inflow from the former British Commonwealth nations, as well as with Arab investors. Across the Pacific, the Koreans and Filipinos are most active in seeking contracts or work abroad, while the Japanese may have to hire more outsiders to take over low-level jobs that have yet to be automated.

In many places, labor is not just absorption of new foreign workers, but of new foreign owners and executives as well. Latin America is the marketing and relocation target for many Americans, Europeans, and Japanese; conversely, millions of Latin Americans have migrated northward seeking prosperity. Everywhere, people are moving beyond their homelands in the search for a better life, creating worker pools that call for cross-culturally sensitive managers. In a sister book in the *Managing Cultural Differences* series, *Transcultural Leadership,* by Simons et al., the term "transcultural manager" was coined to describe that new leader.

In this post-industrial information age, a new work culture is emerging. One of its norms is competence, regardless of one's race, color, creed, or place of origin. High-technology industrial parks around the world are being staffed by technical types of many nationalities, hired because of their scientific ability, regardless of cultural background. Operating high-tech plants requires the best of multicultural management, whether in the "Silicon Valley" of California, Taiwan, Hungary, or India. The same multicultural environment may be observed in academia or in research and development laboratories worldwide.

Blending Organizational Cultures

As McManus and Hergert pointed out in their book, *Surviving Mergers and Acquisitions,* whenever a merger, acquisition, or joint venture is formed by two existing companies, two or more distinct organizational cultures must be combined. It is ineffective when one entity simply tries to impose its culture upon another. It is more productive to seek a cultural synergy between and among the systems involved. But the latter calls for finesse, the practice of sophisticated multicultural management. Nowhere is multicultural management more desirable than in the formation of a consortium made up of several corporations, or of representatives from industry, government, and universities. Again, the managers in such situations have to utilize multicultural skills to create the best in the various organizational cultures and management systems.

Even within a world corporation, one faces cultural diversity among various departments, divisions, and subsidiaries. In reality, every time a project team is assembled, made up of different disciplines and fields of expertise, the project manager must practice multicultural management. Engineers think differently from manufacturing or finance personnel who, in turn, may differ in perspective from marketing or public relations people; each profession or speciality has a unique subculture, often solving problems differently from one another. When such assemblages of personnel are escalated into an international project team or task force, the management challenges are even greater, for then varying macro- and microcultures are participating. Thus, those experienced in intercultural communication and negotiation are more likely to succeed.

Business in the Global Marketplace

International business and professional activity demand movement beyond one particular cultural conditioning into a transcultural arena. Whether one travels overseas for a quick business trip, or becomes an expatriate manager abroad for years, sponsoring organizations should have foreign deployment systems that facilitate acculturation and performance of their representatives. This type of plan is especially helpful when an employee is deployed to an isolated and alien environment, such as an offshore rig, an Arctic petroleum facility, an Antarctic research station, or a desert or mountain scientific outpost. Today, the United Nations, national government agencies, the military, and numerous foundations and nonprofit associations send qualified personnel on assignments to host cultures, often with minimal or no cross-cultural preparation and inadequate knowledge of cultural specifics.

Currently, global industries, including communications, travel, transportation, marketing, food, hotels, and real estate, employ workers outside their native cultures, while providing only rudimentary information about local customs, laws, and practices of the indigenous people, much less any training in foreign language. Not only is multicultural training essential in all management and employee development, it should be a requirement for certain roles. Occupations such as customs and immigration officers, border agents and law enforcement officers, international lawyers, statesmen, health care providers, and so on necessitate cross-cultural education.

Business in New Frontiers

The next generation will be increasingly engaged in space exploration and development. Some 21st-century market opportunities will undoubtedly be in space commerce, industrialization, and settlement. Astrobusiness, whether on the ground or aloft, is an emerging arena for the practice of multicultural management. It is already evident in the aerospace industry, but especially in the areas of communication satellites on which we are so dependent for weather forecasting and control, remote sensing and resource location, and information/entertainment/ banking/postal services.

International spaceports are another example of business in new frontiers. The spaceport proposed for construction in Cape York, Australia, involves a combination of Australian and foreign technical workers, international investors, Russian space technology, and American operations management. In the orbital environment at the Russian station *Mir,* and on the various NASA shuttle orbiters, crews have been composed of diverse cultures—from Russians and Americans to a Saudi prince, a German scientist, a British chemist, and a Japanese journalist. On such spaceflights, both commanders and crews would benefit by multicultural training, especially for longer missions, such as potential future voyages to the new International Space Station (see Appendix B and *Living and Working in Space,* second edition, P. R. Harris).

Multicultural Management at Home

As we move into the 21st century, managers everywhere will be in transition, experimenting with better ways of managing human and material resources during a period of profound change. Many of the forces driving these changes are economic. Domestic enterprises must restructure and renew themselves to meet the challenges of the global marketplace and worldwide customers. As Dr. Woodrow Sears points out in his book *Back in Working Order,* downsizing, mergers, and joint venturing are all examples of local corporations seeking to reposition themselves for a market situation in which capital and credit are scarce, and in which "meaningful work" is available to fewer people every year. Some organizations attempt to survive the turmoil by staying on the leading edge of product development and technology, or by introducing more automation and robotics. Other institutions invest in helping their people to work smarter, so as to better meet customer needs. The latter would seem to be the essence of effective "multicultural management," whether in the private or public sector.

The Multicultural Manager

A manager with cross-cultural sensitivity and skills is much in demand today. The domestic work environment features personnel, customers, and suppliers who come increasingly from diverse cultural and ethnic backgrounds. Foreigners with capital not only buy companies, buildings, and resorts in other countries, but seek partners in joint ventures from those countries. Those who have changed from totalitarianism and centrally planned economies invite representatives from free enterprise nations to do business in their countries, as well as to re-educate their management. The international business scene has truly become a global marketplace that is aided and abetted by communication and transportation technologies. Even small local business types are forced to seek overseas opportunities and to learn about world-trade realities, such as import/export regulations and processes.

Thus, true transcultural managers are more "cosmopolitan"—that is, innovative leaders who are effective intercultural communicators and negotiators. These people are comfortable operating anywhere in the world. Whether representing a business, a government, a foundation, an association, or a profession, these are high performers in the world marketplace. They are capable of functioning readily around their own homeland and its regional groupings, or of moving across borders.

Multicultural managers characteristically

- Think beyond local perceptions, and transform stereotypes into positive views of people
- Prepare for new mindshifts, while eliminating old mindsets
- Re-create cultural assumptions, norms, and practices based on new insights and experiences
- Reprogram their mental maps and constructs
- Adapt readily to new and unusual circumstances and lifestyles
- Welcome and facilitate transitional experiences
- Acquire multicultural competencies and skills, including foreign languages
- Create cultural synergy whenever and wherever feasible
- Operate effectively in multinational/multicultural environments
- Envision transnational opportunities and enterprises
- Create optimistic and doable scenarios for future

Multicultural managers are

- Students of worldwide human relations and values
- Open and flexible in dealing with diversity in people
- Comfortable with those from different disciplines, fields, backgrounds, races, and genders
- Facilitators of newcomers, strangers, minorities, and immigrants to the workplace
- Collaborators in joint ventures, consortia, or coalitions
- Planned change agents and futurists

(Adapted from Simons, Vázquez, and Harris, 1993.)

Why is multicultural competence so essential for these managers? Suppose we take the United States of America as a case in point. Back in the 1970s, the *Atlantic Monthly* ran a feature story on "Uncle Sam—the Deaf and Dumb Giant." It was about findings of a Presidential Commission on Foreign Languages and International Studies (1979), which highlighted how tongue-tied U.S. businesspersons were abroad, and how dependent they were on interpreters. The Commission report stated, "Americans' incompetence in foreign languages is nothing short of scandalous, and it is becoming worse."

More recently, the *Los Angeles Times Magazine* (December 2, 1990) published an article, "A Nation of Know-Nothings—America's Willful Ignorance of the World Puts Us at Peril." It commented on how weak the U.S. government and corporate leaders are in foreign studies—not a prized discipline in this country—while the masses are generally ignorant of the rest of the world. The writer, a *Times* foreign correspondent, Stanley Meisler, cited the U.S. as the most provincial industrialized power on Earth. According to him, Americans generally do not know foreign languages, geography, or international current events, while U.S. public decision- and policy-makers understand little of the cultural and historical forces that shape world events.

A recent *National Geographic* survey also confirmed a woeful lack of educational requirements nationwide in this regard. The report cited a growing benightedness about *international* affairs, economics, and languages, which extends from the State Department to university business schools to industry itself. Isolation and provincialism are seemingly back in style for the 1990s at the very time when American troops serve others abroad.

Ben Wattenberg, the social observer from the American Enterprise Institute, is upbeat about the U.S. becoming the *first universal nation* because of its openness to émigrés and foreign investors. In a recent book on the subject, Wattenberg expounds on the positives resulting from this influx of new talent with multiple skills and languages, as well as new capital, which fuels democratic enterprises. But where do all these foreigners come from, why are they here, and what is the implication for tomorrow's work environment?

The Multicultural Workforce

Like a magnet, North America has been attracting immigrants for many centuries. It may have started when Asian natives migrated across a suspected land bridge over the Bering Sea to what is known today as Alaska and Northern Canada. In the l6th and l7th centuries, the "New World" colonists departed largely from Great Britain, France, and Spain, as well as Africa, which supplied slave labor. In the l8th and l9th centuries, the immigrant trail to "America" expanded to include the Irish, Italians, and other Europeans, in addition to Chinese laborers.

But the 20th century has seen the greatest influx into the U.S. of Hispanics or Latinos, and of Indo-Chinese refugees. In this past century, Canada has received many new arrivals from the British Commonwealth nations, such as India, Pakistan, and Hong Kong, as well as from central Europe and Latin America. In both nations, these varied peoples altered a supposedly homogeneous workforce and made it more heterogeneous and diverse.

Why do these emigrants come to North America? Through the centuries, they have come for two basic reasons—*freedom and opportunity.* The migration pattern has consistently shown that the transplants wished to escape for economic, political, or religious reasons. Rather than accept the status quo in their homelands, the searchers sought a better life for themselves and their families and better environments and prospects to achieve their human potential. For example, the latest arrivals to the U.S. and Canada are students from the People's Republic of China. As reported in the *Los Angeles Times*

Magazine (March 25, 1990), although there were only a handful of Chinese emigrants a decade ago, there are now 43,000 Chinese students in the U.S., the largest segment of foreign students in the U.S.

Among the best and brightest of their generation in Communist China, these people came to absorb knowledge, especially in the sciences and technology, so that they could use it in their impoverished country. They are products of the ancient Confucian culture that for two millennia has etched itself into the soul of Asia, and contributed so much to the human family at large. They also come from the world's most populous nation handicapped by a Third World economy, and from political systems characterized by individual repression and exploitation.

These Chinese students had their dreams shattered by the massacre of their fellow university students at Tianamen Square in June 1989. Within a closed, totalitarian society, the students had peacefully protested for economic and educational reform, calling for more democracy; they dared to rally against widespread corruption and inequity. As a result, most of these students wished to prolong their stay in foreign lands; many of them sought political asylum in Canada and the U.S. Presently, 11,000 of these Chinese youths are legally in the U.S. and will remain here with the American government's permission for at least four more years. Increasingly, they will be assimilated into American society and alienated from China; many will become permanent residents of their adopted lands—the multicultural researchers and managers of tomorrow. Until the Chinese regime and its attitudes change, the North American workforce will be absorbing some of its dislocated younger generation.

Should one of these well-educated persons show up in your office or plant, consider their poignant story and their painful separation from family and friends. In order to utilize their competencies effectively and establish work relationships, try to comprehend their background and fathom their mindset. Don't be surprised if you also find among the new wave of fellow workers refugees from the chaos of Central America, Eastern Europe, and the Middle East. By taking time to reach out and assist foreigners' acculturation, you will enhance your own understanding and knowledge while furthering the competitiveness of your organization.

Leadership in Multicultural Management

Dr. Woodrow Sears, a management consultant in Torrance, California, counsels clients that

- *Leadership* is the creation of structures that permit people to participate effectively in the achievement of worthwhile goals.
- *Management* can be defined as "expect/inspect"—that is, according to Sears, effective managers create and clarify performance expectations with subordinates or colleagues, then they negotiate and conduct inspections to ensure that work is completed successfully. It is an abomination when bias, bigotry, and ignorance within an organization or its management undermine the personnel's fullest contribution and development.

The practice of multicultural management centers around the importance of personnel. In *Human Side of Enterprise,* McGregor makes the point that, for more than forty years, behavioral scientists have been conveying that message to managers, but only now are many of them really beginning to listen and translate the concepts into corporate actions. Many domestic managers relearn such insights when they go abroad and observe management as practiced in other cultures. For example, it was the Japanese application of "quality circles" proposed first by an American industrial engineer, W. E. Deming, that got his countrymen to seriously utilize this group technique. Similarly, current North American management is again relearning about the importance of "human capital" and labor/management cooperation from their Asian counterparts. As Alan Binder, Princeton professor of economics, wrote:

> The Japanese seem to have broken down the "us vs. them barrier" that so impairs labor relations in American and European companies. They do so by creating a feeling that employees and managers share a common fate . . . that a well-run Japanese corporation is of, by, and for its people.
> So Japanese companies train their employees, guarantee job security, and offer career paths that blossom if the company flourishes . . . Japanese CEOs are rarely dictators; many top companies are run by consensus. Work is organized by teams

from the executive suite to the factory floor . . . Consultation
between labor and management is pervasive . . . Japanese
workers cooperate with management because their welfare is
tied up with the company. . . . To a degree that most Americans
would find astonishing, large Japanese companies are run for
the benefit of the employees rather than the stockholders. That
means providing extensive fringe benefits, as well as training
and security; . . . It is in managing people, I believe, that America can learn the most from Japan.
(*Business Week,* November 11, 1991, p. 22.)

The lesson here is the indigenous managers can learn much from
the way foreigners view our own management practices, as well as
from the management systems of other countries.

One of the biggest issues facing North American managers in this
decade is the growing diversity and complexity of the workforce. In
the U.S., demographic reports underscore this new reality:

- Women, minorities, and immigrants will make up 80 percent of
  that workforce by the year 2000.
- Women alone will comprise two-thirds of that labor market
  growth, or 47 percent of the workforce by the turn of this century.
- Native nonwhites and immigrants will equally account for 40 percent of that growth by the 21st century.

In 1991, the U.S. Labor Secretary issued a report on the subject of
the "glass ceiling"—it chided U.S. corporations for placing arbitrary
obstacles to the career advancement of women and minorities, especially into management. Ann Morrison (1982) first utilized that term
in a book co-authored on the subject. In another study on leadership
diversity, Morrison (1992) addressed the following questions:

- How can corporations and other institutions better integrate
  women and people of color into middle and upper management
  ranks?
- Which policies and practices being used in organizations are most
  effective for this purpose, and why?
- What improvements will advance the career prospects for women
  and people of color, especially into management?

Synergy in Organizational Cultures

A critical multicultural management challenge often ignored occurs when two or more systems are reorganized into one enterprise. In the public sector, such realignments occur with changes in administration, policies, and budgets. For example, within today's defense departments everywhere, the end of the Cold War and reductions in military budgets are forces promoting the elimination of some military entities, and the combination of others. Sometimes, a newly elected leader or a government study will recommend streamlining public service and reducing costs by means of uniting several previous departments into a new super agency.

In the private sector, mergers may occur because of a takeover or acquisition by another corporation, or simply through the formation of a joint venture with either a domestic or foreign partner. Again, a consortium may be formed by several companies in a field to create a single firm owned by all (as when several computer manufacturers combine resources to establish an R&D enterprise for the development of a super computer). Macroprojects like a supercollider or a channel tunnel may cause consortia to be formed that bring together government, industry, and universities within a country; at the international level, the members may include several nations, industries, and corporations.

In each case mentioned, the parties not only bring with them a unique organizational history, management, and expertise, but a distinct culture. Too often the executives involved in such undertakings ignore these factors to their own detriment, while concentrating on the task (including its financing) at hand. But managers who have multicultural proficiency take the time to analyze the cultural dimensions of each participating organization in the new venture, then develop strategies to ensure the successful blending of the strengths of each. A good example of this was done within the European aerospace industry, with the creation of Airbus Industry. In this synergistic joint venture, five governments and their companies managed to produce a technological innovation in wide-body jet planes that has successfully penetrated the commercial aircraft market.

In 1996, to meet global competition, Airbus began restructuring into an independent, centralized company. This was a major cultural change as Europe's largest aircraft manufacturer transitioned from a public to a private sector entity, seeking international partners and outside investment. It called for real *multicultural management savvy,* as the following mini case study will reveal about the problems of building a tunnel under the English Channel.

An International Joint Venture Macroproject*

In 1991, all systems were go for the first land link between Britain and the continent since the melting of the Ice Age 10,000 years ago. One of the largest international joint ventures in history was expected to be completed by June 1993. The $15 billion macroproject (double its original estimate), called the "Chunnel Tunnel," celebrated the 1990 meeting of British and French tunnel teams underneath the waters of the English Channel. After centuries of enmity and isolation between the British Isles and its continental neighbors, cultural synergy seemingly triumphed. Since Napoleon's time a century ago, engineers dreamed of penetrating the Atlantic Ocean and creating a direct passage between England and France. The multicultural management of Eurotunnel, a British/ French private company, not only finished the construction of two large train tunnels—one for passengers and the other for freight, as well as a service tunnel—but actually coped with a major fire in the latter and temporary service stoppage. During the planning stages, however, they had to cope with the following multinational problems.

The chunnel enables high-speed trains to make the 27-minute crossing every 10 to 15 minutes. Just as the European Community struggles to come into being, this unique technological venture in cooperation came on line to allow Europeans to travel and trade more easily with the British. Yet it takes *multicultural macromanagement* to operate this enterprise that so impacts the countrysides of Dover and Sangatte. For example, British Rail had projected a direct, high-speed route from the channel to central London, had acquired the necessary

*With credit to Karen Taylor of *FRANCE* magazine, Fall 1990, and William Touhy of the *Los Angeles Times* (Nov. 26, 1991, p. H/3).

right of way, and had enlarged its Waterloo station to receive the new intercontinental trains. Then political and environmental realities interfered—some British industrialists argued for a northeastern route to a Waterloo station terminus, which would be more convenient to shift freight to northern England and Scotland. At the same time, conservationists mounted a major campaign to keep the fast-rail system out of their backyards, and the EC's commission in Brussels questioned whether British Rail's route and terminus would meet environmental standards. As a result, after four years of dithering, the British government overruled the British Rail route in favor of the alternative, which would not only delay the project considerably, but would cost $1 billion more because of the longer distance and needed construction of new London terminals! All this when the British Tunnel Act passed by the Parliament specifically prohibited the government from providing funds for tunnel construction, allowing funds only for road/rail infrastructure that is being built at a laggardly pace.

The route-change decision caused both delay and added expenses to Eurotunnel, the private company that raised its capital by selling shares (three-fourths to French buyers) and by borrowing from 210 banks. Earnings from the expected 15 million passengers were postponed because of a decision made for political, not transport, reasons. With delayed revenues, Eurotunnel was behind on payments to its contractors; both were at loggerheads over who should meet the tunnel's annual budget. For years, intercontinental passengers were inconvenienced because no through route was ready for the opening day of tunnel traffic; travelers to or from London had to take a standard train to a channel port.

Meanwhile, on the other side of the water, the French were disappointed with the British impact on their plans and the disastrous fire in the tunnel during its first year of operation. Yet, when such problems are resolved and the tunnel is fully operational, the economic effect, will be enormous for the peoples of both countries, as well as for the single European market. One beneficiary will be northern France, where the TGV train lines converge, running west to Great Britain and northeast to Belgium, The Netherlands, Germany, and south to France, Italy, and Spain. This transportation crossroad of northwestern Europe will have a sleek new train station at its regional capitol of Lille, close to Brussels. The Euralille centerpiece is a 175-acre ultramodern business and residential park, including a world trade center surrounded by shopping malls and office towers. Here, the link-up will be made with a fully automated subway system and international airport. Le Nord/Pas De Calais region is an educational and research center that attracts other international and high-tech joint ventures, like Rank Xerox, the British/American company with factories here. Such corporations will soon have significant cost advantages in the streamlined European market when the chunnel increases trade and exchange, as between R-X factories in both England and France.

These developments force a change in national mentalities—the British toward the French, the French toward the Belgians, and so forth. The multicultural workforce of France's steel industry in Le Nord—not only the French, but Polish and North African workers—is now being transformed to serve the needs of the tunnel and an emerging metropolitan area. "Synergy" is the new buzzword among local cities, businesses, and universities engaged in regional development there. Because of this worthwhile macroproject, citizens on both sides of the channel are making major psychological, cultural, and economic adjustments. More astuteness in multicultural management among the planners might have lessened the frustrations and delays.

Multicultural Management Abroad

Once a manager, technician, professional, or sales representative leaves the home culture, he or she becomes a "foreigner," literally a guest in a host culture. This situation can be disorienting for some, and even result in "culture shock." Our own culture conditions us—consciously and unconsciously—to the way things are done. In a thousand different situations every day, culture smooths human performance—we know what is expected of us and what we can expect from others. But when we enter an alien environment, we confront a multitude of cultural differences, many of which can be disconcerting. Even when U.S. citizens cross the northern border into Canada, they can be fooled by apparent similarities in the "Anglo" culture—the differences can be subtle in most provinces, but in the Province of Quebec, differences are more apparent, starting with French being the primary language spoken.

However, when the tourist or businessperson from the U.S. crosses the southern border, the cultural dissimilarity is not only more evident, but the economy is vastly different as well. Mexico is a land of great promise and peoples, steeped in Spanish and Indian heritages of ancient civilizations, yet it is still a developing country with elite rich, limited middle class, and masses of poor. Increasingly, the "American" and Mexican cultures have joined forces in border enterprises that truly demand multicultural managers, especially as these plants now employ or are owned by Japanese, Koreans, and Germans. The Mexicans are also geographically North Americans, a fact underscored by the recent North American Free Trade Agreement, which their leaders signed along with the U.S. and Canada (see Appendix A).

To comprehend multicultural management, other chapters in this book provide pragmatic insights for dealing with three major cultural groupings: Americans, Arabs, and Japanese. So in this section, we examine a new arena for cross-cultural skill in business: the People's Republic of China, as well as Eastern and Central Europe. Until recently, this was the domain of the Second World—Communist states, utilizing a centralized, planned, bureaucratic economy. Now the latter is a region in transition, some might even say chaos, as it moves away from totalitarianism toward democracy, from state control to free-market economies and consumerism.

Joint Venture Culture Clashes: Cultural Conditionings In Centralized Planned Economies

When management and workers are products of centralized, planned economies, whether communistic or socialistic, those from democratic, free-enterprise societies may find dramatic differences in viewpoint when attempting joint ventures with them. The former have been culturally conditioned to bureaucratic thinking and acting; they are unused to concepts like customer service, personal responsibility, and profits. Even when the government is in transition to a more open, democratic form, the people suffer effects from decades lived under rigid totalitarianism. Such citizens may seek more humanistic values in the workplace, but for years they have been influenced by a system that required every significant decision to be approved by a higher authority, such as a communist party cell. Consultant Paul Neutz reminds us that once a group decision was made, it was considered absolute, correct, and irreversible—no employee was allowed to question the "truth."

The Economist (March 17–23, 1990, pp. 66– 69) reports on recent joint ventures in the automobile industry that demonstrate the scope of this culture clash. Consider the Shanghai Volkswagen Automotive Company. Operating in the People's Republic of China under a hard-line communist regime can be inscrutable for the West German partner. There is often a mix between the bizarre and the creative—each year fewer cars are produced in this venture with state "enterprises," but Volkswagen's after-tax margin increases. Why? Because it is in the "people's" currency, and in this distorted state economy, the price is often six times higher than the partnership could charge if it exported the cars. Further, the German parent is mandated to use one Chinese machine on the assembly line, but the local product cannot stand up to the demands of the production volume. The result is that only 800 workers are really needed in a factory that employs 2,300.

Official state production declarations are absurd because of the country's austerity program; in addition, only state-owned entities, not individuals, may purchase cars. In Communist China, be prepared to take two or more years to negotiate a contract (it took Volkswagen seven years to do business there). Once up and running, international joint ventures in China face a host of obstacles, including decreasing domestic sales because of tight money policies, and decreasing foreign exports because of inadequate product quality.

Among the local bureaucrats there are few business facilitators, but many officials are willing to attack one's Chinese managing partner if he or she gets too liberal and stray's from the "party line." So why bother to invest and attempt to do business under such conditions? Volkswagen and other foreigners realize that China is the world's most populous country, and someday economic reforms may permit it to have the purchasing power to match. Others are there to take advantage of Chinese technology and to lower prices, such as the American company that recently flew a satellite payload on the Chinese Long-March rocket.

On the other hand, there are former Eastern bloc countries that have freed themselves from communist regimes and centralized control. West European car makers are scrambling east to seize new market opportunities. Germany's Volkswagen and Opel have announced joint ventures to modernize formerly East German plants, while Daimler-Benz has a deal with formerly East German lorry manufacturers to collaborate on development, production, and marketing. To take advantage of the pent-up demand in Eastern Europe for private autos, western companies are expanding cultural ties and economic links there: Italy's Fiat is enhancing its Polski Fiat, a Polish venture started in 1921; French car makers like Renault are increasing operations in former Yugoslavia and the Czech Republic, while Peugeot has big plans for reformed "Mother Russia"; and Britain's Rover Group is negotiating with a Bulgarian engineering group. The media describe the influx of Western business persons into Hungary as "the gold rush of the 1990s"—two hundred joint ventures are already under way. The visitors hope to capitalize on a workforce high on mechanical and mathematical skills, and low on wage costs (about $100 a month to the average worker).

While the emerging democracies of Central and Eastern Europe need western capital and technology, their workforces will require massive re-education to overcome 40 years behind the "Iron Curtain." The same challenges occur when westerners enter into agreements within China or the former U.S.S.R. For example, despite the success of PEPSICO in the U.S.S.R., consider that while 1,300 joint ventures had been signed with the Soviets, only about 300 are actually operational. The mismanagement and mismatch of human and material resources within centralized, planned economies present a formidable hurdle. Yet, somehow, big corporations and small entrepreneurs from the western democracies are managing to overcome these problems. Retraining is the key for success, with talented workers from *transitional societies*. Thus, human resource development must be in more than western management and business practice—it should include training in creativity, innovation, career development incentives and rewards, risk-taking, and learning from failure. To produce cultural synergy in these joint ventures, these emerging "democrats" need to learn about free enterprise cultures and customer service, while at the same time Westerners inform themselves about the socialistic business environment and economic system, and its impact on the inhabitants. These statements can be seen in the media report in the following section.

Challenges in Former U.S.S.R. Joint Ventures

The Economist (March 3, 1990, pp. 78, 80) reminds us of the difficulties foreigners face in doing business in the 15 republics of the former U.S.S.R., especially during its present transition to a market economy. In order to set up shop in Moscow, representatives from McDonald's had to haggle with officials for almost ten years, and practically build a whole food chain from scratch to supply one restaurant. The success of the Canadian entrepreneurs who accomplished this task can be measured in some degree by a Russian cartoon showing a young girl going to her father and saying, "Yuri must be serious about his marriage proposal—he invited me to dinner at McDonald's!"

But the Russians today are interested in more than burgers; they want exchange of capitol investment, scientific and technological knowledge, and guidance in modern management practices. Arthur D. Little of Cambridge, Massachusetts, for example, has been involved with a Russian company, E'West Managers, which transmits basic technologies from their Academy of Science to western institutes and laboratories through a license arrangement for everything from lasers to material science and ceramics. Such companies also channel back royalties and licensing income to Russia.

Despite the chaos within the former Soviet bloc of nations as they transition from a totalitarian to a market economy, many western corporations have set up viable joint ventures in Central and Eastern Europe. This is especially evident in the aerospace industry where both corporate giants, and even NASA, invest in cooperative Russian programs wherein western countries launch their satellites and payloads on Russian rockets (see *New Russian Space Programme,* Brian Harvey and Appendix B).

A newspaper feature, "Culture of Capitalism Gradually Taking Root in Russia" (*Los Angeles Times,* Nov. 27, 1997), described the transformation underway to a society which is more democratic and entrepreneurial. The shift from a passive mentality to an active enthusiasm for moneymaking is evident in the following incidents:

- The engineer who decides to triple his salary by taking a job as a security guard, working all three shifts. . . .
- The young wheeler-dealer who accumulates capital to start a china factory. . . .
- The farmer who seeks more land to expand potato growing. . . .
- The factory worker who moonlights evenings in a bread store to augment his salary. . . .
- The department store workers who leased the sprawling building and turned the store into a semiprivate, joint-stock society, in which 80 percent of the workers own stock.

As the reformers push for radical alterations in sociopolitical structures and systems, Alexander Kondratiev, the Penza region's equivalent of governor, wisely observes: "If they raise you for 70 years to hate the market, you can't change overnight. People have understood what was wrong, but psychologically they have not worked everything through yet." However, the Russians, Ukrainians, Tartars, Ossetians, and myriad other nationalities in the former Soviet empire are beginning to move beyond the Communist conditioning, not just to survive, but eventually to prosper. The millions in these many republics, whether independent or in an economic union, represent a new market opportunity for Western and Japanese management who have patience and multicultural capabilities. Ancient ethnic rivalries that have plagued the regions from the former Yugoslavia to the Balkans can be transformed by cultural synergy into prosperous trade for all. Yet the Europeans, North Americans, and the Japanese who travel there to do business or give aid must model and train the locals in multicultural management.

Summary Insights

The preparation of global leaders today not only takes places in universities and business schools, but within special management institutes worldwide and in training programs of multinational corporations, some of whom sponsor their own "universities." There, adult students not only learn cross-cultural management skills, but how to take advantage of cultural differences when forming partnerships and joint ventures that cross borders, industries, and diciplines (see *Developing the Global Organization,* Moran, Harris, and Stripp). In the emerging work environment, diverse knowledge workers are paramount, along with the practice of entrepreneurialism (see *New Work Culture,* Philip R. Harris). Perhaps this explains why so many high-technology enterprises cluster around great universities, especially those leading on the scientific and technological edge. In this knowledge society, there is a close interplay among university, science, and business personnel. We close this chapter with a quotation to illustrate this important new reality:

> *"The smooth transfer of people and ideas from academe into business, a rare event in Japan and France, is indeed second nature at MIT, whose graduates created companies such as Gillette and Campbell Soup in the 19th century. A recent study by Bank Boston reckons that if the 4,000 or so companies founded by MIT graduates and faculty were turned into an independent nation, the income they would produce would make it the 24th richest in the world. These firms account for annual revenues of some $230 billion and employ more than 1 million people. . . . Many of the companies' founders cite MIT's entrepreneurial spirit as a reason for deciding to start their own business."*
> —*"A Survey of Universities-The Knowledge Factory."* The Economist, *October 4, 1997, p. 14*

Just remember that there are distinct cultural differences to consider between the traditional and entrepreneurial work culture!

CHAPTER 2

Cultural Challenges in Global Management

An Overview

In the growing global marketplace, more and more businesses find themselves confronting new obstacles—obstacles that can endanger the success of global joint ventures. Problems encountered during intercultural business interactions lie in the misunderstanding of basic cultural guidelines present in each of the world's countries. In order to conduct business across cultures, one must be willing to make the effort to understand and work within these guidelines. Each culture has its own unique way of handling business as well as social interactions, and the visitor to particular cultures must recognize the differences. In this chapter, we discuss this important aspect of multicultural business management: the "multicultural clash."

There are a number of situations in global management that can cause friction between managers of different cultures. These situations are simple, common things like personal introductions or telephone conversations. They also include somewhat difficult situations such as business meetings or presentations across cultures, as well as the problems of training and motivation of foreign workers. While these situations all have certain degrees of difficulty, they are everyday occurrences in business and are handled based on each individual's cultural background.

The purpose of this chapter is to overview these types of situations. To facilitate self-learning, we have provided a test on pages 28 and 29, followed by a series of cross-cultural critical incidents or situations that may arise when people from different cultures attempt to work together in joint undertakings. The cultural factors or reasons behind such difficulties are addressed in detail later in this book.

Crossing Regional Cultures—Mr. Chen's Trip to the Far East

Singapore—home base

Mr. Chen, a Singaporean marketing manager, is wondering about the probation note he received after he returned from a four-week overseas sales trip through Asia. He works for a wholesale distribution outlet that supplies its clients with high-quality clothing and garments based on licenses from top American brands. Due to his excellent sales performance in Singapore last year, Mr. Chen had been assigned to head the company's Asia/Middle East sales team.

Hoping to capture numerous sales in one business trip, prior to his leaving Mr. Chen had called numerous contacts in the countries he was to visit and arranged meetings and presentations with them. He scheduled visits to Kuala Lumpur, Jakarta, Seoul, Tokyo, and Cairo. Armed with numerous samples of his company's new product line, including evening gowns, lingerie, cosmetics, and luggage, a confident Mr. Chen sat in his first-class seat on flight SQ 001 en route to Kuala Lumpur.

Malaysia—first stop

On the morning of his arrival in Kuala Lumpur, he phoned his client, Mr. Abdul Magid, to confirm his nine o'clock appointment. This company has been one of his big targets, and he hoped to capture their sale quickly so that he could focus on other clients for the rest of his two-day visit.

Unfortunately, he was told that his meeting was changed to an eleven o'clock lunch with the assistant manager, Mr. Noor Ismail. Although Mr. Chen had already planned a lunch appointment with another client, he had no choice but to agree. He had to shuffle his meeting with the other clients.

Mr. Chen arrived at Mr. Ismail's office on time and quickly began discussing how much profit the Malaysian company could make from his new products. But Mr. Ismail was more interested in learning about the credibility of Mr. Chen's company and Mr. Chen's past activities in Malaysia rather than negotiation details.

After an hour into the meeting, when Mr. Chen was eager to know if the price offer was acceptable, Mr. Ismail said he had to meet with other clients and asked Mr. Chen if he would like to join other members of the company for lunch. Mr. Chen wondered if Mr. Ismail was just passing the buck!

Mr. Chen soon recognized that he needed to show more flexibility when dealing with Malaysian organizations. Their desire to maintain harmony will be shown in their indirect refusal of an offer. They will entertain your offer with a polite smile. Mr. Chen, on the other hand, was used to a direct yes or no when dealing with his clients. The lunch with the assistants went well, but no purchasing contracts were finalized.

To gain the Malaysian company's business, Mr. Chen must maintain further contacts with his clients and continue prodding them for a definite response. To succeed with Malaysians, you must present your company's capabilities, management expertise, and Malaysian clients. You must then maintain ongoing communication with them in order to highlight your products' features and market potential.

Behind a day in his travel plans, Mr. Chen slowed down and began to understand the importance of building relationships with his clients. But his time was up in Malaysia, and a less confident Mr. Chen boarded flight SQ002 to Jakarta. He had worked very hard over the previous six months to recruit an Indonesian marketing agent, who had arranged several marketing meetings and presentations with potentially lucrative companies.

Indonesia—second stop

Marketing to the Indonesian companies proved to be quite rigorous. Mr. Chen and his agent spent a full day with one prospective company, scheduling meetings with three of the important buyers. Each meeting consisted of an hour of waiting and ten minutes of presentation. Mr. Chen tried to make a sale to each of the directors, but ended the meetings by simply giving away samples of his product line. Again, he was surprised that price negotiation did not begin. He thought his low prices would easily clinch the sale.

The agent tried to calm down Mr. Chen's frustrations. He explained that in Indonesia it is customary to make several visits to make sure that everyone involved in the sale approves of it, even before the official submission of the proposal. His agent was just planting the seeds that Mr. Chen would have to water with more samples!

On his last night in Indonesia, Mr. Chen's agent invited him and two other purchasing managers to dinner at Hotel Indonesia. He was now confident about the deal, and after three hours of discussion, the purchasing manager smiled politely and said, "Insha Allah (God Wishes), you may possibly receive our order." The purchasing manager and the agent then left and Mr. Chen found himself with a U.S. $200 dinner bill on his account. No purchase order was made.

When dealing with Indonesians, you must identify key players in the game: a person to introduce you to the highest position in the company, another within the company who will recommend and lobby for your product, and a third who will influence the decision on your behalf. Unfortunately, Mr. Chen's agent did not have the connections he needed.

Korea—third stop

Boarding flight SQ003 to Seoul, Mr. Chen recalled his early negotiations with Koreans. For several weeks prior to the commencement of his overseas trip, Mr. Chen had spent much of his time negotiating a deal to distribute his company's product to a large Korean company. He had begun by contacting the company's sales VP, whom he had met a few months earlier at a garment show. The VP had referred him to a junior manager, with whom he negotiated prices.

At the end of the negotiations, which lasted until just a week prior to his trip, the junior manager confirmed the sales agreement. Before his trip, Mr. Chen asked his company's legal staff to draw up a contract so he could take it with him. While he was on his trip, the marketing staff was to develop promotional materials for the Korean market.

But upon meeting the junior manager in Seoul, Mr. Chen was told that the VP had not actually agreed upon the terms of the contract, and he claimed that another company was offering a similar product line at a reduced price. A done deal was not a done deal! The Korean manager was now asking for another 30 percent discount!

After a few more rounds of negotiation, which lasted two days, a contract was agreed upon, but only after Mr. Chen learned the valuable lesson that, in Korea, only the boss makes the final decision. Like the junior manager, each Korean worker simply tries to satisfy his immediate superior by executing orders in an unquestioning manner. This lesson, though, offered very little consolation: Mr. Chen felt that he would have been a better salesman to Koreans if he would have graduated from a military academy, not a business college!

Japan—fourth stop

Boarding flight SQ004 to Tokyo, Mr. Chen recalled his first attempt to meet his Japanese clients. He had tried to sell his product line to a large corporation that a colleague had previously visited. The colleague gave him the name of a manager in the acquisitions department, Mr. Suzuki.

One month prior to leaving Singapore, Mr. Chen had prepared a marketing packet of his company's services and mailed them to Mr. Suzuki. Two weeks had passed with no response, so Mr. Chen telephoned Mr. Suzuki. The latter remembered the company and product, but said he might be too busy to meet when Mr. Chen was in Japan. He asked Mr. Chen to call him upon arriving in Tokyo.

Mr. Chen reached Mr. Suzuki's secretary when he called from his hotel and was informed that Mr. Suzuki would be too busy to hold a meeting. Mr. Chen wondered about the cold response—it seemed as if Mr. Suzuki wasn't even making an attempt to meet with him. Mr. Chen later learned that Mr. Suzuki was not a close acquaintance of the colleague—the two had simply met at a garment show. Mr. Suzuki declined to do business with him because the two did not have a close mutual acquaintance.

Because Mr. Chen failed to secure a direct sale, he fell back on his Japanese agent, whom he had been working with for several months. Fortunately, his agent's relationship with the contact was a strong one, and a meeting with an important buyer was secured.

When Mr. Chen made his first presentation to a group of high-ranking Japanese buyers, Mr. Chen found himself in a lengthy question and answer period. He was happy the Japanese asked so many questions, and thought it indicated he would secure a good order. Mr. Chen even noticed that the top sales VP had a smile on his face ten minutes into the talk. Mr. Chen thought this smile indicated an appreciation of his products.

Mr. Chen therefore talked with even more enthusiasm for the rest of the hour and made attempts to elicit feedback from the VP. But after his presentation, no offers were made. During his sushi dinner with his clients, he was also bombarded by many questions about the product's quality, his company's ability to meet production quotas, and the order delivery time.

As he sat in the taxi on the way back to the Imperial Hotel in Tokyo at 11:30 P.M., Mr. Chen wondered if the U.S. $400 sushi bill would ever pay off. He wondered aloud to his agent why the company had not made an offer: "You should have seen the expression on the VP's face! He had a mile-wide smile!" His agent then informed him that a smile can indicate not only an appreciation of what one is saying or doing, but can also indicate embarrassment. Mr. Chen felt like a fool upon realizing he had been pandering to the wrong executive!

Most Japanese host meetings with foreigners to ask further questions or to clarify an issue. They will then hold meetings among themselves and decide if they want to proceed further.

Egypt—fifth stop

Mr. Chen then boarded flight SQ005 to Cairo—his last stop, as an Arab distributor there had faxed his office with a request for a price quote on 5,000 of the company's elegant wedding dresses. The Arab had learned of the company through a connection in the U.S. Five-thousand pieces! The Arab distributor must mean business, Mr. Chen thought.

Mr. Chen had quickly faxed the Arab client with a 30 percent discounted price on the products. The Arab's fax had been titled, "Very Urgent," so Chen had assumed that the sale might be completed very soon. He was even happier when the Arab asked for 20 samples to show to clients, samples which Mr. Chen carried with him on the plane to Cairo.

As the Arab met Mr. Chen at the airport in his Mercedes 600c, the Singaporean felt he was in good hands. Upon receiving the samples, the client said "It will take me a couple days to show the product to my clients. We can then make final arrangements." Surprised at this development, Mr. Chen extended his two-day visit to a week and enjoyed himself at the Pyramids Hotel.

After five days of waiting, the Arab finally contacted Mr. Chen. "Thank you for the samples; they are great. My clients are interested in purchasing 500 sets. Can you give them to us at a 20 percent discount from the price you quoted earlier?" A mere 500 gowns with a 20 percent discount from the 5,000 price quote!

If Mr. Chen had been more aware of Arab price negotiation and delay strategy, he would have been in a better position to secure his

---

*For more information on the five cultures and countries described in this mini case, consult the parent book in this series, *Managing Cultural Differences,* Fourth edition, Chapters 12 and 14.

ultimate goal. Most Arabs will lead you to believe they are interested in a large order, ask for samples, gain more time, and then play their cards at the final moment!

A Test of Global Management Skills

The following situations present some of the potential cultural clashes in multicultural management. Try to choose the most appropriate answer in each question, and justify your decision culturally. The response to these common situations will be discussed throughout the book, but the most appropriate answers to these specific cases can be found on page 29.

Situation 1. As soon as an American exchanges business cards with you, he will probably

(a) Admire the quality of the business card paper.
(b) Look at your title to see if you are an important person.
(c) Ask, "What do you do?"
(d) Ask to explain the meaning of your name.

Situation 2. As European General Manager of a production factory in Singapore, you decide to have an open-door policy to receive workers' feedback, but no one comes to talk with you. The reason may be that

(a) The workers will not go over the head of their first-line manager.
(b) The workers do not like you.
(c) It is impolite to meet with the boss without an appointment.
(d) The employees like to work as a team and don't care about the boss.

Situation 3. You are entering a joint venture with a Shanghai enterprise and want to hire a local general manager. You should select this prospective manager on his or her proven ability to

(a) Improve profit by cutting staff.
(b) Acquire more money from the government.
(c) Manage his or her organization.
(d) Learn new technology.

Situation 4. You are invited to give a training seminar in Mexico. The local client representative asks for your fee and terms. Do you

(a) Quote a lower fee since you have never been there before?
(b) Ask how many participants there will be and what they are paying per person?
(c) Quote a lower fee but insist on first-class air travel?
(d) Double your normal fee to leave room for negotiation?

Situation 5. You have just received a fax from an Arab dealer asking for a quotation on 10,000 computers. The potential customer is actually interested in

(a) 10,000 computers.
(b) Your ability to deliver a larger order.
(c) Ten computers.
(d) Your minimum price.

Situation 6. When meeting a Taiwanese friend, it is not appropriate to

(a) Compliment him on how good he looks in his new suit.
(b) Call him by his first name.
(c) Praise his skills for delivering your order on time.
(d) Praise his son's wisdom.

Situation 7. You are sending a new piece of equipment to Japan. Which of the following is most important to send with the equipment?

(a) A detailed technical description in English.
(b) A detailed technical design manual in Japanese.
(c) Audio and video tapes in Japanese on how to use the machine.
(d) A technician to explain how to use the machine.

The most appropriate answers for Situations 1 through 7 are: 1-c, 2-a, 3-b, 4-b, 5-d, 6-d, 7-d.

The Multicultural Clash

This section presents some of the questions that occur across cultures during business introductions, telephone conversations, meetings and presentations, and in training and motivating employees.

Business Introductions

- *What was her name?*
- *Who is the boss?*
- *Why does he keep staring at my card?*
- *Why is he standing so close to me?*
- *Why is she asking about my family? She's never met them.*
- *Should I say, "Nice to meet you, Farid," "Mr. Elashmawi," or "Dr. Elashmawi?"*

Telephone Conversations

- *Did he say his name was Mr. Chen, Chan, or Chou?*
- *I forgot to leave my phone number.*
- *I got the answering machine. What kind of message should I leave?*
- *What was their telephone number again?*
- *I made the call and said what I needed to say. He didn't say much of anything, though.*

Meetings and Presentations

- *Why does he bring everyone in on everything? Can't he make a decision by himself?*
- *Now she's speaking up. Why didn't she raise that point an hour ago when we started this discussion?*
- *How can I commit to monthly meetings? God knows where I'll be on the third Tuesday of November.*
- *He asked the manager for her opinion first. I guess I'd better be quiet.*
- *He's been doing all the talking so I better let him make the decision.*

Training

- *Why are they complaining about working overtime; don't they want to learn about the new machine?*
- *Why doesn't the general manager get involved? After all, this training session is for everyone.*
- *What are they so upset about? I sent them the manual; what more do they want?*
- *A quiz? But I have not had enough time to prepare.*
- *No one has any questions? (Pause.) Good, so everyone understands.*

Motivation

- *How can I get them to work faster? We need to get these machines shipped right away.*
- *Why is she so upset? I thought she would be happy getting a big promotion.*
- *All my ideas have been received with a nice smile and a "thank you."*
- *Why is he so upset? I promoted him to senior manager and he's only twenty-nine!*

These are some of the problems you may face during an encounter with someone from a different culture. Let's now consider the following critical cases during cross-cultural encounters. Put yourself in place of the person(s) in the cases and determine how you would react based on your cultural values.

Time for a Coffee Break

There is a conference at the Tokyo Convention Center involving business executives from all over the world. Mr. John Smith from Texas is one of the attendees, and he is interested in meeting many people from these different countries during the coffee break in the conference.

While walking around looking for someone to talk to, he spots two men—one Japanese and one Arab—who are talking together on the other side of the room; Mr. Smith approaches them.

Smith: Good morning gentlemen, I'm John Smith. (He extends his hand to the Arab man first and then to the Japanese.) Do you mind if I join you?

Mohammed: (As he shakes Smith's hand with both of his.) Welcome, please join us.

Suzuki: (He steps backward and bows slightly. He shakes Mr. Smith's hand without saying anything, ready to exchange business cards.)

Mohammed: Are you enjoying yourself in this wonderful country, Mr. Smith?

Smith:	Oh sure, it's very nice here. What do you do Mr. . . .?
Mohammed:	Mohammed Rageh. I'm from Egypt and the president of my import company. We are here to look at some of the available products and meet our Japanese friends.
Smith:	(Turning to Suzuki.) And your name, sir?
Suzuki:	(He silently hands Smith his business card.)
Smith:	(After looking at it quickly.) Oh, you're Mr. Suzuki.
Suzuki:	Yes, Sany Corporation.
Smith:	I see. (Puts Suzuki's card in his pocket and turns back to Mohammed, reaches into his pocket and hands each his business card.) Do you have a business card, Mohammed?
Mohammed:	(Smiling.) No, I don't carry them with me. Everybody knows me. (Moving closer to John to show his hospitality.) I'm the president.
Smith:	(Stepping back from Mohammed.) Oh, I understand.
Suzuki:	Mr. Smith, you are from the Blackford Company?
Smith:	Yes, I'm the marketing director in charge of the Southwestern Division.
Mohammed:	Well, should we all go have some coffee and enjoy our break time together?
Smith:	I'm sorry, but I have to go talk to some other people. Maybe we'll get together later on. It was very nice to meet you. Goodbye.

Cultural Analysis. John Smith walks away in search of more people to make contact with, as Mohammed and Suzuki look at each other, smiling. They overhear him: "Good morning, gentlemen, I'm John Smith. Do you mind if I join you?"

There are many culture clashes present in this scenario. The first clash was when Mohammed asked John about his stay in the country. John answered quickly, and then asked what Mohammed did. Arabs like to establish a personal relationship with someone before talking about business. Therefore, for John to immediately ask Mohammed what he does went against Mohammed's cultural value system.

The next clash happened when John received Mr. Suzuki's card and almost immediately put it away. In Japan, it is customary to study the business card to determine company name and rank, then become silent for a short time to "feel" the other person's thoughts. So when Mr. Smith didn't bother to look at the card, and, in fact, didn't offer his own card first, he offended Mr. Suzuki.

The third clash occurred when Suzuki asked Smith if he was from a certain company and Smith replied by stating his position in the company and what he was in charge of. Because individual achievement and competition are of great value in the American company, Smith stressed his position and his responsibility in the company. The Japanese, however, valuing the group over the individual, would consider the company first and more important.

When Does Business Start?

Dr. Mohammed Salah, a Kuwaiti businessman, was in Florida visiting his American business associate, Mr. Ed Rutherford, to give a presentation. The day Dr. Salah was to give the presentation, he arrived and was introduced to the staff assembled for the presentation. All levels of management were represented when Mr. Rutherford began the meeting. "Folks, I'd like to introduce to you a man whose company could do great things for us in the future; please welcome Mohammed." Dr. Salah rose to give the presentation, slightly insulted at his introduction. He began by introducing himself, saying "Good morning, I am Dr. Mohammed Salah from Kuwait. I'm very pleased to be here in Florida where I received my doctoral degree from the University of Miami. As you know, Kuwait is rebuilding, and there are many opportunities for your company in my country."

Dr. Salah continued talking further about his country's history and his company's credentials, including recent partnerships with several German organizations. After about thirty minutes, Mr. Rutherford, who was very anxious to get on with business, inter-

rupted Dr. Salah. "Dr. Salah," he said, "this is all interesting background information, but could you please give some specific examples of what we can do for you?" Dr. Salah was confused because he
thought he was doing exactly that.

Hello, What Can I Do For You?

David Pierce, operations manager of an American computer
manufacturer, ordered some computer hard disks from a supplier but they never arrived. He called the supplier, another
American whose name is Bob Wilson, to find out why.
(Telephone rings and Bob picks it up.)

Bob: Bob Wilson.
David: Bob, this is David Pierce from Future Computers.
Bob: Yes, David, what can I do for you?
David: I ordered some hard disks from you last week and
             they haven't arrived yet. Is there some sort of prob-
             lem with the order?
Bob: No, there's no problem. I shipped those off to you
             three days ago.
David: Well, we haven't gotten them yet. How long does it
             usually take?
Bob: Usually two to three days; you'll have to call the
             shipping company.
David: Okay, I will. When did you ship it out?
Bob: October 4, at about three o'clock.
David: Okay, Bob, thanks. I'll get ahold of the shipper right
             away.

David now calls his Japanese supplier to check on a similar
situation.
(Telephone rings and someone picks it up.)

Suzuki: Hello, this is XYZ Distributors, International Depart-
             ment, Suzuki speaking.
David: Hello, Mr. Suzuki, this is David Pierce.

Suzuki:	I'm sorry, what company?
David:	This is David Pierce from Future Computers.
Suzuki:	Oh yes, Future Computers, Mr. Pierce. Did you receive the memory chips?
David:	No, I haven't, that's why I'm calling. Our line is stalled because we're waiting for them.
Suzuki:	Oh, I'm very sorry, Mr. Pierce.
David:	I can't do much with sorry. When did you ship it?
Suzuki:	I must check with my department staff to find out.
David:	Okay, I'll wait here while you check.
Suzuki:	I'm sorry, we must have a meeting to discuss the problem.
David:	Another meeting? Is that all you ever do? (Hangs up the phone in frustration.)

Cross-Cultural Telephone Tips. Trying to conduct business on the telephone can be very difficult. Lack of physical presence when talking with someone can leave you feeling that something was missing from your conversation. When using the telephone for cross-cultural business, however, the problems can be even greater: knowing the cultural guidelines that apply to telephoning a foreign executive, wondering what kind of message to leave on an answering machine, and inquiring if you got your message across to the person on the other end.

It is very likely that when talking to your Japanese contact on the phone, he or she may suddenly become quiet. As we mentioned, conversations in Japan often contain periods of silence during which each participant senses the thoughts and feelings of the other. In other cultures, periods of silence during social interaction are very uncomfortable situations. In Arab cultures, for example, silence is usually reserved for sad occasions such as mourning. Americans may also feel uncomfortable with silence during a telephone call and tend to interrupt the silence with self-disclosure or arguments to press for a response.

The end of the telephone call is equally unique across cultural lines. In Arab cultures, the telephone call is usually ended by the expression of continuing long-term relationships, the exchange of good wishes, and the wish to hear from the other caller again. These lines follow the same values of personal relationship and trust so vital in Arab culture. The Japanese frequently end a business call by saying that they will discuss the details with the group, and get back to you when an agreement is reached, but no commitment will be offered.

In contrast to the Japanese value to wait and seek group consensus (of which you saw an example in David Pierce's call to Mr. Suzuki), Americans tend to end telephone conversations by more definite terms. In keeping with their values of directness, action, and independence, Americans usually end phone calls by pressing for answers or a commitment to action. People from other cultures can be uncomfortable with American actions in this regard, because Americans can appear too abrupt and pushy compared to the value systems of others.

Just as all cultures have particular ways of talking on the telephone, they use the same mannerisms when leaving messages on answering machines. The following are a few examples of messages left by people from different cultures. Try to figure out from which culture they come:

"This is Bill Fletcher from Bison Industries. Thank you for sending the fax, very interesting. I'll be in touch, probably within the month based on whatever happens. Again, I appreciate your quick response to my request."

"Hello, Dr. Farid, this is Manuel calling to say hello and to ask for your fax number. I guess you're not in so I'm calling to say I will be sending by mail some of the information we've been talking about. I wish you well, and have a nice trip. You should be getting my letter sometime next week. Thank you."

Have you figured out the differences in cultures between the two callers? Which one is most probably an American?

Getting Into Business

Tom Baxter is the program manager for new products at Silicon Data Corporation in California. He has called a meeting with his designers to review the progress of the "Global Telephone" project his company is introducing.

At two o'clock, Tom; John Ericson, the American hardware design engineer; Chen Tang, the Chinese software engineer; Paula Ghandi, from India, the system integration engineer; and Saed Shabah, the marketing manager from Saudi Arabia, are present.

At ten minutes past two, Tom glances at his watch as Saed arrives at the meeting. Saed enters, greeting everyone and, looking at Ms. Ghandi, asks, "How was your lunch?"

"It was great. Thank you again for inviting me. Do you have any plans for dinner?"

Tom is anxious to start the meeting and says, "I believe everyone has received a copy of the agenda. Does anyone want to add any items?" Immediately, John says, "Tom, I think we should include the issue of documentation, which Mr. Chen is handling." Tom looks at Mr. Chen and says, "Do you have any objections?" Mr. Chen replies by smiling politely and shaking his head "no."

Tom goes through the meeting listening to each member's progress. Toward the end of the meeting, Ms. Ghandi interrupts and asks, "What about the issue of delivery?" Tom replies, "You should have put that on the agenda when we started the meeting." Ms. Ghandi assumes that Tom doesn't want to discuss the issue and she sits down without saying anything else.

Cultural Analysis. The potential for cultural clash in this common multicultural business situation is quite high. In each culture, every aspect of business is handled differently. The Americans start conversations differently than the Arabs or Indians, and the Chinese have different reasons for holding a meeting than the others. As we discussed, clashes between businesspeople from different cultures are inevitable without proper knowledge of each other's cultural values.

Again, valuing directness and action orientation, the American program manager was anxious to get into business. However, he is faced with the indirect, nonconfronting approach of the Chinese and the time frame of the Indian engineer.

Will "Call Me John" Make the Sale?

John Smith is an American executive giving a presentation to a multinational group of businesspeople at his company headquarters in Los Angeles. He begins his presentation by telling his audience about himself.

Smith: Good afternoon everyone, I'm John Smith, director of marketing and sales for Goodman and Smith; please call me John. I've gathered everybody together today to discuss our new products and, I hope, send you home with one of them. Before I get started, though, I'd like to go around the room and ask everyone to introduce themselves. (Turns to another American in the room.) Let's start with you, Bob.

Bob: Okay, my name is Bob Wilson and I'm the marketing manager for Global Advertisements, and I'm here to learn about your products in order to develop a market plan.

(This process goes around the room stopping next at Mr. Suzuki from Japan.)

Suzuki: Thank you very much. I'm sorry for my English. I am with the Suzuki Motor Corporation. I work in the International Department, Tokyo office.

Mohammed: I come from Saudi Arabia from the Mohammed Ali family, and I'm the president of my company. I have a Ph.D. from Stanford University. If you come to Saudi Arabia please visit our home and have dinner with us.

Chen: I am G. C. Chen from Taiwan; my American name is Gary. I am pleased to be in California, and I am looking for a mutual profitable relationship with your esteemed company, Mr. Smith.

Smith: Great, please call me John. It's getting very warm in here. Please feel free to take off your jackets to get comfortable.

All the Americans immediately follow Smith's advice and take off their coats. Other participants, waiting for an indication from their senior member, do not.

John starts his colorful presentation and proceeds along point by point for about fifteen minutes. When he asks the general audience for questions, this conversation takes place:

Bob: John, could you tell me again how many of those you could produce in a month?

Smith: Two thousand, Bob. (Looks around room.) Do our associates from Japan have any questions?

(They nod their heads, "yes, yes," but don't say anything, so John continues with his presentation, assuming they have no questions. After about an hour, John ends his presentation by asking the audience again if they have any questions. From the silence, John assumes no one does, so he thanks everyone for their time, and closes the presentation. Afterward, John is curious how his presentation went, so he decides to ask Mr. Suzuki for his opinion.)

Smith: Do you think your company would have an interest in buying some of our products?

Suzuki: Yes, yes.

Smith: That's wonderful. I'm sure you'll be happy with them. (Turns to the Chinese executive, Mr. Chen.) How about you, Mr. Chen? Would your company be interested in any of these products?

(As a junior executive, Mr. Chen looks to his boss for some assistance in answering the question. The senior executive looks at John and silently smiles. John then looks at Mohammed.)

| **Smith:** | Dr. Mohammed, do you think you would be interested in buying some of our items? |
| **Mohammed:** | *In sha Allah* (God willing), we will do a great deal of business with your company. However, we have to see you in Saudi Arabia first. |

That night John went home believing he had scored at least three sales. How many sales do you think he made? One, two, three . . . None?

Cultural Analysis. Similar clashes between cultures can occur in many parts of meetings or presentations. From the seating arrangement to the decision-making process, each culture conducts it in a specific way. For example, in Japan, the seating is prearranged, and although there is no particular order in regard to status, everyone must sit in their assigned seats.

This is quite different from the way Arabs arrange their seating. In Arab culture, the oldest or most senior executive present sits at a place of obvious importance, to show his status to the other participants.

Different still is the American seating arrangement, or rather, lack of arrangement. In an American meeting or presentation, everyone generally sits where they wish, or where there is an available space. This custom demonstrates the American value of equality.

It's Time for a Meeting

Participation is another aspect of the business meeting with potential for causing a cultural clash. Determining who gets involved in the proceedings and how questions are asked varies in each culture.

In some cultures, even deciding who should or should not attend a meeting follows a specific pattern. Arab managers expect only high ranking personnel at important meetings. Senior executives do not feel comfortable discussing substantive issues in the presence of technicians because of Arabs' extreme status consciousness. However, the Japanese will invite all those concerned with an issue to a meeting regardless of title because group participation and consensus are key values in Japanese business.

When making presentations to Arabs, after a while you may notice that no one is asking questions. In an American conference room, it is acceptable for the presenter to ask the audience for questions. In Saudi Arabia, however, the senior member has the highest status and must be addressed first before anyone else may speak.

In Japan, business meetings are highly participatory, with everyone present getting involved in the discussion. When meeting with foreign executives, however, the meeting is seen as being held for informational purposes, and the participants sit quietly and listen to you. This makes it difficult for the American or Arab presenter to determine whether or not their material has been understood.

Determining if an audience understands your message is achieved through the use of feedback. When making a presentation or conducting a business meeting, there is a certain amount of information you give out and a certain amount you expect your audience to give back. The amount of feedback you receive changes from culture to culture. In Japan, when meeting with foreigners, direct feedback is almost nonexistent. This is because Japanese meetings are designed solely for gathering information about whatever subject is being discussed. The group then takes that information and discusses it at a later time. Therefore, an extremely small amount of feedback is given, which can be quite confusing to the foreign presenter.

The American feedback process is quite different from the Japanese method in that feedback is instantaneous. From start to finish, the participants in an American business meeting give their opinions on the material being discussed in an effort to show their ability to think independently and to acquire all the facts.

The Japanese would find the American model of the business meeting, where the main function is to reach a decision and set a plan of action, too confrontational. The Japanese business meeting is one with a defined hierarchy and a solemn atmosphere where direct answers are never given. Because of this apparent lack of commitment, executives from other cultures often incorrectly assume their message has been misunderstood.

The way time is valued can be a major source of frustration and a cultural clash as well. In Malaysia, for example, employees show up for a meeting at different times. Your appearance at a Malaysian meeting is based on your position in the company. If you are the most senior member you arrive last and start the meeting.

In American business "time is money." This means that time spent extraneously to finish the task at hand is wasting time and, therefore, wasting money. Americans feel it is very important to be punctual and show up at the stated time of a meeting or other business function. Punctuality is highly valued because it demonstrates the individual's desire to use the available time efficiently. This factor also relates to showing respect for the value of the other participants' time. If you show up late for an American meeting, oftentimes the group will start without you, and you will be left behind trying to understand what was missed.

Say What You Mean

In the course of the meeting or presentation, the language used by each culture may not always have the same meaning. An excellent example is the American and Japanese usage of the word "yes." In American culture, when you say "yes," you are indicating that you agree with or accept the previous statement. When talking with the Japanese, they often use the word "hai" which translates to "yes." It does not mean they agree with you, however, only that they understand the point you are making.

Language can be a cause of cultural clashes in many other ways besides misunderstanding the word "yes." The use of language reflects the self-image of each culture as well. Americans use direct words and sentences in an effort to reach a conclusion quickly. This situation would not sit well with Japanese or Arab executives, however, because of their value of group harmony and long-term relationships.

Arabs' use of language reflects their sense of hospitality and interest in maintaining a long-term relationship. To rush the process of a meeting by asking for a commitment or setting a specific deadline would be insulting, and could possibly result in the termination of any future business plans.

Although English has become the international language of business, a language barrier still exists. In order to solve this problem, an interpreter is sometimes used to help overcome the language barrier. An interpreter is not always a sure way to get your message across, though. If the individual is unfamiliar with the material you are presenting, you run the risk of confusing your audience. This problem is especially true when your presentation contains technical language or slang with which the interpreter is unfamiliar. It is a good practice, therefore, to provide your interpreter with a copy of your material beforehand.

While language is an important tool in meetings and presentations, nonverbal communication is equally crucial, especially in situations where persuasion is necessary. A perfect example is the American trait of making direct eye contact when speaking to others, which gives Americans a feeling of sincerity and equality. The Japanese, however, especially those who are not in superior positions, hardly ever look each other in the eye. Therefore, the direct American style would be considered too forward and out of line with maintaining group harmony.

Cultural Training Taboos

The following eight critical incidents are presented for your own cultural analysis. Each one has a short commentary at the end to stimulate your thinking.

1) A Jordanian engineer flies to Tokyo to orient a group of Japanese workers on Arab management before they leave to build a new factory in Amman, Jordan. He has prepared the material to address three different groups: the senior managers, the junior members, and, finally, the workers.

   On the first day, the engineer notices something unusual about the group's composition: The Japanese group is made up of twenty employees from all different levels of seniority. Since his first training session is designed for the senior managers, and there are members of all three groups here, he is unsure how to start. Now he has to deliver his orientation to all levels at one time, which never happened in companies back home.

As companies establish offices and plants in countries overseas, the problem of training local personnel who will be working with the equipment arises. How to meet the needs of both the workers and the managers without insulting anyone's ego is of great importance. In addition, knowing how to approach a training session with Japanese, Arabs, Americans, or people of other cultures and using the type of methods to which they are accustomed is important. It is crucial to understand the composition of the group, time allowed for the training sessions, expected employee preparation, and the materials used in the process. Without a basic understanding of these guidelines, cultural clashes will often occur. In the previous example, for instance, if the Jordanian engineer had known of the Japanese training style, which typically involves workers from all levels of management, he could have been prepared to conduct effective training. Instead he started from a disadvantage because of his lack of knowledge of their cultural differences.

2) In another example, a group of ten Egyptian engineers and technicians, led by Dr. Rageb, the chief engineer, had been invited by their Japanese associates to come to Osaka for a training program. On Monday morning, Dr. Rageb arrived for the first training session. When he located his seat he found he was placed next to one of his company's technicians. Dr. Rageb then noticed that the Japanese instructor intends to conduct the training to all the team members together. Since Arab culture is very status conscious, Dr. Rageb was disturbed by his placement next to someone with less seniority who will receive the same information and training as the other technicians. After a short time, Dr. Rageb found the situation too uncomfortable, got up, and left the room. The Japanese instructor and program coordinator were confused by Dr. Rageb's behavior; had they been aware of the cultural differences between Japan and Arabia, they would have been able to more suitably seat Dr. Rageb.

3) In the meantime, Frank Crawford, an American businessman, is sent to Japan to give a three-day training session concerning a letter-sorting machine his company sold to a Japanese corporation. Mr. Crawford starts the training at nine o'clock, breaks the session at noon for lunch, and wraps everything up at five o'clock. A few of the participants have more questions, and he

answers them respectfully. He then says goodbye, and goes to his room in the hotel where the seminar is taking place, which also happens to be where the trainees are staying.

Two hours later, as Mr. Crawford is preparing for the next day's program, the telephone rings: it is the program manager asking him to join him at the hotel bar. Mr. Crawford agrees to the invitation and heads downstairs. When he arrives, he is shocked to find all the trainees sitting there waiting for him. They had all showered, had dinner, and were ready to continue discussing details of the training topic, as in the Japanese custom.

At eleven o'clock, Mr. Crawford finally made it back to his hotel room. He was tired, but far wiser about Japanese training methods.

4) Mr. Yamamoto from Japan is at his Mexico headquarters to train the local workers how to use a new product. At nine o'clock, he begins the session. Seventy-five minutes later, Mr. Yamamoto calls for a break. During the break, he notices the participants are talking about their families and other personal matters, but are not discussing the product he has been demonstrating. Mr. Yamamoto resumes the training session, has a break, and at about three o'clock, breaks a third time. This time everyone thanks him and wishes him well, and starts to walk out the door to go home. Mr. Yamamoto stops one participant and asks, "Where is everybody going?" The person answers, "We are going to pick up our children and go home to eat with our families."

Confused, and quite suddenly alone, Mr. Yamamoto packs up his things, thinking, "I'd better call the head office to tell them I will be back at least two days later than planned." He assumed the participants would devote time even beyond the scheduled sessions, as the Japanese do; had he studied Mexican culture, he would have realized up front the need for additional training time.

5) Bill Johnson arrives in Japan to train the employees of a Japanese company on the use of some new equipment. Since he sent dozens of copies of the instruction manual for the equipment two weeks ago, he expects the training session to be simple, consisting mainly of explaining sections of the manual that the employees didn't understand.

When the Japanese employees arrive, Mr. Johnson notices that no one has a copy of the manual with them. "They must have already memorized it," he thinks. Mr. Johnson begins the session with a video showing how the product operates. After the video ends, he asks the participants if they have any questions. No one speaks up, so Mr. Johnson assumes they understand everything. He says, "thank you," and starts putting away his materials. Then a voice says, "I'm sorry, Mr. Johnson, do you have this machine with you?"

"No, I didn't bring one with me, but your company will be receiving the one you ordered any day now."

Later that evening, Mr. Johnson gets an angry phone call from his boss back in the United States. "What happened over there, Bill? The marketing manager for their company just called me and said they are reconsidering buying the equipment because he says we didn't give them a chance to be trained properly." Because of the Japanese training method of learning by doing, the employees expected to be trained on the machine, a fact that Mr. Johnson, with his American cultural values, had not even considered.

This process would not be an acceptable procedure, however, even in Arab cultures. Arabs rely more on theoretical training programs than on material that needs to be memorized. In American culture, you learn by yourself, but in Arab cultures, the trainer has all the responsibility, while in Japan, training is accomplished by working together in a group.

6) Mohammed Ali, an Arab trainer, has been sent to his American factory to train the workers on a new machine. The employees arrive at the session, and he begins to demonstrate how the machine works. After a few minutes, the Americans appear confused, and one of them asks, "Don't we get a handbook for this?" The Arab, because of his culture's procedure of relying on the trainer to explain everything, did not expect to be required to give out the manual. The American workers, however, with their independence-oriented culture, expected to have materials describing the product before the training started.

7) Mr. Schmidt has been sent by his German company to Japan to train five Japanese workers on how to use a new machine. He only has five days to finish the training program, so he

makes plans to train one employee on each of the five days. On the first day of training, though, all five trainees show up, prepared to be trained as a group. Confused, Mr. Schmidt tells one of the employees to stay, and he sends the rest back to work. The workers, looking perplexed as well, talk among themselves. A short time later, the manager of the group approaches Mr. Schmidt and says, "I'm sorry, we are a group and expect to be trained together. Please, could you show us, as a group, how to use the machine?"

The Japanese evaluate their training and testing experience as members of a group. For instance: Group A has been training all week on a new machine that their company will soon be using. Today, the trainer has planned a test for each group to evaluate their progress. To do this, Group A is given the machine they have been training on all week, and are told the machine has a problem. The group discovers the source of the problem, fixes it, and is given a score reflecting their effort.

Evaluating the results of training programs for American groups relies on the cultural importance of individuality, competition, and self-reliance. Americans do not hesitate to take individual responsibility for their answers in front of a group. For example, the instructor may ask one of the participants at random spontaneous questions, or ask a question to the general group, and someone in that group will usually volunteer an answer.

8) In an Arab company, Mr. Jones, an American consultant, has been conducting a training program on a new computer for the past five days. On Friday, as soon as the employees arrive, Mr. Jones hands them a test on the use of this computer. The workers all appear to be upset with Mr. Jones, but he figures they haven't slept much. Later that afternoon, Mr. Jones finishes grading the tests and comes to a disturbing conclusion: not one person passed the exam, despite the fact they had been discussing the topic for the entire week.

Arabs, contrary to the American system of pop quizzes and oral examinations, expect at least two days' notice before an exam. Also, Arab tests consist of direct questions, based on facts they have learned. Without ample time to study the material, they will not be prepared for any test, no matter how well the subject is explained.

Motivation by Money, Words, or Status

The motivation of human performance differs somewhat by culture; our culture influences behavior by confirming what to value. The following eight critical incidents illustrate these cross-cultural differences, requiring you to do your own cultural analysis of how you might act in each situation.

1) Mr. Mahyidin Bin Omar, one of three Malaysian workers at a Japanese plant in Kuala Lumpur, has been working on a production machine and has an idea. He thinks that production could be improved if one aspect of the process was changed slightly. So Mr. Omar meets with his Japanese supervisor, Mr. Tanaka, to discuss the idea. While Mahyidin was explaining his plan, Mr. Tanaka just sat quietly, smiling and nodding—as if only slightly interested. After that short meeting, Mahyidin left feeling as if he was just politely listened to by his supervisor, since he did not get any response of encouragement. He was inclined not to even submit new ideas to his boss, Mr. Tanaka.

Most Malaysian workers are motivated by immediate positive feedback and encouragement by their supervisors. However, Japanese managers tend to give little immediate feedback, especially to foreigners, sometimes causing them to feel unappreciated and, therefore, less motivated. However, Mr. Tanaka will probably discuss Omar's ideas with his Japanese colleagues.

Motivating employees to work harder, or to develop new ideas, is difficult. When trying to motivate foreign workers, though, the process can not only be confusing, but divisive and counterproductive as well.

2) On the other side, Fred Johnson, the new operations manager for a French company in Saudi Arabia, had a problem. He wanted to ship the product on which his five employees were working. It was almost five o'clock, though, which was quitting time, and the workers were already starting to put things away. Fred thought that if they worked a little longer, they could finish the job. He called them together and said, "Listen, I think we can get this finished tonight. If you stay for forty-five minutes more, I'll buy each of you a drink."

At five o'clock sharp, the whistle blew and everyone left. Mr. Johnson was not happy with this situation and wondered why no one thought his offer was enough motivation. Unhappy, he went to the bar that night to drink by himself, not realizing that Arabs do not drink alcohol.

3) When Mr. Swenson, a new shift supervisor of a Swedish company in Taiwan, observes Betty Hu, a new employee on the assembly line in the factory, he notices that she is having trouble putting the units together properly. He wonders what the problem is, so he shouts across the room to her, "Betty, do you need some help? Your line is getting slow." Betty looks up; her face begins to turn red with embarrassment. The workers around her start smiling and laughing. Later that afternoon, Betty comes to Mr. Swenson's office and says she wants to quit that line. Mr. Swenson, wondering what caused this sudden desire, says, "Why do you want to leave? You're doing fine, you just need a little more time to learn everything." Betty immediately starts crying, and Mr. Swenson wonders what he did wrong.

4) Tran Nguyen from Vietnam was doing an excellent job in the American factory in California where she worked. As a reward, her American manager, Mrs. Brownstone, decided to promote her to the next level. This new job would put her at the same level in the company as her husband, who also worked at the factory. Tran quietly declined the promotion, which left Mrs. Brownstone confused. Mrs. Brownstone didn't realize that Vietnamese husbands must have a higher status than their wives.

5) Jane Barton was an American employee working in a Japanese company in New York City. She worked there for two-and-a-half years before she became pregnant. Her immediate Japanese supervisor, Mr. Suzuki, heard the news, congratulated her, and asked when she was going to leave the company. Jane told him that she would probably stay for about seven more months and then take three months' leave before coming back. The Japanese supervisor looked surprised and said, "Oh, seven months. I think leaving sooner might be better for your baby." Jane, confused, went back to work thinking he was just concerned about her health. A month went by, and Jane's supervisor suggested to her again that she quit, saying that it

would be best to go home to prepare to have the baby and take care of the family. Jane looked angrily at him and said, "I'm not leaving yet." Two weeks later, the supervisor called her into his office and told her that a pregnant woman is not a valuable part of an efficient team, and she was assigned to a less responsible job. Mr. Suzuki's actions were based on his old traditional Japanese cultural norms that a pregnant woman's place is in the home.

6) Mr. Huang from Taiwan was working for an American company. He graduated from a top American university and, because of his accomplishments, was hired by Tran-Tech, a high-technology firm in California. During his first year with the company, Mr. Huang exhibited excellent and creative work. At his annual performance review, his boss, Brian August, told him he was very pleased with Mr. Huang's work. During this review, Mr. August asked, "Where would you like to be a year from now?" Mr. Huang smiled and said, "Thank you Mr. August," and became silent.

Mr. August was confused when, the following week, he found out that Mr. Huang had resigned and moved to a competitor's company. He failed to realize that Vietnamese expect the boss to take care of their career plans.

7) Mr. Franzen is the managing director of a German tire subsidiary in Japan. After one year, Mr. Franzen decided to reorganize his division, and called a meeting of his five Japanese second-line managers. At the meeting, he announced that he was appointing Mr. Nakashima to head the newly reorganized department. During the course of his announcement, Mr. Franzen commended Mr. Nakashima for his "hard work, creativity, and competitive attitude, especially at the age of twenty-nine."

After the meeting, Mr. Franzen noticed that two of the other, older managers were angry with the decision, and within a month, one of the older managers had requested to be transferred into a different subsidiary. Further, productivity in the department dropped significantly, leaving Mr. Franzen perplexed. Mr. Franzen had, in fact, selected Mr. Nakashima from the group, ignoring the Japanese group harmony and surprising them with his own decision.

8) Pierre Gorgan, a French engineer, was hired by a Japanese company based in Japan because of his Ph.D. and ten years of semiconductor design experience. During the first three months, he showed some very creative work and was able to produce excellent new design features.

Pierre also brought his wife and children with him to Japan, so every day after work he took the six o'clock train home to have quality family time. One afternoon at work, his manager asked him to go with him to the coffee shop. He told Pierre that he didn't spend enough time with his team members, especially after work during drinking hours. Pierre replied, "You know I don't drink, and I would rather spend my free time after work with my family. Besides, my results are appreciated and the new product will be ready for the production line very soon." The Japanese manager smiled at Pierre and nodded his head.

After his initial six-month probation period with the company, Pierre wondered why his contract was not renewed. He was a creative, results-oriented, hard-working engineer who was greatly appreciated in his home country. Pierre apparently had missed many other Japanese cultural values related to group interaction that his boss valued more highly than his creativity.

Mr. Bell's First Trip to Arabia—What Went Wrong?

John Bell is the Middle East sales manager for a medium-sized American company. He was making his first trip to Cairo, the capital of Egypt. His mission was to introduce his company's new product line to the president of a major local import/distribution company, and to secure a large order.

At eight o'clock the morning after his arrival, Mr. Bell telephoned Mr. Hassan, the president of the local distribution company, to confirm his appointment at one o'clock in the afternoon. Mr. Hassan's secretary welcomed him and told him she would call him as soon as Mr. Hassan arrived in the office. By ten o'clock, Mr. Bell had not heard from Mr. Hassan's office, so he called back. This time a different person answered the phone and informed Mr. Bell that Mr. Hassan was still in the market and he would call him right back. Finally, at eleven o'clock, Mr. Hassan's personal secretary called and told Mr. Bell that Mr. Hassan would be happy to have tea with him tomorrow at ten o'clock. Mr. Bell hung up the telephone disappointed to have lost a whole day and upset that Mr. Hassan only wanted to have tea with him.

The next day at ten o'clock sharp, Mr. Bell arrived at Mr. Hassan's office, where he introduced himself to the secretary, who was talking on the telephone. When she finished the phone call, the secretary asked Mr. Bell to sit down, and she offered him a cup of tea. After fifteen minutes, Mr. Hassan arrived in the office, and with him were two Western salesmen. Mr. Hassan opened his arms to greet him, but Mr. Bell was not sure if he should give him a hug or a handshake, so he stood at a distance, extending his hand. Mr. Hassan invited all of his guests into his office, and offered everyone coffee. Mr. Bell refused, saying he had just had some tea and was ready now to give Mr. Hassan a full presentation on his company's new product line.

Mr. Hassan was not ready to discuss business, however, and asked Mr. Bell about his trip and how he liked Cairo. Mr. Bell replied that it had been a long trip and that he had stayed in his hotel room for practically the entire day yesterday. Then Mr. Hassan started asking his other guests about the prices of their products. Soon, he asked Mr. Bell about his new products and his company's potential commission. Mr. Bell felt uncomfortable discussing prices in front of other people, and had expected a face-to-face meeting with Mr. Hassan. During this time, Mr. Hassan answered some phone calls and signed some documents. He seemed very adept at handling several things at once.

Finally, when Mr. Hassan's other guests had left with his assistant and Mr. Bell was ready to make his technical presentation, Mr. Hassan asked his secretary to bring another cup of coffee. Apparently, Mr. Hassan wanted to relax Mr. Bell, who was anxious to make his presentation. The secretary brought in the coffee, and Mr. Bell asked if he could have some milk with it. The secretary smiled and said, "Arabian coffee tastes better without milk." By now it was about noon, and Mr. Hassan asked Mr. Bell if he would like to join him and his assistant for dinner tonight; tomorrow Mr. Bell could make his presentation to the technical director and the marketing manager. Mr. Bell agreed and went to his hotel to book his room for two more nights. He then called his headquarters to postpone his next appointment in Italy. It was becoming clear that he might have to stay the entire week.

By this time, Mr. Bell had recognized and felt the sense of time in the Arab business world. He now understood it was necessary for him to slow down when discussing business matters with his Arab partners.

His dinner appointment was not until seven-thirty so he reorganized his presentation for the next day, and then went to the market and bought a nice Arab shirt. Around seven o'clock, he went down to the hotel bar for a drink, where he was soon joined by several other Western businesspeople. Mr. Bell started talking with them and lost track of time. At seven forty-five, Mr. Bell looked at his watch and, realizing he was late, left the bar quickly. While leaving the bar, he met Mr. Hassan and his assistant, who were both formally dressed. Mr. Bell felt uncomfortable not only because he was dressed casually, but he was also late for their appointment.

The next day, Mr. Bell arrived at Mr. Hassan's office at eight forty-five. He was prepared to make his presentation to the marketing manager and the technical director at nine o'clock. Mr. Bell greeted the secretary, calling her by name and using some flattering Arabic phrases he had learned the night before. He also presented Mr. Hassan's assistant with a gift. The assistant thanked him for the gift and put it aside.

Mr. Bell came to the presentation wearing the same Arab shirt he had purchased and worn the night before. He thought he would fit in better if he looked more Arab, but everyone in the office was looking at him strangely. At nine o'clock, Mr. Hassan's assistant accompanied Mr. Bell into a medium-sized conference room. In the room were 15 people waiting to hear Mr. Bell's presentation.

He opened his presentation with a few words in Arabic, and discussed his company's background for 15 minutes. Then he started to show some of his company's products, and everyone moved in very close to look at them, which made Mr. Bell uncomfortable. After that, Mr. Bell moved on to give technical details of the products. Soon after he started, a young man in the audience started questioning him about the specifications. Mr. Bell had not expected to be asked these questions, and therefore did not know the answers.

Then the marketing manager pointed out that several of the products were not applicable to local markets because they didn't fit in with consumer habits. The manager felt that the new product line would have to be adapted to the local markets before he would accept it in his distribution channels.

At this point, Mr. Bell realized that his presentation was the same one he had given in Germany the month before; his marketing department had not made any modifications to reflect the local culture.

At the end of the presentation, Mr. Hassan's assistant accompanied Mr. Bell to Mr. Hassan's office where another guest was in the room. Mr. Hassan greeted him and asked his guest to sit beside him. Mr. Bell was very anxious to close a sale and asked if Mr. Hassan would like to place an order. Mr. Hassan politely told him, "*In sha Allah* (if God wishes), we will do some business." Not knowing this common Arabic phrase, Mr. Bell was unsure if it meant yes or no.

At the end of their meeting, Mr. Hassan told Mr. Bell that his company would write him soon with some good news. Mr. Bell left the office very happy and headed to the airport for his next assignment.

Three months have passed since Mr. Bell visited Cairo, and he has not heard any response from Mr. Hassan's company. He has written twice, received no response, and he wonders what went wrong!

Mr. Bell acted throughout his encounter based on specific American cultural values: directness, action-oriented, and results-oriented. His time frame was not in line with that of his Arab counterpart. Without knowledge of the Arab values of hospitality and building upon personal relations, he continuously encountered culture clashes he could have avoided if he had made an earlier effort to become aware of the differences in American and Arab values. Chapter 3 discusses these differences in detail.

Summary Insights

In this chapter, we presented several examples of challenges often met in business by management, technical, and marketing personnel during intercultural business interactions.

From the moment two people shake hands in a personal introduction to the close of a sale, cultural values influence us and affect the way we do business with others. The examples presented, which included telephone calls, meetings and presentations, as well as training and motivation, indicate the importance of awareness, understanding, and respect of others' cultural values and differences. We expand upon these themes especially in Chapters 5 and 6.

In the next chapter, we explore in greater detail the cultural reasons behind the behaviors that we have discussed.

CHAPTER 3

Valuing Multicultural Diversity

An Overview

To successfully deal with a new culture, whether with a person from a specific company or a different country, you must make an effort to identify their cultural values and inherent priorities, and how they differ from your own. This chapter introduces a new way of evaluating cultural dimensions, thereby expanding understanding of values and how they are different from others. In addition, we present the results of our extensive studies and training among business executive groups from different cultures, and how they define their cultural values and set their priorities.

Following the discovery of one's own values comes the ability to identify the values of others and their priorities. This chapter presents a cultural competence and synergy model, showing how to successfully interact with other cultures.

This chapter also discusses other important elements in our cultural dimensions, such as nonverbal communication, the use of language, space and time orientation, and how these things influence our success or failure in communication across cultures.

Throughout the chapter, we explain the cultural reasons and the roots of "proper" responses according to each person. When you interact cross-culturally, culturally-based responses will make your encounter more successful and enjoyable.

We offer a short quiz, followed by a series of critical incidents to facilitate your understanding of cultural differences.

A Test of Cultural Awareness

True or False

_____ 1. In most Asian cultures, self-sacrifice is important and expected.

_____ 2. When a Chinese person asks if you have had lunch or dinner, he plans to invite you out.

_____ 3. Your educational credentials will be enough when dealing with American executives.

_____ 4. In Arab culture, gifts should be opened in the presence of the giver.

_____ 5. Most of the time, when a Japanese person says "yes, yes," she is confirming her agreement.

_____ 6. Most Americans tend to value spiritual enlightenment more than material possessions.

_____ 7. In Malaysian culture, group achievement is not as important as individual achievement.

_____ 8. In order to work successfully with your Singaporean team, you must first exhibit your technical capability, and then gain their trust.

_____ 9. Most Swedes value risk-taking more than cooperation.

_____ 10. Compliments and well-presented flattery are generally not appreciated in South America.

The response to any of the above and other similar situations is directly related to cultural values. The most appropriate answers to these questions are 1-T, 2-F, 3-F, 4-F, 5-F, 6-F, 7-F, 8-F, 9-F, 10-F.

Defining Culture

- *What is culture? Is it music, art, food . . . ?*
- *What do you value most? Money, freedom, family . . . ?*
- *How do Japanese perceive what Americans value most?*
- *How do Americans perceive what Japanese value most?*

Mr. Tanaka, a Japanese business executive, is meeting with Mr. Mohammed from Saudi Arabia, Mr. McCoy from the United States, and Mr. Rimbaud from France to discuss a possible joint venture. Each person is carrying his own set of cultural baggage, and within each of these bags is a particular type of cultural value. The first bag contains the cultural values of his own country. In the second bag are the values that his company finds most important for successful business. The third bag reflects the cultural values of the person's family, which were learned through observance and teaching by the family members. The fourth bag contains the individual values of each executive, based on his or her personal life experience.

Although each culture has a similar framework for developing cultural values, the priority of these values may differ in each culture. For example, the Japanese would probably put more importance on the company's values because being part of the group in business is generally of higher importance than individual values. In contrast, the American may hold greater regard for personal values instead of the company value system because personal independence is considered important. The Arab executive might do exactly the opposite, however, because his family values are an important guide in Arab culture.

This section introduces you to some critical dimensions of culture, as well as the elements within them—elements that shape our behavior in life and influence our business interactions and success.

Many business executives searching for global success today are embarking on joint ventures in order to expand their market share. This involves technology transfer, training multicultural personnel, extensive cross-cultural telephone communication, and negotiations. Often a person tries to deal with other cultures using his or her own set of cultural values, which have been rewarded all through his or her life. The failure of many of these ventures is not usually due to lack of money or technology, but rather to the cultural difference and misunderstanding of the values of the other person, company, or country.

How would you respond to the question, "What is culture?" Think about this for a minute before you proceed. Is it clothing, food, art . . . ?

During our experiences training executives from many of the world's companies and cultures, we asked the participating managers that same question. We asked them to give their response in a couple of words or short sentences. This question usually surprises the participants and they take time to think about it. After considering many possibilities, most participants came up with the following responses about what defines culture:

- A way of life
- Tradition
- A set of rules
- Art
- Beliefs
- A set of values
- Language
- Food
- Religion

What was your answer? Does it appear on the list above? Which one of the above responses is the "right one?" In everyday life, we cross-culturally communicate with someone, interculturally communicate with a few people, or multiculturally communicate with many people from different cultures. Without a full understanding of that definition and scope of culture, we misinterpret and ignore many cultural dimensions.

All of the responses to the above question are, in fact, true, because culture includes every one of them. From our observations and interaction with so many cultures, we can conclude that the definition of culture is really *culturally defined* based on each person's experience. Moreover, we have noticed that most Asians and Arabs, for example, put more emphasis on past events, using words like "food," "clothes," "art," and "religion," while American and western societies focus more on the present with an eye on the future, mentioning "values," "beliefs," and "behaviors." This explains the time frame by which each society is measured and defined. In American culture, an hour is sixty minutes, but in Arab or Asian cultures, it could last an entire day. When Arabs or South Americans meet, they both start the conversation by mentioning past events. Americans, however, generally focus on current events and keep looking ahead, as evidenced by the common American phrase, "How's it going?" rather than "What did you do last night?"

The European response to the culture question usually includes "art," "music," or "food." Each of these definitions is perfectly correct within each society, but if the European travels outside his boundaries without understanding others' cultures, problems can occur. In order to achieve global success, we must now expand our horizons and understanding of the deep dimensions of culture.

Based on the response of many participants, we suggest that culture is *"The behavioral norms that a group of people, at a certain time and place, have agreed upon to survive and coexist."*

The following list shows the various phrases that the word "culture" brings to mind:

- Language
- Nonverbal communication
- Space and time orientations
- Religion and belief systems
- Pattern of thinking
- Self-images
- Set of values
- Material culture
- Aesthetics

For example, Japanese speak Japanese, Arabs speak Arabic, and Americans speak American English, reflecting one aspect of each of their cultures.

Nonverbal communication is communication in any form other than words that can produce shared meaning and elicit a response. One aspect of this communication is the use of spatial relationships, including the distance people maintain between themselves and others in social interactions, the physical orientation of the body toward others, and the arrangement of environmental space.

For instance, spatial orientations are different in each culture. An American, when speaking with another American in person, will stand about one arm's length away. An Arab, on the other hand, may stand much closer, which tends to make the American uncomfortable. A Japanese may stand further away than either an American or an Arab.

- Steve Johnson, an American business executive, was assigned to his company's Tokyo office. He would be leaving in one year, so he could have time to prepare for life in Japan. In that year, Steve vigorously studied the Japanese language with his American team until he had a good understanding of it. However, when he finally arrived in Japan, he found himself in numerous cultural clashes responding to Japanese nonverbal communication such as bowing or smiling back even before he left the Tokyo airport. All he thought it took to work effectively in Japan was to just learn the language. Apparently, he didn't consider many of the other cultural dimensions listed.

In American culture, religion is not usually discussed and is considered a private pursuit. However, as you'll see in the next example, religion plays a vital role in Arab culture, influencing most decisions in life or business.

When Professor Murayama left his university office in Osaka for Cairo, he had studied some of the history of Egypt and learned a great deal of the language. Upon arriving in Cairo, though, Professor Murayama discovered that there was a strong emphasis on religion for which he was not prepared. Lunch breaks usually took over ninety minutes, to allow time for midday prayer. He had to adjust his working schedule accordingly. Professor Murayama didn't realize that Arabs use faith as an important motivational tool.

Another cultural dimension is the pattern of thinking used by each culture. Most Americans, for example, are logical and straightforward in their thinking. Many Japanese, however, pattern their thinking around group interaction, while those in Arab cultures use emotion to form their thoughts.

The self-image of each culture is another aspect to consider. Most Japanese think of themselves as being members of a group, company, nation, and family rather than as independent individuals. Americans, conversely, think of themselves as unique individuals, independent and equal. Arabs have a self-image of being part of a family, a religious group, and a rich cultural heritage.

The set of cultural values are an abstract set of ideals that represent what is expected, required, or forbidden. Values affect a person's priorities and attitudes about which forms of behavior are appropriate in any given situation.

Within specific cultures there exist many subcultures. As we mentioned earlier in this section, Mr. McCoy is an American, carrying American cultural baggage, but he also works for United Steel, which has its own set of company values. Moreover, he is affected by the cultural norms of his family, school, and unique life experiences.

- On the other side, Mr. Tanaka was born in Japan and since birth, he has been affected by a different set of cultural norms through his family, school, and so forth. In cross-cultural interactions, he naturally uses the values he learned throughout his life, and because they are so instinctive to him, he is convinced that they are the right values. Naturally, another person will feel that his own cultural norms are correct. This can lead to a cultural clash because both parties expect the other to conform.

As stated, culture is not a word, but rather "behavioral norms that a group of people, at a certain time and place, have agreed upon to survive or coexist." However, this norm must change for that group to survive in new environments. Even within one culture, cultural values change between generations in order to adjust and survive in new environments.

Material culture is the set of cultural habits built around products we have based on new technology. Items such as televisions, computers, and cars are all things that change our behavioral norms and therefore influence our cultural values. In the near future, advances in computer-interface technology may change education from group to individual learning values.

Although all human beings have a natural love for beauty and fine arts, their reflection of these also varies across cultures. Looking at Japanese art, for example, gives you insight into that culture.

In the next section, we focus on and discuss important elements of our culture: value systems, self-image, nonverbal communication, use of language, and space and time orientation, and we examine the contrasts of different cultures in order to demonstrate the differences, but not to choose a definite right or wrong culture.

Cultural Values

- *What are three top American values?*
- *What are three top Japanese values?*
- *Why do differences exist between the two?*
- *Why do many Arabs begin business interactions by mentioning past relationships?*
- *Why do most Japanese managers often respond to your request by saying "yes, yes"?*

Let us examine the following situations in order to point out the differences in values across cultures and their influence on daily business interactions:

- Scott Thompson, marketing director for a high-tech firm in California, holds a meeting between himself, Mr. Noguchi from Japan, and Mr. Samir, the local manager of a Japanese company in Saudi Arabia, to discuss a new marketing plan for Global Telephone.

During the discussion, Mr. Thompson asks Mr. Noguchi if he approves of the new product feature that he designed in California. Mr. Noguchi replies, "Yes, it's very interesting." "Does that mean you like it?" Mr. Thompson asked. Mr. Noguchi answers, while looking to his team members, "I must discuss this with my group." While Mr. Thompson tries to extract an answer from Mr. Noguchi, Mr. Samir interrupts to try to mediate the conflict between the other two. Mr. Samir changes the subject to future market shares and proposes that Mr. Thompson and Mr. Noguchi visit Saudi Arabia to further explore the market.

This scenario is typical of multicultural business clashes that occur between people from diverse cultural backgrounds. What was in Mr. Thompson's cultural baggage that influenced him during that short interaction? Was it group harmony, directness, or privacy? In fact, Mr. Thompson has been applying his values of openness, directness, and action orientation. How about Mr. Noguchi? Why was he reluctant to give an immediate direct response to Mr. Thompson? What was it that influenced him? Seniority, formality, reputation, or group consensus? Group harmony and consensus are important to Mr. Noguchi and so he abstained from giving his answer until he had the chance to discuss the matter with his Japanese team. Why did Mr. Samir interrupt to suggest a visit to his country? Was it because his baggage valued competition, compromising, risk-taking, or hospitality? Relationship and compromising were important to Mr. Samir and so he was trying to mediate the situation to avoid loss of face.

Most of life's interactions are based on several sets of cultural values developed since childhood. This set of values has been accumulated, rewarded, and enforced by our family, our community, our company, and our country. These values differ from country to country, and even within a country, its companies, and finally each person.

Let us now discover the following:

- *What do Americans value most?*
- *What do Japanese value most?*
- *What do Malaysians value most?*
- *What do Chinese value most?*
- *What do Arabs value most?*

During our multicultural management skills development training for business managers, we asked participants to list some of the important values in their society, as well as what they felt other societies valued. Table 3.1a lists some answers we obtained from both a Japanese group and a Malaysian group who were each asked what they thought were important Japanese values.

Table 3.1a
Values of Culture

What Japanese Value Most, According To Themselves and Malaysians	
Japanese	Malaysians
Information	Technology
Harmony	Lasting friendship
Honesty	Loyalty
Options	Excellence
Loyalty	Achievement
Social status	Tradition
Tradition	Consensus
Respect	Group harmony
Company	Respect
Status	Supremacy
Relationship	Pride
Job	Productivity
Cooperation	Integrity
Society	Profit
Hard work	Country loyalty
Politeness	Sacrifices
Family	Economic power
Modesty	Trust
Uniformity	Hard work
Adjustment	Group decision

As you may notice from the Table 3.1a, the Japanese have certain ideas about what they value, and the Malaysians reiterated some of the same values. However, the Malaysians also mentioned some other values about the Japanese that are not on the Japanese list. For example, the Japanese participants list the values of harmony, loyalty, and relationship. The Malaysians concur with these items. The Malaysians, however, also list profit, self-pride, and supremacy as important Japanese values. These are values that the Japanese apparently didn't think they valued as much, but the Malaysians thought they did. These differences involving perception can cause many of the cultural clashes.

Table 3.1b presents what a Japanese group felt were the top American, Chinese, and Arab cultural values. As noted in the table, this group probably knows more about American culture and less about Chinese and Arab cultures. When Japan closed its doors to

Table 3.1b
Values of Culture

What Japanese Say Other Cultures Value		
Americans	Chinese	Arabs
Personal life	Bicycles	Religion
Wealth	History	Allah
Fairness	Health	Koran
One answer	Obeying power	Status
Family	Family	History
Liberty	Money	Family
Materials	Age	Nationality
Education	Civilization	Islam
Time	Gold	Moustache
Frontier spirit	Relationships	Gold
Success	Respect	
Dreams	Group	
Freedom	Food	
Directness		
Money		
Reasons		
Religion		
Power		

the outside world for a 300-year period, it conformed to one culture—Japanese. When the doors were reopened, the main cultural influence on them was from American sources, so the culture most familiar to the Japanese other than their own is the "American Way."

Reviewing the Japanese list of American values, we find it is fairly accurate, especially in listing success, directness, frontier spirit, and such. Looking at the Japanese list of Chinese values, however, it is obvious that the Japanese view of the Chinese is limited to tradition, history, money, and controlling power.

On the other side of the world, we find that the Japanese people's knowledge of Arab culture is almost entirely limited to religion. This response gives us an indication of the reason for the cultural clashes that Japanese businesspeople encounter when traveling to Arabia without proper multicultural training and preparation. In fact, when they leave Japan with such limited perceptions, many of the Japanese try to deal with Chinese and Arabs by applying American values that they see as applicable to most other cultures, but which are not. Then the Japanese are faced with unpredictable responses, as clearly the Arab and Chinese people have different cultural values than the Americans.

The knowledge and feelings of the Malaysian culture, based on what they know about the values of the American, Chinese, and Arab cultures, are shown in Table 3.1c.

In this context, Malaysians, like the Japanese, have fairly accurately predicted many of the American values, such as openness, individuality, freedom, human rights, and so on. We see that the Malaysians were able, due to their historical relationship, to list some important Chinese values as well: self-sacrifice, status, survival, and affiliation—that the Japanese group failed to predict; the Malaysians also pointed out the Chinese desire for superiority and material prosperity.

On the Arab list, the Malaysians came up with more basic Arab values than the Japanese, such as family security, social grouping, status, and, of course, religion.

This expanded knowledge of the Malaysians about other cultures may be a factor in their current success when communicating and attracting foreign investors, such as Chinese, American, Japanese, Arab, and so on.

Table 3.1c
Values of Culture

What Malaysians Say Other Cultures Value		
Americans	Chinese	Arabs
Success	Money	Family
Power	Wealth	Community
Adherence	Hard work	Wealth
Material possessions	Facing hardships	Brotherhood
Openness	Gambling/investing	Respect
Profit	Status	Power
Individualism	Self-sacrifices	Social-grouping
Time	Business	Religion
Commitments	Success	Status
Individual freedom	Survival	Leisure
Money	Affiliation	Traditions
Aggression	Group interaction	Self-image
Realism	Material prosperity	Friendship
Logic	Superiority	
Ultimate power		
Innovation		
Human rights		
Progress		

Priorities of Cultural Values

What do you value most? How do your priorities influence your day-to-day activities, especially those relating to your business work? Begin answering these questions by filling out Table 3.2, which lists values that are common to most international cultures, but their importance varies from group to group.

In the column titled "10," select your ten highest values. From these ten, choose the top five that are most important to you; mark these in the column titled "5." From these five mark the top three, and from these three decide on your top value. Keep these values in mind as you proceed through this chapter.

During our management training we asked participants to prioritize the 20 values mentioned in the above exercise. Tables 3.2a-e list the top five values of several cultures; the values were obtained from surveys. Compare the values with those you selected for yourself.

Table 3.2
Shared Cultural Values

	10	5	3	1
1. Group harmony	—	—	—	—
2. Competition	—	—	—	—
3. Seniority	—	—	—	—
4. Cooperation	—	—	—	—
5. Privacy	—	—	—	—
6. Openness	—	—	—	—
7. Equality	—	—	—	—
8. Formality	—	—	—	—
9. Risk-taking	—	—	—	—
10. Reputation	—	—	—	—
11. Freedom	—	—	—	—
12. Family security	—	—	—	—
13. Relationships	—	—	—	—
14. Self-reliance	—	—	—	—
15. Time	—	—	—	—
16. Group consensus	—	—	—	—
17. Authority	—	—	—	—
18. Material possession	—	—	—	—
19. Spirituality	—	—	—	—
20. Group achievement	—	—	—	—

Table 3.2a presents the contrasts in the priority of values among Americans, Swedes, Russians, and French. What is most startling about Table 3.2a is the similarity of the values of each country. First, each western nation values freedom. While it is not surprising that

Table 3.2a
Priority of Values

American	Swedish	Russian	French
Equality	Freedom	Family	Self-reliance
Freedom	Relationships	Freedom	Freedom
Openness	Cooperation	Self-reliance	Openness
Self-reliance	Family	Openness	Relationships
Cooperation	Openness	Possessions	Time

Americans should do so, note that even Russia, the most powerful component of the former Soviet Union, cherishes freedom.

Each culture also places high priority on openness. This may have a serious effect on cross-cultural business relationships: Foreign companies expanding their operations into these countries will want to be frank with their employees; they will also benefit from honest negotiations. Drastic changes in objectives, which indicate behind-the-scenes instability, will upset western partners and associates.

Also, the importance of self-reliance cannot be over stressed. And so when working with Americans, French, and Russians, allow them to express their individuality and creativity. Self-reliance leads, after all, to problem-solving: Your western employees may not expect your advice for certain tasks and will most likely contact their superiors directly when they need assistance.

American cultural values can be seen in television and film, as well as in laws and institutions. These values include directness, openness, self-reliance, and independence.

Let's compare the values of the five eastern groups covered in Table 3.2b with western values. Whereas self-reliance is of great importance to westerners, easterners, in general, place emphasis on relationships, group harmony, cooperation, family, and spirituality.

Also take note of relationships and group harmony, values which can greatly effect organizational dynamics. If your Japanese or Indonesian joint venture partners expect group harmony, be careful not to upset them by emphasizing open conflict. On the other hand,

Table 3.2b
Priority of Values

Japanese	Korean	Indonesian	Malaysian	Filipino
Relationships	Family	Relationships	Family	Family
Group harmony	Cooperation	Family	Group harmony	Spirituality
Family	Relationships	Reputation	Cooperation	Reputation
Freedom	Group harmony	Cooperation	Relationships	Cooperation
Cooperation	Spirituality	Group harmony	Spirituality	Freedom

constructive conflict with cooperative attitude can produce effective results, so avoid allowing group harmony to develop into group think.

As with all cultures, successfully interacting with your Asian partners and associates requires the ability to balance several opposing cultural tendencies.

Arabs and Thais, as shown in Table 3.2c, are more inclined to put their trust in senior authorities. Therefore, a western company beginning operations in the Middle East or Thailand, for example, may need to change its current culture and implement different procedures for managing new employees. Whereas American employees may feel intruded upon by watchful supervisors, their Arab and Thai peers will expect more advice and feedback.

Table 3.2c
Priority of Values

Thai	Arab
Seniority	Seniority
Reputation	Spirituality
Relationships	Reputation
Cooperation	Family
Authority	Authority

The values listed in Table 3.2d are those of the four main groups of Chinese in Asia. Note that although there are many common values, such as reputation, family security, cooperation, and relationships, the values do vary quite significantly.

Table 3.2d
Priority of Values

Chinese	Taiwanese	Hong Kong	Singaporean
Equality	Competition	Competition	Relationships
Freedom	Family security	Relationships	Family security
Family security	Reputation	Reputation	Openness
Group harmony	Seniority	Time	Cooperation
Cooperation	Authority	Possessions	Freedom

Chinese from Taiwan and Hong Kong, for example, both classify competition as most important, and reputation as third. Both also value wealth and authority. As the list from Singapore indicates, the culture of that tiny island republic is the most westernized of the groups: It places great values on openness, freedom, and equality.

It's important to understand, moreover, that these values can have quite different meanings as a result of the divergent ways in which they are interpreted by the various social systems. In Singapore, for example, freedom and equality are best understood in terms of western influence. The mainland Chinese also value equality, but only in the sense of the equal sharing of work and profit under the current social system.

This definition of equality contrasts with the American notion (adopted by Singaporeans), which really involves equality of opportunity. To the Chinese in China, freedom may be a reflection of their desire to free themselves of their current economy and move toward an open-market system. While Americans also place freedom second, they interpret it as freedom of individual choice.

All across national boundaries, most Chinese adhere to traditional values of family, group harmony, and cooperation. These contrast with the American emphasis on openness and self-reliance. The value of family is listed in all the Chinese groups except Hong Kong, a fast-paced environment in which there is less time to value family. In fact, Hong Kong is the only Chinese culture to place a high priority on time.

Singaporean Chinese value relationships highly, probably as a result of their living in a diverse culture with Malay and Indian elements. Singapore's open-market society and advanced modernization are probable reasons why Singapore Chinese place a greater value on openness, equality, and freedom than do respondents from Hong Kong or Taiwan.

In Taiwan, competition is regarded highly, a reflection of the emphasis on hard work. This is a traditional Confucian value, but it is not high on the value list of Chinese from the mainland, where the current social system guarantees social services.

The Taiwanese regard for reputation, seniority, and authority are best understood as a reflection of the fact that Taiwan is a small country that survives under strong leadership and the constant threat of extinction from the mainland. Although Americans have been in Taiwan for decades, few American values have been incorporated by the Taiwanese, in strong contrast to the situation in Singapore.

The variance in values among Chinese from the mainland, Hong Kong, Singapore, and Taiwan reflects diverse patterns of social change, economic policy, and political history. Westerners, as well as Chinese, must attune themselves to the subtle impact of these diverse values if they hope to establish business relationships and take advantage of opportunities with the Chinese.

As Table 3.2e shows, the new generation of managers from Japan and Thailand have assimilated western values pervasive in international business. These include self-reliance, freedom, and equality.

This trend should not be a surprise. For as international businesses have grown, they have often adopted western corporate models, as well as western technologies. This change in values must be addressed before working with Asian companies. You may have to expand your understanding of Japanese culture, for example, to include not only the traits of senior and traditional leaders, but also the young middle managers and associates whose input is often quite important to decision makers. Cultures change over time in order to survive in new environments.

Values Across Cultures

To explain the cultural value contrast more clearly, we developed Table 3.3, which compares specific contrasting values of American,

Table 3.2e
Priority of Values

Japanese		Thais	
Traditional	**New Generation**	**Traditional**	**New Generation**
Relationships	Freedom	Seniority	Reputation
Group harmony	Relationships	Reputation	Family security
Family	Family	Relationships	Relationships
Freedom	Equality	Cooperation	Cooperation
Cooperation	Self-reliance	Authority	Self-reliance

Japanese, and Arab cultures. Reading across the table from left to right provides perspective on the values of each culture.

In examining Table 3.3, we note that one of the top American values listed is freedom—freedom to choose your own destiny—whether it leads to success or failure. Japanese culture, on the other hand, finds a higher value in belonging. In this culture, you must belong to and support a group(s) to survive. Belonging to a group is more important to Japanese culture than individualism. Arab culture is less concerned with individualism or belonging to a group, concentrating instead on maintaining their own family security and relying on Allah for destiny. Individual identity is usually based on the background and position of each person's family.

Table 3.3
Cultural Contrasts in Value

Americans	Japanese	Arabs
1. Freedom	1. Belonging	1. Family security
2. Independence	2. Group harmony	2. Family harmony
3. Self-reliance	3. Collectiveness	3. Parental guidance
4. Equality	4. Age/seniority	4. Age
5. Individualism	5. Group consensus	5. Authority
6. Competition	6. Cooperation	6. Compromise
7. Efficiency	7. Quality	7. Devotion
8. Time	8. Patience	8. Very patient
9. Directness	9. Indirectness	9. Indirectness
10. Openness	10. Go-between	10. Hospitality
11. Aggressiveness	11. Interpersonal	11. Friendship
12. Informality	12. Hierarchy	12. Formal/ admiration
13. Future-orientation	13. Continuation	13. Past and present
14. Risk-taking	14. Conservative	14. Religious belief
15. Creativity	15. Information	15. Tradition
16. Self-accomplishment	16. Group achievement	16. Social recognition
17. Winning	17. Success	17. Reputation
18. Money	18. Relationship	18. Friendship
19. Material possessions	19. Harmony with nature	19. Belonging
20. Privacy	20. Networking	20. Family network

The value American culture places on independence and individual freedom of choice naturally leads to the idea that everyone is equal regardless of age, social status, or authority. Japanese and Arab cultures, however, place more value on age and seniority. The Japanese individual will always give way to the feelings of the group, while Arabs respect authority and admire seniority and status.

In most business situations, Americans would come with a competitive attitude. The Japanese, conversely, value group cooperation in the pursuit of success. An Arab will make compromises in order to achieve a shared goal between two parties.

In American culture, the phrase "time is money" is commonly accepted as a framework for the desire to finish a task in the shortest amount of time with the greatest profit. If a process is considered inefficient, it "wastes" time and money, and possibly will be abandoned. The Japanese, however, value high quality over immediate gain, and they patiently wait for the best possible result. Arab culture also values quality more than immediacy, but the trust in the business relationship is the most important value.

Americans emphasize individual achievement and are results-oriented; therefore, they value directness and openness when dealing with others, enabling individuals to finish tasks more quickly. Because of these values of directness and equality, Americans tend to be informal when speaking and writing, often using first names. The Japanese prefer to follow an indirect, harmonious style when dealing with others. Go-betweens help to move the process along, and interpersonal harmony is considered more important than confrontation. The Arab culture, like the Japanese, avoids direct confrontation. However, Arabs prefer to negotiate directly in the spirit of hospitality and friendship until a compromise is reached.

Americans tend to be oriented toward the present and immediate gains, which explains why Americans value taking risks. To an American, accomplishing a task as quickly as possible brings the future closer. The Japanese, however, view time as a continuum, and are long-term oriented. As a result of their value of a long-term, quality-based relationship, the Japanese tend to be conservative and patient. The Arab culture believes that the present is a continuation of the past and that whatever happens in the future is due to fate and the will of Allah.

A principal value of American culture is individual achievement. When someone accomplishes something by him or herself, he or she expects and receives recognition for being a creative person, or the one who developed the best idea. The Japanese, because of their value of group achievement, seek information in order to help the entire group succeed. In Arab culture, the individual is not as important as preserving tradition. An Arab measures success by social recognition, status, honor, and reputation.

Images of Cultures

Self-image, or how we see ourselves, is a way of expressing our cultural identity. Cultural self-image tells us who we think we are and how we can distinguish "us" from "them." By asking someone from a culture what it means to be an American, Japanese, or Arab, a list of cultural characteristics emerges that gives us a good description of what that particular culture values and how it sees itself in relation to other cultures.

Of course, how we see ourselves is not the same thing as how others see us. What we see as natural, normal, and even ideal, other cultures see as different. To the extent that "your cultural values overlap with mine, your image of my culture will be positive. To the extent that our values differ or conflict, your image of my culture will be negative."

To clarify the differences in each culture's set of priorities, and how these sets influence our cultural behavior, we asked several groups of manager-participants to draw what we call a "cultural postcard." The postcard was designed to represent what someone from a particular culture thinks of other cultures as well as their own.

The images drawn by the participants clearly represented the perceptions of a person or group from outside that culture. In our daily interaction with people or groups from different cultures, we may have certain stereotyped images of the other culture. However, the deeper one interacts with and becomes a part of a different cultural group, the more one understands the norms and priorities of that culture, and in turn, is able to interact successfully with them.

Cultural Competence

From the outside, a tree grown in California would probably look just like a tree grown in Japan. However, the growth of each tree is largely dependent on the soil that the roots of the trees have to "interact" with to grow. The strength of the roots is also dependent on the environment the tree is exposed to, from sunshine to thunderstorms. Imagine the values of a particular culture represented as the roots of a tree. These roots (values) are the source of strength needed by the tree to survive in the surrounding environment (society). Of course, we don't really see the roots, but we are constantly exposed to the tree nevertheless. The type of fertilizer and water fed to the tree contributes significantly to the growth of it (reward). In addition, you cannot transplant a tree into other soil unless you prepare the roots for the new soil.

The roots of each tree may have a different form, much like the cultures they represent. The Japanese roots are twisted together because they may have rockier soil and need the combined strength of the roots to support the tree during rough weather. The American roots, however, are individual, separate, straight, and deep, responding to their soil condition.

Using this model, we see that these roots present the sets of individual, company, or country values, which produce a certain type of society (branches, leaves, and flowers). In that sense you cannot ask a Swede or Russian used to being rewarded/punished by a specific set of values to immediately comply with a new set. In the same way, an American executive cannot ask a Malaysian company worker to comply fully with his American set of values while dealing with him.

A successful culturally competent person must be aware of his or her own priorities, as well as those of his or her country or society, and reorganize them properly to achieve group success. That person must also make an attempt, in initial dealings with the other culture, to adhere to and respect the other system. When they are accepted by the group, then they can slowly introduce their own set of values to the other group. If both sides recognize the new values as necessary for coexistence, then they will be accepted, and cultural synergy will naturally occur.

Figure 3.1 proposes that all of our behaviors in business or social life are influenced by both our belief systems, such as life, death, religion, and nature, plus our rewarded values. These beliefs are taken by human beings as accepted norms, and it takes a major crisis to change them.

However, our set of values changes according to the group or societal system of rewards and punishment. In the American system, for example, the values of independence, competition, and risk-taking are rewarded, enhanced, and encouraged by the group. If an executive working in the United States tries to introduce group harmony, seniority, and status as prime values for his business success, he will probably be discouraged and be forced to comply with the

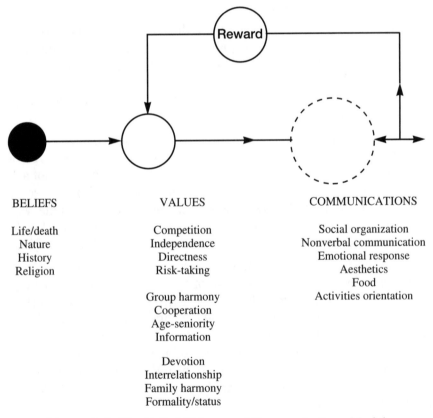

BELIEFS	VALUES	COMMUNICATIONS
Life/death	Competition	Social organization
Nature	Independence	Nonverbal communication
History	Directness	Emotional response
Religion	Risk-taking	Aesthetics
		Food
	Group harmony	Activities orientation
	Cooperation	
	Age-seniority	
	Information	
	Devotion	
	Interrelationship	
	Family harmony	
	Formality/status	

Figure 3.1. The Belief, Values, and Communications Model.

more valued system of American independence, openness, direct-ness, and risk-taking.

By contrast, many of the Japanese reward systems are based on group harmony, group consensus, and group achievement. If a Japanese executive were to attempt to introduce self-reliance, indi-vidual competition, and risk-taking into the Japanese work environ-ment, he would more than likely be disparaged within his culture.

Building one's cultural sensitivity requires that we enhance three important input sensors of the human being. As shown in Figure 3.2, these are listening, watching, and feelings, or Phase I. During our interactions, most of us filter the messages coming to us, either verbal or nonverbal. We usually like to hear what we want and filter out what we don't like. As discussed, the use of language and non-verbal communication plays an important factor in our cross-cultural encounters and understanding.

In addition to listening, we must expand our vision to see beyond what is directly in front of us. However, the most important feature in building cultural competence is to stimulate our feelings when we interact with other people, even within our own cultural group. These three elements represent a dynamic process that we must use to expand our understanding of other cultures. If this input is sufficient then it must be followed by Phase II, in which we react and participate with other persons or groups.

A good analogy is the food and water that our physical body requires: If it is the proper food, our body takes the time to digest it

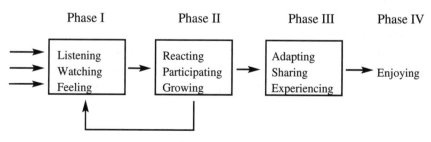

Figure 3.2. The Cross-cultural Joy Model.

and this results in physical growth. If Phases I and II are successful, then in Phase III a person should be able to adapt and, most importantly, to share the experience with others in a more enjoyable way, demonstrated by the output of the dynamic cross-cultural joy model.

In some cultures, such as the Japanese, the elements of Phase I— listening, watching, and feeling—are highly valued and practiced. In business meetings, for example, most Japanese would listen, watch, and sense the thoughts of their foreign partner more than they would respond directly. Within the Japanese culture, in Phase II, they will participate, react to new ideas, and come up with agreed-upon decisions adapted to their own values.

On the other hand, American cultural values may put less emphasis on listening and watching, and instead put more on Phase II, fast reaction and participation, which again would not necessarily result in a true cultural synergy due to an inability to adapt adequately to other cultures, most often due to the wrong input. The proposed process is, in fact, an ideal way to achieve cultural synergy and requires extensive awareness and skill development.

Nonverbal Communication

- *Why does she keep raising her voice? I can hear her perfectly.*
- *This is just a working meeting. Why is he wearing a suit?*
- *He keeps staring at me. What's wrong?*
- *Every time I meet him, he wants to shake my hand.*

Nonverbal communication represents an important element of our cultural dimension. Each culture has its own unique system of nonverbal messages, whether it is the use of hand gestures, tone of voice, or even physical contact such as a pat on the back or a handshake. Let us now discover some elements of cross-cultural nonverbal messages.

Shaking hands is a form of nonverbal communication that nearly every businessperson uses. When, and in what context, the handshake is used shows the difference between cultures. For example:

Most Americans expect to shake hands

(a) When they meet for the first time.
(b) Before they leave for work.
(c) In the morning.
(d) Only if you extend your hand first.

In American culture, first-time greetings are almost always accompanied by a firm handshake. This is used to show a sense of equality and sincerity between the two people involved in the greeting.

Americans use hand and arm gestures sparingly to add emphasis, but in most gestures the elbow does not go above shoulder level, as it may in other cultures. Americans tend to make eye contact when beginning and ending their speech. This factor establishes their directness, sincerity, and equality, which are important values in American culture.

Within the Japanese culture, the proper form of nonverbal expression during a greeting is not a handshake, but a bow. The depth, duration, and repetition of the bow reflect the communicator's social status. Physical distance between those involved is maintained, and contact is avoided.

In Arab culture a greeting between close friends often consists of the two people hugging each other. A greeting between strangers, however, is usually just a handshake.

Other forms of nonverbal communication in American culture that demonstrate the value of equality can be measured in many different ways. Consider this situation:

You are visiting the United States for the first time. You notice that most Americans stand in line at theaters, supermarkets, bus stations, etc. This indicates that they

(a) Are formal and believe in one status.
(b) Like to maintain harmony with everyone.
(c) Do not believe in competition.
(d) Believe in equality.

Americans wait in line with others because one of their top cultural values is equality. Standing in line demonstrates a value that Americans learn in childhood—that every person has the same chance at something. They wait for their turn when others before them are waiting for the same thing. The line scenario would probably not happen in Arabic cultures, where status is a top value. Someone who has higher status than another would not wait in line with the other person because he would feel uncomfortable.

Japanese culture also has many forms of nonverbal communication that are also unique to their way of life and which are used as values to guide them through every situation. What role does smiling play in Japanese culture, for example?

In a meeting with a Japanese team, you notice that one of the managers has a continuous smile on his face. This means

(a) He likes what you are saying.
(b) He feels sorry for you.
(c) You should smile back.
(d) He is reacting to what you are saying.

The Japanese tend to communicate with little eye contact, few facial expressions, and almost no hand gestures. Especially in negative situations, an expressionless face is considered highly desirable. A smile, however, is often used to mask embarrassment or discomfort in certain situations.

On the other hand, an Arab smiles to show hospitality and a desire for friendship. Americans have essentially the same use for smiling.

Nonverbal messages do not always have to be visual, as this situation demonstrates:

You are discussing a subject with a Japanese team. Suddenly everyone is quiet. You should

(a) Tell a joke to wake them up.
(b) Give your discount now.
(c) Be quiet too.
(d) Ask them what the problem is.

In Japan, silence is a virtue, and most conversations contain periods of silence during which each participant tries to sense the thoughts and feelings of the other. Therefore, the answer is to be quiet too. Such use of silence would probably not work in American culture, however, because Americans, with their directness and openness, feel uncomfortable with prolonged periods of silence.

Arabs, on the other hand, value hospitality, family, friendship, and religion, and use these values when making decisions. The Arab culture has many nonverbal messages as well, such as the use of hand gestures and tone of voice. For example, consider this scenario:

You are discussing a business proposal with two Arabs in their office. You notice that their tone of voice changes depending on the subject matter. Should you

(a) Keep your tone of voice quiet?
(b) Go along with their high/low tone?
(c) Use a higher tone to impress them further?
(d) Tell them they are speaking too loudly?

In Arab culture, increased pitch or volume while speaking indicates heightened emotional involvement or interest in the subject. Therefore, to interact successfully with them, it would be a good idea to follow their high/low speech style.

Another Arab nonverbal message involves the important Arab value of hospitality, as in the following case:

After finishing your visit to an Arab company, the president offers to escort you to your car. He is offering this gesture in order to

(a) Discuss privately the final commissions.
(b) Further express his hospitality.
(c) Show his competitors next door that he has a contract with you.
(d) Give you a last chance to offer that discount he has been seeking.

Hospitality is a top Arab value. The president wishes to establish a relationship with you and, therefore, is friendly and hospitable in order to achieve his goal. An American company president, using his cultural value of privacy, may make the offer to walk you to your car, but will most likely do so to discuss the deal with you out of earshot of the other staff members.

Use of Language

- *Hi, how are you?*
- *Drop by my house for a visit sometime.*
- *Yes, yes.*
- *What can I do for you?*
- *Please, have a cup of coffee.*

Use of language is perhaps one of the most obvious barriers in cross-cultural communication—the problems of communicating in a language different than your own go beyond learning to translate a set of words. Language defines culture and structures our patterns of thinking, our perceptions, and our very concepts of reality. Ideally, each of us should know at least something about our intercultural partners' language. Of course, it is impossible to speak every language, but being aware of the differences is the first step to increasing the effectiveness of that communication. Let us consider the following:

This is your first week in an American office. Your American co-worker says to you, "Let's get together sometime this week." You should

(a) Accept it as a friendly comment.
(b) Invite him to your house to meet your family.
(c) Tell your spouse to prepare to have dinner with your co-worker.
(d) Expect the American to invite you to play tennis this weekend.

Americans often say things just to be friendly, sometimes without actually intending to follow through. When they say, "Let's get together," it could mean they want to do something with you, but it is generally used to indicate their desire to keep in touch with you or as a polite ending to a conversation, so you should accept the statement as a friendly comment.

In contrast, if an American said, "Let's get together" to a Japanese acquaintance, the Japanese person would probably plan to have dinner or do some other activity with the American soon. The formal way the Japanese use language is quite the opposite of the casual American style.

You are calling an American businesswoman on the telephone. She immediately says, "Yes, what can I do for you?" You should respond by saying

(a) "Thank you, I don't need your help."
(b) "Where is the order you promised me?"
(c) "You are too impersonal."
(d) "How was your weekend?"

Because American culture places a high value on directness, your answer should be geared toward finding out where your order is, if that is the reason for your call. A response to the point would be the expected procedure for dealing in American business, and would not be considered rude. In Arab culture, a person might begin the conversation by asking how your weekend was, but in American culture that is not related to the task at hand and would be considered irrelevant. Let's explore the way the Japanese might approach the following:

On your visit to Japan, you noticed that most Japanese people say "Excuse me" when they approach you or begin a conversation. This is common because

(a) Japanese value independence.
(b) They are always in a rush.
(c) They try to maintain harmony.
(d) Japanese do not like surprises.

Many Japanese may say "Excuse me" when beginning conversations because they do not like surprises, and prefacing a comment with "Excuse me" helps to maintain group harmony.

In a discussion with a Japanese businessman, if he nods his head and says, "Yes, yes," he

(a) Understands what you are saying.
(b) Agrees with what you are saying.

(c) Is listening.
(d) Is bored.

When a Japanese person says "yes, yes," he is usually indicating that he is listening to what you are saying or follows along with your train of thought. It doesn't necessarily mean, as in American culture, that he agrees with your statement.

You are calling your Arab business contact on the telephone. He says "When will I see you?" You answer,

(a) "God willing we will meet again soon."
(b) "Any time you wish."
(c) "I will call you when I am ready."
(d) "Give me an order and I will come to deliver it myself."

Arab culture values religion and hospitality, therefore your response should be along those lines of "God willing we will meet again soon." An American, who values directness, might say something like, "I will call you when I've got the information." This would be insulting to the Arab person, though, because he was showing his hospitality to the caller, and to not reciprocate the same sentiment would be rude.

In discussing commissions with your Arab partner, he will probably

(a) Tell you straightforwardly that he wants a 25 percent commission.
(b) Talk about the expense of distribution systems in Saudi Arabia.
(c) Tell his assistant to inform you how much he is willing to accept.
(d) Give you his requested commission in writing.

Arab business values the indirect approach when conducting business. Therefore, when discussing commissions, instead of saying straight out what he feels, he will often discuss the general market value of the product, and then indirectly come to an agreement. How would the answer differ between two Americans?

Space and Time Orientation

- *Our meeting was at ten o'clock but it's ten forty-five, and he's still talking with the previous visitor. Should I wait or leave?*
- *The invitation was for dinner at seven o'clock. What time should I show up?*
- *Time is money. Does that mean save it or spend it?*
- *When she said, "I'll get back to you," does that mean in an hour, a day, a week? When?*

How space is used and what that use signifies vary from culture to culture. Some cultures require a larger "comfort zone" of interpersonal space than others. Most people are unaware of how their own culture structures spatial relationships, and therefore do not take this factor into account when interacting with other cultures in business. Crosscultural violations of spatial requirements can produce discomfort, anxiety, hostility, and even conflict, often without the participants understanding why they feel their territory has been invaded.

Like space, time has different meanings in each culture. How the culture defines time, and what value it gives to the past, present, and future, communicates just as surely as words. The vocabulary, grammar, and meaning of time vary widely around the world.

In this section, we discuss both space and time orientation by offering different scenarios using the American, Arab, and Japanese cultures.

You are visiting your American partner's office, and have seated yourself in the conference room. When he joins you he will probably

(a) Sit on your right side.
(b) Sit on your left side.
(c) Sit in front of you.
(d) Wait for your invitation to sit.

The seating in American business meetings is usually set up in a face-to-face manner, placing the participants directly across from each other, exhibiting equality and competition. In Arab culture, your business contact, depending on his status, will probably sit next to you.

You have received a fax from an American company asking for a price quotation. They are expecting your reply

(a) By return fax.
(b) By phone.
(c) By regular mail.
(d) In about one week.

Most Americans, as you know by now, value directness and often use the phrase "time is money." This means that when dealing in business, any time not spent directly on solving the task at hand is considered wasted. Therefore, the Americans probably expect you to fax or even call back as soon as possible. In dealing with Japanese or Arabs, it will take a longer time for the response, and will probably be by mail.

Japanese culture values modesty, group achievement, and group harmony, which can be seen in their use of open space in the business environment. It is different than workplaces in other cultures, and has the potential to cause a cultural clash as seen from the following example:

You are on a training assignment at a Japanese company in Tokyo. They offer you a desk in the middle of a big hall with 15 other staff members. Will you

(a) Ask for a special room because you are used to working in a quiet office?
(b) Ask for a portable wall to keep others from looking at you?
(c) Accept the offer?
(d) Ask for a corner location away from traffic?

The Japanese workplace is usually a large hall with many desks in it. The open space plan in most Japanese companies reflects their inner harmony, and promotes sharing and group discussion. To ask for your own office would be interpreted as antisocial and would be considered nonproductive for the company.

This is your second visit to your Arab business contact's office. He asks you to come from ten o'clock to eleven o'clock in the morning to continue your discussion. You should arrive at:

(a) Nine-thirty.
(b) Ten o'clock.
(c) Eleven o'clock.
(d) Ten-thirty.

An Arab's time frame is generally much longer than most other cultures'. In Arab culture, the present is an extension of the past, and the future depends very much on the will of Allah. Regular clock time is not as highly valued as in the American culture, and in the above situation, ten o'clock to eleven o'clock means your discussion will continue sometime within that hour. The Arab businessman will most likely have a few other people in his office during the same time period you are there, so the loose time structure fits within the cultural value of time.

Summary Insights

In this chapter, we have introduced a new definition of culture as "the behavioral norms that a group of people, at a certain time and place, have agreed upon to survive/coexist." This definition has been supported by many statements and examples from different cultures. We have also explored several elements in these behavioral norms, such as language usage, nonverbal communication, and space and time orientation across cultures.

Based on our own interviews with participants from many countries, cultural values and their priorities have been defined. Group harmony and relationships are the top values of Japanese culture, while in contrast, equality and openness are more important for Americans, and family security for Malaysians and Arabs. Many of these values directly or indirectly influence daily behavior, especially in business dealings.

Perceptions of different cultures by others reflect the stereotyping that can occur. Stereotyping must be avoided to successfully communicate cross-culturally.

Building cultural sensitivity and competence requires an enhancement of the physical sensors: listening, watching, and feeling. This task is necessary in order to respect, participate, and share knowledge and experiences with so many global cultures.

In the next chapter, we present how sub-cultures exist between and within worldwide organizations—as a reflection of a particular country-based culture.

CHAPTER 4

Corporate Multicultural Values

An Overview

- *What is "corporate culture"?*
- *How do the values of Apple Computer employees in the U.S. differ from their counterparts in Singapore?*
- *What are the differences between engineering and marketing cultures?*

Just as we can study the macrocultures of countries and their inhabitants, so we may analyze the macroculture of an institution or system and its members. In studying organizational cultures, we may apply the cultural values identified in Chapter 3.

In the previous chapter, we defined culture as "behavioral norms that a group of people, at a certain time and place, have agreed upon to survive or coexist." In this chapter, we apply this definition in search of corporate subcultures as perceived by employee groups within business organizations—as opposed to what may be stated or recommended by top-level management.

To demonstrate these corporate values, we selected data from our global management training programs in the United States, Japan, and Malaysia. Using this data, we present examples of subcultural values within these organizations as defined by engineers, marketing, and middle-line managers. We also summarize the cultural value contrasts between American, Japanese, and Asian companies as a reflection of their society's cultural values and the norms the companies use to survive in business.

The data provided in this chapter are a result of training sessions conducted with personnel from a variety of organizations. Through exploration of their corporate cultures, the participants became aware of the cultural values and priorities discussed in the previous chapter. The sessions helped to expand the participants' awareness and apply learning experiences to define their own organization's corporate cultures.

Apple Computer-USA

This first case involves Apple Computer, an American entrepreneurial company. We developed this information during our multicultural skills development programs, which were given to several groups within the company. Our objective was to increase the level of employees' awareness across cultures. The participants had been exposed to most of the material presented in the previous chapter and had learned to value multicultural diversity. It was felt that the participants would recognize the cultural elements of, then fully discuss, their organization's inner culture and corporate values.

The Corporate Culture

To promote a commonly shared value system within the ranks of its employees and subsidiaries worldwide, Apple management has circulated within the company what is known as "Apple Values." These corporate values are as follows:

- Empathy for customers/users
- Achievement/aggressiveness
- Positive social contribution
- Innovation/vision
- Individual performance
- Team spirit
- Quality/excellence
- Individual reward
- Good management

This list is intended to act as Apple's code of working values, considered necessary by top management to survive within the company, as well as to respond to the market.

How many of these values are in common with the American values discussed earlier? How many of these reflect common values of Apple's manufacturing subsidiaries in Europe and Asia? As a business priority, empathy for customers is at the top of the Apple list.

Achievement, aggressiveness, and individual reward are clearly American values that lead to success within American society, and in turn, the American market. As an entrepreneurial company, management encourages innovation and vision, quality and excellence, team spirit and good management.

The Employee Culture

To explore how employees perceive, share, and value these statements-of-management-value guidelines, we asked several of the employee-participants to respond to the question, "What are Apple's cultural values?" Following are some of the participants' responses:

- Group achievement
- Competition
- Risk-taking
- Technology
- Creativity
- Innovation
- Empowerment
- Diversity
- Caring
- Openness
- Open-door policy
- Recognition
- Informality
- Flexibility
- Sense of belonging

Innovation, creativity, and technology are major corporate cultural strengths according to the participants. What other norms do the employees follow, but are not stated in the previous corporate culture list? In the list above, employees indicate informality, openness, risk-taking, and empowerment as the norms that these groups agree with to coexist and survive. The response represents additional cultural norms of the organization that are shared by Apple working groups.

We also asked the participants to list the important cultural values they felt would enhance Apple's global business success, as follows:

- Diversity
- Customer satisfaction

- Empowerment
- Total quality
- Vision

The Engineering Culture

As we discussed, within a corporate culture there exist many sub-cultures, such as those in management, engineering, and marketing. Each of these subgroups develops its own set of values that the team members strive to adhere to in order to succeed. We asked a group of engineers from Apple to list the most important values to them as engineers, and they were as follows:

- Result-orientation
- Cooperation/Teamwork
- Innovation
- Total quality management
- Long-term vision
- Open communication
- Visibility
- Individual empowerment
- Self-directed work group
- Equality

Apple Computer: American versus Singaporean Corporate Cultures

To demonstrate another subculture within the Apple organization, we asked Apple workers in Singapore to list what they felt were the value differences between them and their American counterparts. Table 4.1 lists the differences.

Examining Singaporean versus American values clearly shows that American employees are more likely to adhere to the corporate values listed by Apple itself than are the Singaporean employees; Americans are more inclined to follow the value system that reflects the values of their country, and since Apple was started in the United States, the stated "corporate" values reflect American ideals.

Table 4.1 demonstrates the existence within the organization of a different value system among its Singaporean workers than the one

Table 4.1
Apple's Diverse Values

What Apple's Employees Value	
Singaporean	American
Teamwork	Individualism
Reserve	Openness
Long-term gains	Short-term gains
Analysis	Zealousness
Team rewards	Individual rewards
Listeners	Talkers
Seldom questions	Questions/brainstorming
Implementation	Innovation

instituted by the head office. Ideally, the corporate culture statement should reflect the common values of all subcultures locally as well as globally, responding to inner group and outer business needs.

In the next section, we present another company's values, and demonstrate its response to its corporate subcultures.

Petronas-Malaysia

In this case, we discuss the corporate and subcultures of Petronas, one of the leading oil exploration and distribution companies in Malaysia. The data presented also came from our multicultural diversity training of a group of managers from the organization.

No data were available from top management on the subject of "corporate culture," so we had to ask the group what Petronas' subcultural values were in order to define its corporate culture.

The participants again came from engineering, marketing, and management. Each group worked independently, applying the cultural values we discussed in the previous chapter to develop their perception of the company's subcultures.

The Management Culture

Following are the values that the middle-line management group feels are being adhered to within the company:

- Status conscious
- Submissive ("hammer and nail")
- Effective
- Management by meeting (MBM)
- Territorial
- Caring/welfare
- Visionary
- Top-down communication
- Civil-servant mentality
- Lack of upward mobility

This information shows that Malaysian management values status, such as title, position, degree, and so forth. Caring about the welfare of the employees is also valued highly. This value was combined with top-down communication, or the "hammer and nail" approach. Management by meeting, with territorial responsibility, seems to be a part of Malaysian corporate culture. In general, most of the values stated reflect a subculture of Malaysian society. However, it's clear that Malaysian corporate culture differs to a great extent from Apple's in America.

The Engineering Culture

We also asked a group of engineers from Petronas to list the cultural values or norms of the engineering division.

The values the engineers perceived to be important were as follows:

- Teamwork/cooperation
- High work ethic
- Seniority
- Good project management
- Risk-taking
- Group harmony
- Integrity
- Relationship
- Current technology
- Self-reliance

Teamwork, seniority, relationship, and integrity are important values that the engineering culture shares with the management culture. However, as engineers, they also listed cooperation, self-reliance, group harmony, and technology as unique cultural values that were not necessarily important to the management group.

What happens then if a manager directly overseeing an engineering group ignores or simply is unaware of the engineering culture's values? He or she will naturally face many cultural clashes from the engineers, as they clearly value a different set of norms.

The Marketing Culture

Finally, we asked a Petronas marketing group to discuss and prioritize the values perceived by them as important in their marketing activities. They were as follows:

- Maximize revenue/minimize costs
- Self-reliance
- Relationships
- Group harmony
- Competitiveness
- Cooperation
- Professionalism
- Sensitivity
- Reputable image
- Authority

The marketing group thought that their functional responsibility required them to focus more on maximizing revenue and minimizing costs, which they realized through the importance of relationships. The group also felt their top values were supported and enhanced by competitiveness and self-reliance. Reputable image, professionalism, and sensitivity to clients' needs were also seen as important values in their marketing activities.

What would happen, then, if Apple entered a joint venture with Petronas? Try to determine the expected culture clash between the marketing, engineering, and management groups. These different cultural values should create an awareness of the difficulties encountered in joint ventures or mergers that are insensitive to subcultures within organizations.

Global Culture

If your organization is expanding its activities overseas, what are the important cultural values you should bring to the new site? We asked participants from Petronas what cultural values their company should carry with them on the road to global expansion, and they responded with the list below:

- Professionalism
- Integrity
- Relationships
- Friendliness
- Openness
- Reputation
- Religion
- Dedication
- Cohesiveness
- Harmony

As a Malaysian group from a diverse local culture (Malay, Chinese, Indians), harmony, professionalism, integrity, and relationships were mentioned as important. Reputation, dedication, and cohesiveness reflect their business values. Openness and friendliness would probably help them in dealing with western clients.

What do you think the response of your company's staff and management would be to the same question? Would the perceptions be similar or different than those of the Malaysian group?

Advanced Micro Devices-USA

The Management Culture

During a training program we conducted for Advanced Micro Devices, a U.S.-based company, we asked three groups of employee-participants to discuss and state their company's cultural values. Again, the groups came from management, engineering, and marketing departments; they were all Americans. AMD does not have a published corporate values list. Let's look at input from the management group, keeping in mind the set of values presented by the Malaysian and Apple groups.

This is what a middle-line management group felt were their company's most important values:

- Aggressiveness
- Risk-taking
- Informality
- Independence
- Ego-driven
- Confrontations
- Improvement
- Profit-driven
- Youthfulness
- Meritocracy

These values reflect how the group feels success is achieved within their company: being aggressive, risk-taking, confrontation, short-term orientation, and independence. Within such an entrepreneurial organization, management learns also to be profit-driven, informal, and meritocratic (a system where advancement is based on achievement).

In American culture, it is common for management to try to use these identified cultural values in operations overseas. Environments such as Japan, Saudi Arabia, or Malaysia may resist these imposed values in joint-venture activities, and cultural friction will certainly occur.

The Engineering and Production Culture

We also asked two groups from within AMD—the engineering and production divisions—to list the cultural values they follow to succeed in their daily work. The engineering group listed these cultural values:

- Profits
- Top-down decision-making
- Competitiveness
- Autonomous business units
- Customer-driven
- Multinational company
- Partnership

- Technological competitiveness
- Meritocracy

The production division's values included:

- Time
- Competition
- Privacy
- Risk-taking
- Freedom
- Relationships
- Self-reliance
- Authority
- Group achievement
- Quality

   As an entrepreneurial company, values such as being profit-driven and sensitive to customers are listed as important to the engineering group, while the production group lists time, privacy, and group achievement as important. Compare these values to those of Apple's Singaporean group or the Malaysian group and you will note the differences that are naturally reflected in each country's and company's business cultural values.

The Marketing Culture

   Let's now examine another set of values that reflects American culture within an American company. Following are the values that the group of marketing managers from AMD listed as most important in their marketing activities:

- Charisma
- AMD —"The Conqueror"
- U.S. pride
- Market-driven
- Status conscious
- Meritocracy
- Pride in technical support
- Focus on PC market

- Independence
- Animosity toward competitors

The importance of high visibility, the ability to conquer, and maintaining independence reflect part of the American marketing culture. Other values listed come from the entrepreneurial culture. How do these values compare with the Malaysian marketing values presented earlier? It is clear that both American and Malaysian groups reflect their country's values, their organizational norms, and their own group values. Each group's behavior reflects the cultural norms and values that help them survive within their own business environments. Again, different behaviors are simply different, not right or wrong, because the business environment is different for each group. Many of the problems we have discussed occur because people are unaware of such differences and/or are disrespectful of others' values and priorities.

Japanese Corporate Cultures

This section presents specific cultural-value data from diverse Japanese organizations. These data demonstrate that company culture is a reflection of country culture, and that people within an organization must agree upon specific norms for business survival.

Examine what groups from each of the following Japanese companies see as important values for business success.

Mitsui Corporate Values

- Group harmony
- Long-term relationships
- High quality
- Cooperation
- Conservation

Matsushita Corporate Values

- Policy-orientation
- Customer satisfaction
- Contribution to society
- Coexistence
- Coprosperity

Mitsubishi Corporate Values

- Fair play in business
- Employee orientation
- High morale
- Concern for individuals
- Non-risk-taking

From examining each set of values from these three leading Japanese companies, we see that they again strongly reflect Japanese societal values. Group harmony, long-term relationships, quality, customer service, contributing to society, and coexistence emerge as definite ingredients for success in any Japanese company.

Comparing these important Japanese corporate values, we note that they are very different from those of American companies like Apple or AMD, whose values are successful tools in the American market. Both the Japanese and American corporate values are a reflection of the local norms that each group has agreed upon to survive and succeed in business.

Sony Corporate Values

In working with the Sony group, we asked participants to list important values they felt that Sony's corporate culture held. These are the results of their input:

- Liberalism
- Internationalism
- Positive toward change
- "Me"-ism
- Risk-taking
- Challenges
- Zealousness

These values clearly put Sony in what we call a very entrepreneurial culture, which is unusual for the Japanese; liberalism, risk-taking, a positive attitude toward change, zealousness, and internationalism are not typical Japanese values. These values are more characteristic of American entrepreneurial companies. This may explain why Sony has been so successful in the U.S. and global markets.

It has been necessary for Sony to develop a set of values such as these to increase the company's ability to succeed not only in Japan, but worldwide. These values have certainly enabled Sony to successfully undertake joint ventures with many American organizations. In a joint venture, Sony would probably be more successful with American companies than would the three other Japanese companies mentioned. The current joint venture between Sony and Apple Computer is an example of a successful story.

Of course, corporate culture is manifested in more than just *values,* and is influenced by where a facility is located and with whom it interfaces. For example, the Sony plant and operation in San Diego, California, has a bi-cultural environment that is unique and different from its counterparts in Japan or nearby Mexico. It is not just the manufacturing process and management—the culture is altered by the locale and its multicultural workforce, by American laws and regulations about the workplace and worker, and by the type of consultants brought into this regional facility. The Sony twin plant in Baja California again is impacted by local traditions of Tijuana, the Mexican culture, and indigeneous employees, as well as by border business practices.

Motorola-USA

Let's now examine the values of another American entrepreneurial global company—Motorola. What are Motorola management's goals and how do they implement these initiatives? Keep in mind the cultural values of the companies discussed in the previous section, and how each one has succeeded using the agreed-upon values.

Corporate management's key beliefs, goals, and initiatives were circulated to their employees. They are as follows:

Motorola Management Goals

Key Beliefs—How we will always act:

- Constant respect for people.
- Uncompromising integrity.

Key Goals—What we must accomplish:

- Increased global market share.

- Best in class:
  —people.
  —marketing.
  —technology.
  —product.
  —manufacturing.
  —service.
- Superior financial results.

Key Initiatives—How we will do it:

- High-quality products.
- Total cycle-time reduction.
- Product and manufacturing leadership.
- Profit improvement.
- Participative management.
- Cooperation between organizations.

As listed, respect for people and integrity is at the top of management's belief list. As an American company with an American culture, they predictably listed specific goals, such as increased market share and superior financial results. Management believes success could be accomplished through action-oriented, high-quality productivity, manufacturing excellence, and participatory management.

While working with members of Motorola, we asked them to discuss and list the cultural values they perceive as important for their success. Let's now see how the above goals reach the working level groups:

- Respect
- Integrity
- Manufacturing
- Customer satisfaction
- Conservatism
- Technology
- Inward focus
- Broad-based suppliers
- Competition
- Long-term relationships

- Global development
- Quality

As seen from the employee-value list, respect for people and integrity are important values. Customer satisfaction through quality and excellence in manufacturing reflects the general corporate values. However, conservativeness, inward focus, and long-term relationships were not mentioned directly by management, but stated as an important value by the employee. This is a reflection of the working cultural norms the group developed for their success.

We also asked a group of Asian employees working within the company, with Malay and Chinese cultural backgrounds, to list their perception of their company's corporate values.

The employees listed these as the cultural values they share:

- Excellence
- Ethics and integrity
- Respect
- Harmony and racial sensitivity
- Empowering the workforce
- Care for employees
- Risk-taking
- Cooperation
- Seniority
- Family

The values that were important to them included excellence, integrity, and ethics. They also listed qualities that most Asian cultures value, such as harmony, racial sensitivity, caring, and cooperation, reflecting their own cultural background.

These shared values represent the combination of Motorola corporate values with local Asian values, indicating a successful operation, as the employees are able to feel and understand these cultural values. However, this mentality is slightly different from the initial set of beliefs, goals, and initiatives initiated by Motorola management. It is a successful step toward cultural synergy between American and Asian cultures in business, however.

Contrasts in Corporate Cultures

The previous cases have given us insight into several corporate cultures in the United States, Japan, and Malaysia. Subcultures exist within each of these organizations, which reflect the functional activities of the groups, such as marketing, engineering, and management.

Here we summarize the main values of the three leading American companies discussed: Apple, Motorola, and Advanced Micro Devices (AMD). Table 4.2 lists specific values upon which each company depends to survive. By examining these sets of values, you can see a general reflection of many American and entrepreneurial cultures. These are the ingredients that make for a successful company in an American environment.

Table 4.2
American Corporate Values

Apple	Motorola	AMD
Creativity	Integrity	Aggressiveness
Innovation	Respect	Informality
Group	Customer	Independence
achievement	satisfaction	
Competition	Conservative	Youthfulness
Technology	Competitiveness	Meritocracy
Empowerment	Global development	Profit-driven
Diversity	Manufacturing	Quality
Openness	Technology	Charisma
Informality	Quality-driven	Freedom
Caring	Inward focus	Top-down decisions

Furthermore, in Table 4.3, we summarize the cultural values of these leading American organizations versus those of the three Japanese companies and the Malaysian organization. By examining this list of values, it is clear that, in general, they reflect each country's culture. This table gives us the first clue to the causes of cultural clashes and challenges that American, Japanese, Malaysian, or any other nationality may face in global joint ventures.

Let's assume AMD, with its listed set of values, is starting a joint venture with a Japanese firm having the listed Japanese values. John

Table 4.3
Corporate Cultural Values

American	Japanese	Malaysian
Competition	Group harmony	Status-conscious
Innovation	Long-term	Management
	relationships	by meeting
Quality	Quality	Territorial
Informality	Customer satisfaction	Teamwork
Technology	Conservative	Seniority
Openness	Employees	Group harmony
Creativity	High morale	Authority
Customer needs	Concern for individual	Visionary
Empowerment	Non-gambling	Professionalism
Profits	Contribution to society	Competition

Smith, project manager at AMD, along with a five-person support team, will be stationed at the Matsushita offices to develop a new project. John is also managing a five-person Japanese team. John approaches the project carrying his American cultural values, enforced by those from AMD's corporate culture. He is in Japan with his engineers working with his counterpart Japanese engineers. Similarly, the five-person team from Matsushita carry their Japanese values enhanced by Japanese company values.

Each value represents a source of cultural friction, from conducting meetings to negotiation, motivation, and training.

In successful joint ventures, John Smith's team should be aware of his own company's values and how they influence his management style. He, and each member of his team, should also recognize the set of values that each member of the Japanese team carries. Daily clashes will occur if any or both parties don't recognize and respect the other's values and create a common value set for the project to proceed.

What usually happens, for example, is that a member of an American company goes to Japan and vice versa and tries to force the employees to adhere to his own and his company's set of values (assuming he is holding a high position or has a large stake in ownership). Cultural clashes would then occur, limiting his effectiveness. He must recognize that he must first work within the existing culture and accept it. These are the norms to which the others are accustomed. Both sides can then work to integrate the new common sets of values.

Contrasts in Asian Corporate Cultures

The corporations highlighted in the next section have corporate values common to the Southeast Asian business environment. Participants in our management training programs chose the values listed.

Table 4.4a
Asian Corporate Cultures

Thailand: Phonelink	Singapore: Telkom	Hong Kong: Hutchison
Group harmony Parenthood Flexibility Being informed Patience Reputation	International outlook In transition Focused on relationships Customer oriented Self-reliance Cost conscious	Bottom line Authoritarian style Loyalty is expected Adhere to policy Commitments

So what do these values indicate? What can we learn from them? First we can see that these values are reflective of the national cultures presented in Chapter 3. Comparing them to corporate values of American companies and other cultures, we can note that there are some major differences between these values and those of Apple, AMD, and Motorola.

However, some of Singapore Telcom's values may mix well with American values. Self-reliance and an international outlook certainly describe many American corporations, as do a customer-oriented focus and cost-consciousness.

Thus, companies looking to work with existing companies in Southeast Asia might look to Singapore: They are certain to find some core values from which to build a prosperous relationship. This may explain why Singapore has attracted many foreign investors from the west. Many companies in Singapore are also deemed receptive to American corporate values.

On the other hand, in Thailand, most companies operate within value systems emphasizing group harmony and cohesion. From the values listed, in fact, one may infer that the Japanese will have an easier time adapting Thai workers to their values. This said, one must keep in mind that successful international business often involves the art of compromise. Upon adapting to the values of Thais, many business we have worked with have found that their employees are just as productive as those of other regions and areas.

Examining the values listed for the Hong Kong organization, it is clear that the Chinese and British values of authority, loyalty, and policy have influenced the company's cultures. Let us now examine the values of a different group of companies in Asia: Samsung, Indosat, and Renong.

Again, as Table 4.4b shows, corporate values reflect in the national culture of the organization. In Korea, most companies' management will adhere to strict rules, which show respect to status and authority. Business is conducted conservatively, with strong internal connections among family members. This is reflected in large Korean organizations that have expanded through family supports.

In contrast, an Indonesian company, such as Indosat, focuses on teamwork and satisfying employees and customers. Loyalty is expected and rewarded. As an emerging global organization, clear management and high ethical standards are also expected.

In the case of Malaysia, we notice the mix of eastern and British values in centralized management, image, the value of training, and

Table 4.4b
Asian Corporate Cultures

Korean: Samsung	Indonesia: Indosat	Malaysia: Renong
Status conscious	Teamwork	Centralized management
Visionary	"We care more" motto	Result-oriented
Internal relationships	Sustainable customer	Image-oriented
Competition	Satisfaction	Focus on training
Short-term objectives	Quality	Personal networking
Conservative	High standard of ethics	Conservative
Formality	Loyalty	Checks and balances

conservativeness. Because many Malaysian managers were educated in Britain, these values are reflected in their businesses.

Aptitude Tests

The following self-assessment questions have been developed and provided to help corporate managers identify their organizations' competitive priorities. As we have seen from the previous discussions, companies have to create their own cultures as well as respond to the market/client culture. If these values and their priorities are not defined, top management may pull in one direction while workers pull in another, especially in multicultural joint ventures, ultimately ending in failure for all parties involved.

The boxed material shows ten important competitive strategies that management or employees might employ to gain business success. You may introduce this test to your organization's top management, middle management, and workers, and ask each group to rate the ten strategies: low, average, or high. In some leading entrepre-

---

Competitive Edge Strategies

What priority does your firm give in business?

	LOW	AVERAGE	HIGH
1. Developing new technology	___	___	___
2. Applying new technology to produce new products	___	___	___
3. Low manufacturing costs	___	___	___
4. High-quality products	___	___	___
5. Low-price products	___	___	___
6. Wide distribution system	___	___	___
7. Extensive advertising	___	___	___
8. Quality of service	___	___	___
9. Employee loyalty	___	___	___
10. Global expansion	___	___	___

neurial companies, management stresses developing new technology and applying it to new products. Other organizations, once past the initial stage in developing their business, may be focusing on high-quality products with low manufacturing costs.

The important data you should get from participants' answers, however, is to see how top managers, middle managers, and working personnel view their company's priorities differently in a competitive market. This will allow you to more clearly define your overall corporate culture.

The Technology Group Assessment below distinguishes values that personnel involved in research, development, and innovation value in their work environment.

This test can be taken by any individual or group within the organization. People with competence in technology development will naturally value most items highly. However, if people within a technology development group don't score very well, then they are probably not really effective members of that team and should perhaps be transferred to another function such as production or marketing.

This set of values, such as listening openly to new ideas, acceptance of criticism, tolerance for failure, and future orientation, are basic values of a successful researcher or innovation group. Such a

---

Technology Group Assessment

How do you value each of the following?

(Low 0 - High 10)

1. Listening to new ideas   ____
2. Implementation of new ideas   ____
3. Acceptance of criticism   ____
4. Tolerance for failure   ____
5. Positive attitude toward change ____
6. Orientation to the future   ____
7. Willingness to work extended hours ____
8. Open access to information   ____
9. Celebration of accomplishment   ____
10. Reward personal achievement   ____

TOTAL SCORE   ____

Production Group Assessment

How do you value each of the following?

(Low 0 - High 10)

1. Membership in organization   ____
2. Teamwork   ____
3. Sharing work credit   ____
4. Group reward   ____
5. Mutual respect and trust   ____
6. Shared responsibility   ____
7. Decentralized procedures   ____
8. Quick decision making   ____
9. Immediate results   ____
10. Hard work   ____

TOTAL SCORE   ____

group needs these qualities to succeed in an innovative and technologically developed environment.

The Production Group Assessment lists another set of values common to a production or manufacturing group. To be an effective member of the team, you must value these qualities highly; otherwise, you will not fit well into such a group.

Summary Insights

This chapter presents data that support the definition that culture is the behavioral norms that a group of people have agreed on to survive or coexist. Culture is not what others would like to impose on another group. Workers, middle-line managers, engineers, and marketing personnel have their own set of working values that oftentimes differ from the direction top management thinks the company should go.

Moreover, subcultures exist within each organization. These subsets must be clearly defined and agreed upon, and must be shared by the group for success. If you don't share the values within a group, you will be unable to change the group's attitudes; conflict will exist, decreasing productivity and quality.

CHAPTER 5

Managing Intercultural Business Encounters

An Overview

In this chapter, we apply our knowledge and awareness of existing differences in cultures to specific, daily situations that most business-people encounter in the course of their business interactions. We start by presenting cultural differences encountered when people meet for the first time. We follow by showing cultural contrasts during normal telephone communications, as well as during meetings and business presentations. Finally, we point out how culture influences written messages and letters and how the way they are written reflects upon different cultures. In discussing these important business situations, we again show the contrasts between American, Japanese, and Arab cultures. We demonstrate and explain these differences through several real-life business situations to enhance your skills in multicultural business communication.

As in previous chapters, keep in mind your own cultural values and priorities, and how you would respond differently to each of the situations presented.

Intercultural Business Introductions

- *What sort of greeting should you expect during your first meeting with an Arab executive?*
- *How much space should you keep between yourself and an American?*
- *When introducing yourself to a Japanese executive which of your qualities should you emphasize?*

First impressions are very important. The way you present yourself during the first encounter may open or close the door to many other opportunities. In the business world, how you are perceived usually determines how much, if any, business you will do with someone. Making a good first impression usually depends on how clearly you understand the cultural differences and apply that knowledge to avoid misunderstandings.

People from every culture have different procedures they follow and different expectations when interacting with others the first time. These are based on the beliefs of each culture and are additionally derived from the individual value system of each person. This is why the initial meeting with an executive from a different culture must be approached with care and understanding.

Cultural Contrasts in Business Introductions

In the first meeting between executives from different backgrounds, it is important to understand each other's cultural objectives. As shown in Table 5.1, during a typical business introduction, members of different cultures often have completely different objectives. To most Americans, for example, the objective of such an encounter is to find out what you do and to add you to a list of contacts. Typically, the Japanese will try to first find what company you work for, which department you are with, and your individual position within the company. Arabs, on the other hand, will first make an effort to establish personal rapport before discussing any business prospects.

The following are typical examples of what may happen during a personal business introduction. Try to identify the most culturally appropriate answer for each question in these situations. (Keep in mind the cultural values of Americans, Japanese, and Arabs that were discussed in Chapter 3.) The scenarios presented are also designed to help you gain an understanding of the different aspects of the intercultural business introduction.

Apart from these three target cultures, think of other cultures in which you have encountered differences in introductions. For example, in place of the handshake, managers in India may first bow their heads slightly, hold their two hands together as in a prayer-like mode, and say as a form of greeting, "Nameste." Furthermore, they will be indirect before getting down to business communications. Impersonal talk about how you like their country, the pleasantness of your trip, where you have traveled, etc., may precede serious conversation.

Table 5.1
Cultural Contrasts During Business Introductions

	Americans	Japanese	Arabs
Cultural Objective	Find out who you are; Add to network of contacts; Gain control	Discover your position in the company and your mission; Maintain harmony	Establish personal rapport
Business Cards	A formality; a record of contact	Important to show company affiliation and level	Formality; No intrinsic value
Opening	What do you do?; Job identity crucial	Put yourself in group context: 1. company 2. department 3. individual	Establish personal status/family context; General conversation
Self-image	Independence	Member of group	Part of rich culture
Use of Language	First name; Informal; Friendly	Little talking	Expression of admiration; Flattery; Formal greeting
Nonverbal Messages	Direct eye contact; Firm handshake	Bowing level; Minimal facial expression	Facial expression; Body language
Spatial Orientation	Individual space; Maintain distance	Groups maintain distance; Structured	Close distance; Informal
Time Orientation	Short period of introduction	Give lead to others	Long range; Take initiative
Information Exchange	Business-related; Level of responsibility	Company-related	Personal
Closing	Get down to business; Take the initiative	Period of harmony; Response to initiative	Expression of hospitality/personal relationship
Applied Cultural Values	Informality; Openness; Directness; Action-oriented	Harmony; Respect; Listening; Non-emotional	Religious harmony; Hospitality; Emotional support; Status/ritual

In all first encounters with strangers, each is projecting an image to the other; each is evaluating the other. Thus, first impressions are important and worthy of your effort to be sensitive to the verbal and non-verbal cues you are receiving.

Opening Introductions and Cultural Self-Image. Cultural differences in a business introduction become apparent starting with the exchange of business cards. After receiving someone else's card, most Americans will probably glance briefly at it, then put it away for future reference. Americans often consider the business card exchange a formality, done simply to be able to contact the person again. Conversely, the Japanese consider the business card important to show your company affiliation and your level in the company.

Situation 1. After receiving a Japanese business card, you should take time to

(a) Put it in your wallet or shirt pocket.
(b) Examine it carefully.
(c) Ask how to pronounce the name in Japanese.
(d) Find out the person's department and title in the company.

After looking at your business card, a Japanese executive will usually allow a period of silence in respect for your company and will try to feel your thoughts and establish harmony, so in Situation 1, the best thing to do is to examine the business card carefully and acknowledge the company name. In contrast, the Arab, to whom the exchange of business cards is simply a formality with no intrinsic value, will immediately engage in general conversation to establish a friendly rapport, without paying attention to the card.

Situation 2. An American businessman arrives at your office. Within the first five minutes he will probably

(a) Tell you about his long trip and the trouble he had finding your office.
(b) Ask you for a hot cup of coffee.

(c) Ask you, "What do you do?"
(d) Inquire about your children.

Americans consider it important to be time-conscious, action-oriented, and direct. In keeping with this self-image, Americans like to start business immediately. With the business card quickly put away, the first question generally asked is, "What do you do?" In this culture, business and family are usually separated because most Americans equate job with personal identity. Americans will not ask you about your children or spouse, because they consider it a private matter, and would feel uncomfortable sharing this information with you until they know you better. In contrast, Arabs may begin by talking about their trip to your office and their families, and would expect and accept a cup of coffee or tea, reflecting their values of hospitality.

Situation 3. When introducing yourself to the Japanese, you should emphasize your

(a) Managerial capability.
(b) Technical know-how.
(c) Interest in closing the sale before you leave.
(d) Company's capabilities and long-range market share.

Most Japanese executives will probably be more interested, first, in your company's capabilities and future market share. A westerner may try to emphasize his individual managerial or technical abilities, but this approach would be out of line with the Japanese values of group harmony. Japanese executives will also resist any pressure to close a sale before they have discussed the details within their group.

Use of Language, Nonverbal Messages, and Spatial Orientation. The words you use when meeting someone for the first time is also crucial to the overall impression you make. The American value of equality comes through when speaking with them. Their informality is exhibited by the use of first names and general friendliness. Arabs, on the other hand, usually use eloquent words and flattery as expressions of hospitality and friendship, for Arabs place a high value on maintaining personal relationships. The Japanese will do just the opposite of the Arabs, however. They tend to be very conservative in verbal expression, preferring to communicate nonverbally, reinforcing their values of modesty.

Nonverbal messages are often what a person meeting you for the first time will notice. These messages are among the most important aspects of introductions. The Japanese bow when meeting others, using a minimum of facial expression. Arabs may use body language, such as opening their arms in greeting, to show hospitality or friendship. American nonverbal messages include direct eye contact, a firm handshake, and physical distance between the people meeting, bringing us to Situation 4 and the topic of spatial orientation.

Situation 4. In talking with Americans you should

(a) Keep two-arms' length away.
(b) Keep a half-arm's length away.
(c) Keep one arm's length away.
(d) Put your left hand in your pocket.

The majority of Americans value their individual space, and stay about an arm's length apart from each other. In contrast, Arabs exhibit their value of hospitality by standing closer together.

Situation 5. In your first encounter with an Arab businessman, you should

(a) Open both your arms to receive his hug.
(b) Give him your business card with your left hand and extend your right hand for a handshake.
(c) Shake hands, and give him your business card after you sit down.
(d) Give him your business card only if he asks for it.

In Arab culture, hospitality is highly valued, especially with personal encounters with foreigners. Among Arabs, a hug is normal, but for first-time meetings with foreigners, a handshake is expected. Business cards, as discussed, are not as important as in other cultures. Offering items with your left hand is inappropriate in Arab culture: Always use your right hand when offering or accepting.

Information Exchange and Closing Introductions. The exchange of information between parties is, again, directly tied to the inherent cultural values of each individual. Both the Japanese and Arabs spend considerable time and expense building a relationship with someone they may do business with. Both value the long-term payoffs they can gain from time invested up front establishing personal rapport and trust. This value is shown in Situation 6, meeting an Arab executive.

Situation 6. An Arab businessman offers you a cup of Arabian coffee at his office. You don't drink coffee. You should say

(a) "No, thank you."
(b) "Thank you, but I don't drink coffee."
(c) "Thank you," and accept the cup of coffee.
(d) "No, thank you. Coffee makes me nervous."

The situation asks what to do if an Arab offers you a cup of coffee; he is in fact extending his hospitality to you. If you refuse the offer, he may be insulted. If you would rather not drink the coffee, take a small sip, and set the cup aside. Your host will understand and will not be offended.

In contrast to the Arabs and Japanese, Americans typically spend a short time building a personal relationship with business associates. They tend to be more oriented toward short-term goals. Many Americans value their independence and personal freedom over commitments to personal relationships in business.

Applied Cultural Values. At this point, it is clear that many of the cultural values mentioned dictate the way people from each culture conduct their business. Americans apply their identified values of openness, informality, directness, and action-orientation in every aspect of business, including personal introductions. People from an Arab culture, on the other hand, apply their values of hospitality, religious harmony, emotional support, and long-term relationships. The Japanese use group harmony, respectfulness, and listening to form their decisions and conduct their business.

Intercultural Telephone Communications

- *What does a visiting American business associate expect from you when calling to set up a meeting?*
- *When phoning your Arab distributor, how should you begin the conversation?*
- *What do you do if, while talking to your Japanese business contact, she suddenly becomes quiet?*

Due to increases in telecommunication technology and new sophistication in equipment, telephone usage in business has become a major communication medium. Discussing business transactions by telephone has become a replacement for in-person business conversations. Therefore, the cultural guidelines used in face-to-face meetings must be applied in order to achieve similar results on the telephone to avoid disappointing results.

First, we discuss the cultural objectives of each culture, and the common way people from these cultures start a phone conversation. We then explore how the process of intercultural telephone conversation works.

Cultural Contrasts in Telephone Conversations

As outlined in Table 5.2, an American makes a business phone call with a specific result in mind—either to get information or to initiate action. The American caller usually starts conversations by giving his or her full name, followed by the company's name, and then immediately stating the purpose of the call. "This is Jane Smith from Xerox. Could you please tell me the status of our order?" This reflects the American value of directness.

People from different cultures use the telephone based on their cultural values. To be able to use telecommunication technologies to your advantage, you must understand these values, and work within the guidelines of each culture. The following situations are examples of possible intercultural telephone encounters. These situations give you an idea of what actually occurs during a typical intercultural business telephone conversation. Try to select the most appropriate cultural response in each.

Table 5.2
Cultural Contrasts During Telephone Conversations

	American	Japanese	Arab
Objective	Information/action	Information	Personal relationship; Commitments
Opening	Full name; Purpose of call	Company name	Personal greeting
Process	Task-oriented; Direct question	Information gathering by listening	Indirect approach; Inquire first about self/family, then get to business
Use of Language	Direct objective	Generally conservative	Flattery
Nonverbal Communication	Urgency	Silence/harmony; Nonconfrontational	Conveys emotion with tone of voice
Time Orientation	Time is money	Time controlled by caller	Longer time span
Information Exchange	Step-by-step	Always seeking; Minimum given	Looping to objectives
Closing	Seek commitment; Assign responsibility; Will be in touch	No commitments; Will discuss; Call us back	Greeting; "Wishing peace;" Reiterates long-term relation-ship; Let us hear from you again
Applied Cultural Values	Directness; Privacy, Action/task-oriented	Listening; Informative; Company; Harmony	Religious harmony; Emotional support; Social organization; Process orientation

Situation 7. Your American business partner phones from her hotel to tell you that she has arrived from overseas and is ready to meet. You should

(a) Tell her that you will send the company limousine to pick her up.
(b) Ask her if she needs directions to your office.
(c) Ask her to take a taxi on your company's expense.
(d) Ask her where she would like to meet you.

If an American calls from her hotel, she probably expects to find her own way to your office. She will most likely ask directions on how to get there. This reflects the American values of independence, learning by doing, and action-orientation. An Arab executive has different expectations. Because of the Arab values of hospitality and status, in the same situation you should offer to meet her at her hotel or arrange transportation for her. Of course, an American would not turn down an offer of a ride, but she may not expect it either.

Most Japanese business callers seek information, but not necessarily results. The Japanese caller identifies his company first, his department next, and then his name: "This is Fujitsu Corporation, Engineering Department, Maruyama speaking." Stating the name of the company first shows the Japanese values of company affiliation, personal modesty, and group harmony.

The Arab business call builds interpersonal rapport and establishes a basis of trust between the two people. The Arabs indirectly approach the purpose of the call after all the background information is discussed.

Situation 8. You are calling your Arab distributor from your home office. You may start the conversation by

(a) Asking about his wife.
(b) Asking if he has mailed his late payment.
(c) Hoping that he and his family are well.
(d) Asking how his business is doing.

With Arabs, you should open the conversation with general background questions about the last meeting, his health, and his family. Direct questions about late delivery or payments are not good openers because they may cause uneasiness. After the initial conversation, a detailed business discussion will occur. In Arab countries, a business relationship that is based on trusted friendship is of greater value than one based strictly on business.

Use of Language, Time Orientation, and Information Exchange. After the opening of the conversation, each caller has a distinct process for the rest of the phone conversation. Language used is important to the success of the telephone conversation. Americans are task-oriented and will generally proceed step-by-step without being sidetracked by personal interactions. Even if two people have already met, only one or two references to some common interest will be mentioned; then it's on to the business at hand.

Situation 9. You telephone your American business associate. After you identify yourself, she says, "What can I do for you?" You respond

(a) "Where is my order?"
(b) "How is the weather in your city?"
(c) "How is business?"
(d) "There's nothing you can do for me."

When talking with an American on the phone, you will probably immediately sense action orientation. To the American, a response such as "Where is my order?" is perfectly acceptable. Direct, step-by-step action to reach a goal is the most appropriate problem-solving technique in American culture. People from other cultures, such as Japan, must reach group consensus before proceeding.

Even in telephone conversations, where you cannot see the person with whom you are negotiating, nonverbal communication plays an important role. Arabs use a certain tone of voice to convey emotions to persuade the other person. Americans use a particular tone of voice to convey a sense of urgency, to play on the idea that time is money and, if you don't act soon, you might lose your chance. The Japanese use a different attitude during phone conversations: they wait and listen in order to gather information they can use to make decisions. They often use periods of silence on the phone to establish harmony and to avoid confrontation or argument.

Closing Telephone Conversations and Applied Cultural Values. Situation 10. At the end of your telephone discussion with your Japanese friend, you ask him if the price is acceptable. He answers, "Yes, yes," meaning

(a) He is confirming his acceptance of your price.
(b) He has heard and understood your offer.
(c) You should give a deeper discount.
(d) He is politely saying no.

In Situation 10, if, at the end of your phone conversation with your Japanese business associate, you ask him if the price is acceptable, and if he says, "yes, yes," what does he mean? To most westerners, the word "yes" means agreement or confirmation. Most Japanese and Asians use the word *"hai,"* or "yes," to affirm that they are listening and are following your line of thought, not necessarily that they are agreeing with you.

This formality goes along with the way the Japanese close a business telephone conversation. They do not offer any commitments, but say they will discuss the matter and call you back when they reach a group agreement. This response typifies the basic Japanese cultural value system designed around listening, gathering information, and maintaining group harmony.

The Arab executive may close the conversation somewhat differently than the others. Arabs finish by reaffirming their desire for a long-term relationship, exchanging good wishes, and expressing a desire to hear from you again. This ties in with the Arab cultural values of religious harmony, emotional support, and establishing long-term relationships.

Americans, in keeping the cultural values of directness, task- and action-orientation, and privacy, end phone conversations by pressing for answers or committing to action. At the end of the conversation, both parties confirm their individual responsibilities and commitment to the agreed-upon plan of action. The following two scenarios demonstrate some of the contrasts discussed.

Moshi, moshi ("hello, hello")

Mr. John Smith, an American, is the marketing manager for Weyerhaeuser. He is calling Mr. Yamamoto, marketing director for the Rising Sun Company in Japan, to inquire about his latest proposal.
(Telephone rings, a woman answers.)

Woman: *Moshi, moshi* ("hello, hello")
Smith: Hello, this is John Smith, may I speak to Mr. Yamamoto please?
Woman: Oh, I'm sorry, who is calling please?
Smith: This is John Smith calling for Mr. Yamamoto.

Woman: I'm sorry, what is the name of your company?
Smith: I'm calling from Weyerhaeuser.
Woman: I'm sorry, could you spell that please?
Smith: W-E...
Woman: I'm sorry, "W-Z"?
Smith: No, W-E-Y-E-R-H-A-E-U-S-E-R. Is Mr. Yamamoto there?
Woman: Oh, Weyerhaeuser. Thank you very much, your name please?
Smith: John Smith.
Woman: And who do you wish to speak to?
Smith: I said, Mr. Yamamoto.
Woman: I'm sorry, which department? We have many Yamamotos.
Smith: Oh, of course. Mr. Yamamoto from the international marketing department.
Woman: Thank you very much, wait just a minute please.

(Music plays during hold. A telephone rings in a big hall, where many people are working at desks. There is only one telephone. Someone passing by picks up the phone.)

Man: Moshi, moshi.
Smith: Hello, Mr. Yamamoto?
Man: Oh no, this is Suzuki. Who is calling please?
Smith: This is John Smith calling for Mr. Yamamoto.
Man: I'm sorry, what is the name of your company?
Smith: Weyerhaeuser.
Man: Could you spell that please?
Smith: W-E-Y-E-R-H-A-E-U-S-E-R
Man: Thank you very much. Just a minute please.

(Music plays again.)

Man: I'm very sorry but Mr. Yamamoto is in a meeting. Could you call again later?

(Smith hangs the phone up in frustration after an eight-minute long-distance call.)

This situation reflects the contrasts that exist between the two cultures, and the problems that can arise due to a lack of understanding. As mentioned, in Japan the company is valued the most, then the department, and finally the individual. This reflects the Japanese cultural values of group belonging.

The American culture, however, recognizes the individual first, then the individual's position, and lastly, the company. Americans value independence, equality, and competition, and therefore consider the individual to be of more value than the group.

When John Smith called his Japanese counterpart, he acted in the same way as he would if calling someone from his own American culture. He didn't understand the values that are crucial to working within the Japanese business world. He did not show respect for the company he was calling by simply asking for Mr. Yamamoto. In addition, he failed to identify the name of his company before his own name. John Smith's actions may be considered unacceptable in Japanese culture, and immediately put him in a less important place in the minds of the Japanese counterpart.

Let us now look at the next scenario demonstrating the telephone techniques of a different culture.

In sha allah ("if God wishes")

In his attempt to get a response to his written correspondence with an Egyptian import company, Mr. Clark, the Middle East regional manager in New York, called Mr. Saber, the Egyptian company's president.

Clark: Hello, Mr. Saber, this is Bill Clark.

Saber: Good morning, Mr. Clark. It is nice to hear your voice. How is your family and everyone in New York?

Clark: We are fine, thank you. I'm calling to see if you received my letter about starting a partnership with your company?

Saber: Yes sir, we got every letter, and we welcome you to visit us in Cairo, the historical city of Egypt. Have

> you ever been to Cairo before?
> **Clark:** No, actually I haven't. Have you had a chance to look over our offer?
> **Saber:** *In sha Allah*, we will do good business together. The weather is very beautiful in Cairo these days, so if you come to visit us, don't bring that heavy clothing you need in New York.
> **Clark:** Well, maybe I could come to Cairo if it would help. When is a good time for me to come?
> **Saber:** You are welcome any day, Mr. Clark, and please bring with you several samples of your company's products.
> **Clark:** Okay, Mr. Saber, *in sha Allah* I will be in Cairo next week.
> **Saber:** All in Cairo will be waiting for you!

Both Mr. Clark and Mr. Saber approached this conversation with different objectives, and that is where the conflict began. Mr. Clark had specific reasons for his phone call. He wanted to find out if the company had received his correspondence and if Mr. Saber was interested in the product.

Mr. Clark was unsuccessful in reaching his objectives because he failed to understand the Arab cultural values of personal rapport when conducting business. He should have recognized and acknowledged the time frame Mr. Saber was using in order to establish personal contact and trust before going into the details of business. Since Mr. Saber could not reach these objectives over the phone, Mr. Clark found himself having to go all the way to Cairo to negotiate face-to-face with the Arab businessman.

Multicultural Meetings

- *What do the Japanese expect to solve during a business meeting?*
- *Will asking an Arab executive for his opinion help stimulate discussion?*
- *Whose view do you ask for first in a Malaysian meeting? The oldest? Perhaps the junior member? The senior member?*
- *How is an American business meeting structured?*

Within each culture, business meetings are everyday occurrences. The process of conducting business and the expected
results, however, can vary greatly. These processes come from the
expectations of each individual culture. Every society has a unique
cultural value system that acts as a guideline for behavior in every
situation. These values are the unwritten rules that every member
of a culture learns and applies to individual situations in life. Business, which has been known to imitate life, follows a similar path.

When these guidelines are used within a culture, business is conducted in a certain way along preestablished cultural paths. As businesses expand into foreign countries and societies though, it is
important to recognize and understand the other's value system. If a
business meeting takes place between people from contrasting cultures, and one or both of the people don't know each other's cultural
guidelines, conflicts will most likely arise. This dilemma demonstrates, as business becomes more global, the need for greater cultural understanding, especially in face-to-face situations such as the
business meeting.

Cultural Contrasts in Multicultural Meetings

In any multicultural meeting, you will be faced with certain cultural contrasts, from the opening of the meeting through the participation of those in attendance, and ending with the decision being made
and the close of the meeting. The self-image of each culture, the
proper way to use and understand the language and nonverbal cues
of a particular culture, and the use of space and time are all vital elements of a meeting. In Table 5.3, we list these main points of cultural
contrast focusing on three cultures: American, Japanese, and Arab.

The most important aspect to remember in meeting with executives from other cultures is that each one approaches business differently. In an American meeting, for example, everything that
needs to be discussed is usually written out beforehand in order to
address and solve each problem quickly. In contrast, the Japanese
business meeting is not for immediate solutions, but instead for
information gathering to make future decisions, especially when
meeting with foreigners. Different still is the Arab meeting, in which
the purpose is to establish a relationship with the client before business is conducted.

Table 5.3
Cultural Contrasts During Multicultural Meetings

	American	Japanese	Arab
Cultural Objective	Formulate plan of action	Seek information; No conclusion	Build rapport and Establish trust base
Opening	Direct to objective	Identification of seniority; Period of silence for harmony	An introductory period to warm up—expression of hospitality
Participation	Expected from all in attendance	Led by seniors; Seek feelings of group; More listening	By seniority; Specialist involved; Indirect to task
Self-image	Equality; Independence; Competition	Part of group; Modesty	Rich culture; Generosity
Use of Language	Statement direct; To the point	Indirect no; Yes/no	Flattering; Looping
Nonverbal Communication	Informal; Minimum emotional expression	Hierarchy; Occasional silence	Seniority/age; Dress level; Emotion
Spatial Orientation	Opposite — across the table	Circle; Pre-arranged	By status and age
Time Orientation	Always punctual; Future-oriented	On time for first meeting important	Historical context
Decision Making	Fact-based; Risk-taking; Appeal to reason	Information-based; Group consensus	Intuition; Religious background
Closing	Conclusion; Plan of action; Responsibility	Will discuss with others; No commitments	Future meeting oriented/open loop
Applied Cultural Values	Cultural directness; Action-oriented; Individuality; Future-oriented; Risk-taking; Achievement; Accomplishment	Information-seeking; Hierarchy; Group harmony; Listening/observing; Patience	Hospitality; Religious belief; Age/seniority; Flattering/admiration

Conflicts in the process or purpose of a business meeting are based on the cultural value systems of the particular country. For example, in an American meeting the focus is on formulating a plan of action. The highest priority is placed on finding out what has to be done and finishing it as quickly as possible.

Situation 11. You are attending an American business meeting. If you disagree with one of the points being discussed, you should

    (a) Wait until the last five minutes to bring up the discrepancy.
    (b) Address it as soon as possible.
    (c) Write it down and pass it discreetly to the coordinator.
    (d) Just sit quietly until someone brings up the subject.

Recognizing the cultural objective helps show the way to proceed in Situation 11. Since one of the most important values in American culture is directness, you should bring up any disagreement you have with the plans as soon as the opportunity presents itself. This action demonstrates your openness, competitiveness, and willingness to take risks in order to get the job done right. Waiting until later to bring up a disagreement would be counterproductive.

In some Asian cultures, it is considered normal to write down any disagreement and pass it to the coordinator, or to wait until after the meeting to discuss it. This illustrates the Asian culture's recognition of seniority and personal modesty in pursuit of group harmony and consensus. The Arab cultural objective is different still. Arab culture suggests the purpose of a business meeting is to establish trust and to show hospitality. In addition, Arab meetings are dictated by status and seniority.

Situation 12. When you introduce yourself at an American meeting you should emphasize your

    (a) Educational credentials and the schools you attended, especially if they are prestigious.
    (b) Level of responsibility in your organization.
    (c) Current salary.
    (d) Latest accomplishments.

The objectives based on the cultural values of each country have an effect on the opening of the meeting as well. Because achievement is valued in American culture, it would be fine to discuss your level of responsibility in your organization and to discuss your past achievements as well. In Arab and Japanese cultures, however, it would be more beneficial to describe your educational credentials and current responsibilities.

Situation 13. You are starting a meeting with a Japanese team. The team leader asks you, "What is the purpose of your visit?" You answer

(a) "To learn more about your company's product."
(b) "To exchange information about our products and potential market."
(c) "To present my company's product line."
(d) "To secure an agreement on a joint venture with your company."

While Americans want to make a deal and Arabs wish to establish a relationship, most often the focus of Japanese business meetings is to gather information, or (b).

Meeting Participation and Cultural Self-Image

Situation 14. You are conducting a meeting with ten Arab managers and workers. Everyone is participating except one manager. Will you

(a) Not worry about him?
(b) Ask who has any more comments before the meeting ends?
(c) Look at that particular manager and ask if he has something to say?
(d) Tell him that this is his last chance to talk?

As the meeting progresses, a situation may occur where a participant may have a disagreement or question, as shown in Situation 14. In American culture, you would speak up immediately, but in Arab culture that method would not be acceptable. In Arab culture, when you disagree with something, you usually remain silent. In order to get each person involved in the discussion, you must first address the senior member in the group. Once the top-level executive starts talking, the junior members will follow. In Japan, conversely, the senior executive usually speaks last. However, in this case the most appropriate answer is (c).

All of the values mentioned are based on each culture's ideas of how situations are supposed to function. History and culture dictate how you interact with people in all aspects of life, including business. A large part of why these cultural guidelines are followed is due to how each culture views itself—its "self-image."

We have already discussed certain self-images. Americans take pride in independence, equality, and competition. These images can be demonstrated by their greetings, seating arrangements in a meeting, and use of language. Japanese conduct meetings and make decisions as a group, and always strive to be a strong and cohesive unit. On the other hand, the cultural objective of the Arab business meeting is to establish rapport and mutual trust between the persons involved.

The Use of Language and Nonverbal Communication. Understanding a cultural self-image is important to understanding a person from a particular culture. To know how an individual thinks of him or herself or his or her culture is directly related to how he or she conducts business. The language used in each culture is deeply rooted in its history and traditions.

In Arab culture, the language used is hospitable and flattering, and the same attitude holds true when forming business relationships. Arab executives use language to establish and maintain long-lasting relationships.

The Japanese use language that is noncommittal and that takes an indirect approach to addressing issues.

The American businessperson is exactly the opposite of the Japanese in many ways, but especially in their use of language. Americans value the ability to say what they mean directly, in order to get to the point and therefore reach a decision.

To get your message across cultures in business, it is crucial to use the right language. Without the proper words, nothing will be accomplished. How and what you say is important, but what you don't say can be just as important.

The Japanese may use the established hierarchy in the company to give a certain mood to the meeting. This hierarchy also dictates how a meeting is conducted because of seniority. Arabs use seniority or status level as a form of nonverbal communication. The seniority of a person in the meeting establishes the individual as important, and the impact of what he says is directly related to seniority. Americans often use an informal hierarchy setting (as nonverbal communication) in business meetings to show equality. This informality helps those involved in the meeting feel more equal in status and responsibility. By using a minimum of emotional expression, Americans create a mood in which everyone deals with problems equally to come to a conclusion as quickly as possible.

Space and Time Orientation. Another cultural aspect somewhat related to nonverbal communication is spatial orientation. The seating arrangement says a lot about how each culture conducts business. In an American meeting, the participants are placed across the table from each other in a direct, almost confrontational setting. In an Arab meeting, the seating arrangement is quite different. Those involved in the meeting are arranged specifically by status and age, showing the Arab respect for seniority. In Japan, the seating is prearranged in a circle with no particular order, especially during discussion periods with other Japanese.

Some cultures value time differently than others and use it in different ways. In Arab culture, for example, your arrival at the meeting is, again, directly related to your seniority and status in the company. On the other hand, Japanese executives are on time for meetings. Americans value punctuality, in an effort to move along swiftly in the completion of the meeting.

Decision-making. The purpose of holding meetings, of course, is to eventually make a decision. Some cultures reach it sooner than others, but eventually all come to some conclusion. In the American business meeting, decisions are made based on facts, risk-taking, and by personal appeal. The Japanese generally base their business decisions on information received during the meeting, then they try to reach the full consensus of the group afterwards. The Arab decision-making process is much less exact than the other two, but equally as effective. In Arab culture, decisions are made with the executives' position, intuition, and religious beliefs in mind.

Closing a Meeting and Applied Values. People from each culture end a meeting in a distinct way, again, based heavily on the individual cultures of the participants. In Japanese culture, the meeting usually closes with no commitments (to further discuss the information with other parties involved). The Arab meeting ends with a promise to continue the relationship established in their meeting. In the American conference, a definite conclusion, plan of action, or delegation of responsibility is reached, and commitments are received from each participant.

Though each culture is different than the other, it is important to realize that no one is right or wrong; each is simply different. Each culture maintains its own value system that works well within their society. The American values of independence and competition are no better or worse than the Japanese values of group harmony and patience, or the Arab values of hospitality and religious beliefs. In order to work well within the other culture, however, you must be able to recognize, respect, and adapt to the style of that particular culture to succeed.

Cross-Cultural Presentations

- *What kind of materials do Americans expect to have in hand when you begin your presentation?*
- *How do you keep your Japanese hosts interested in what you are talking about?*
- *What should you seek toward the end of your presentation to Arab executives?*

The most difficult aspect of conducting business with someone from a different culture is presenting your information. This difficulty often arises from not understanding your host's cultural guidelines. When making presentations to audiences from different cultural backgrounds, it is crucial to adapt to their values in order to make your objectives understood. The way we present ourselves, the material we use, and the way we conduct our discussions are all culturally oriented.

Cultural Contrasts During Multicultural Presentations

Presentations, like any other multicultural business situation, are based on the individual cultural values of the audience. To make a presentation within the boundaries of a particular culture is very important to cross-cultural understanding. To understand the overall process of the presentation, from the opening to the closing, based on each culture's self-image, is vital. The proper use of verbal and nonverbal communication, space and time orientation, and persuasive techniques are all important to the complete cross-culturally successful presentation. Table 5.4 lists the main contrasts in presentations among American, Japanese, and Arab cultures.

Cultural Objectives and Presentations. To make an effective cross-cultural presentation, it is necessary to understand the cultural objectives of each audience. The Japanese goals in a presentation are to present status and seek supportive information from the audience. In Arab culture, the presentation is used to present a specific problem and to ask for participants' views. In American culture, the facts are presented, and an agreement is reached.

Situation 15. You are making a presentation to executives of an American company. They are expecting

(a) To receive an outline of your presentation in advance.
(b) You to hand them a copy of your presentation before the meeting starts.
(c) To receive a copy of your chart part-by-part as you go through your talk.
(d) No copy of your material.

These objectives are a natural result of each culture's value system and act as the blueprint for each aspect of the presentation. In keeping with their cultural values of directness, Americans come to presentations prepared to discuss issues and to come to a specific conclusion. Americans usually expect advance notice about presentation outlines and objectives. Americans will also often expect to receive written materials at the beginning of the presentation so they can scrutinize the material and be ready to ask questions.

Situation 16. You are conducting a presentation to Japanese managers. You should start by

(a) Talking about the school you attended and your latest accomplishments.

Table 5.4
Cultural Contrasts During Presentations

	American	Japanese	Arab
Cultural Objectives	Present facts; Reach agreement	Present status; Seek supportive information	Present problem; Seek views
Opening	Very short; Direct to task	Information exchange	Background information
Process	Objectives; Justification; Sense of needs; Conclusion; Action	Participative	Status controlled; Input from specialists
Self-image	Self-reliant	Group belonging; Modest	Family affliction
Use of Language	Very direct	Conservative	Elaborate; Emotional
Persuasion Tools	Loss of opportunity; Short-term gain; Factual data; Team up	Maintain harmony; Group competition; Long-term gain; Go-between	Crisis; Religious; National
Nonverbal Communication	Eye contact; Dynamic	Silence; Modesty	Status
Spatial Orientation	Equal	Farther	Closer
Time Orientation	Use time pressure; Short-term result	Emphasis on quality	Long-range cooperation
Information Exchange	Open and expected from all participants	Seek more than give	Indirect to task
Media	Use of multimedia for persuasion	More visual than written	Highly verbal
Closing	Seek agreement; Set up action plan	Maintaining harmony	Future relationship; Need judgment of older/senior person
Applied Cultural Values	Logical; Factual; Directness; Equality	Nonverbal; Group-oriented; Information exchange	Status-oriented; Nonverbal message; Indirect to task

(b) Apologizing for not speaking Japanese.
(c) Asking everyone to introduce themselves.
(d) Reminding them that you need a firm answer on your proposal before the end of the meeting.

When starting a presentation to Japanese executives, the style is often completely different than the American process. In contrast to the direct American style, when starting a presentation to a Japanese group, you should be in line with their value of modesty. Reflect this culture by being polite, apologetic, and thankful. It is important to not discuss your personal achievements or to ask them for their immediate direct commitment, for directness is not in their cultural guidelines.

Situation 17. You are starting your presentation to Arab managers. You should

(a) Recite words from the Muslim holy book, the *Koran*.
(b) Give a brief introduction about your company's worldwide activities.
(c) Introduce your technical qualifications and point out that you are a graduate of a prestigious school.
(d) Ask your hosts to introduce themselves.

An Arab making a presentation will most likely express his appreciation for hospitality. When among other Arabs, he may begin with an appeal to religious harmony by wishing for God's help and blessing. An Arab may also be interested in your company's technical and financial references, as well as your in-country references. The Arab values of trust and reputation are demonstrated by their desire to establish a personal relationship with those with whom they do business.

Verbal and Nonverbal Communication. When making any presentation, use of language is an important element. The Japanese are very conservative in their use of language, keeping with their value of modesty. Arabs use elaborate and eloquent language as a persuasive tool, to appeal to their audience on an emotional level. Americans use direct, simple words and sentences.

The presence of nonverbal communication in each culture mirrors that culture's self-image. The Americans consider themselves independent, the Japanese interdependent, and Arabs religious and trusting.

Presenters from the three target cultures convey different nonverbal messages to gain audience support. Americans may use the force of a dynamic personality or individual style conveyed by voice level and tone, direct eye contact, and body language. The Japanese will attempt to sense the audience's thoughts and feelings and establish harmony through a period of silence. Arabs may vary their tone of voice, emotional appeal, and personal status to gain support.

Persuasion is a common practice throughout the world, but the individual techniques vary. Americans tend to persuade by discussing the possible loss or gain of opportunity. Print and television advertisements are constantly appealing to Americans in that way to save money, or gain power and appeal. "If you don't act right now, you'll lose your chance," or "Come on down right now; prices may never be this low again." The possibility of lost opportunity is a great motivator for most Americans.

In a business meeting, an American might make an offer and establish a deadline for the deal. This process is in complete contrast to the Japanese style of persuasion, which focuses on maintaining group harmony. They look to establish long-term relationships and maintain that relationship as a persuasion technique. Pressure on price or deadline is usually not exhibited; rather, quality and a reflection of consumer need are presented as the foremost concerns.

Arabs, on the other hand, will appeal more to religious or national beliefs, or even friendship and emotion. This is why they take more time establishing personal/business rapport in order to ease into the situation.

During presentations, Americans reflect their cultural values of directness and openness in their communication with participants. For example, if an American asks the audience, "Are there any questions?," and no one responds, it is assumed there are no questions. In contrast, if the same question was asked in a Japanese meeting, no one would respond either, but for a different reason: the Japanese value of group harmony—not wanting the other participants' time to be wasted. The Japanese also demonstrate their care not to embarrass the presenter if they don't know the answer, or if the question is of less value to the other participants.

Situation 18. During your presentation, one of the Americans in the audience questions the data you are presenting. You then

(a) Ask, "Why?," and justify your data.
(b) Say, "Okay," and proceed.
(c) Say, "We can talk about this issue after the meeting."
(d) Respond, "Put your concern in writing."

In keeping with the American value of directness, the right thing to do would be to ask why the person disagrees and back up your position with data. This factor shows your ability and willingness to compete, and helps the Americans with their fact-based decision-making process.

Situation 19. It is almost one hour into the two-hour Arab company presentation and no one has asked a question. Will you

(a) Keep going?
(b) Tell them it's time for questions?
(c) Look at the manager and ask, "Do you have any questions?"
(d) Call for a break and discuss the subject informally?

Another problem related to information exchange is the one presented in Situation 19. Here, the question asks what to do if, after an hour or two into your presentation to an Arab audience, no one has asked a question. Arab cultural values stress the importance of status and age, which is directly related to how questions are asked. The senior member of the group often speaks before anyone else. To get input from the other participants, you must address the senior member directly for input; the others can then follow.

Closing the Presentation and Applied Cultural Values. The close of a presentation reflects the cultural values of society just as much as any other part. The American will come to a conclusion, seek an agreement, and set up a plan for future action. The Japanese presentation ends naturally with the exchange of information and group harmony. The Arab presentation closes by looking to the future as a continuation of the past. The senior leader indicates the direction to follow.

Being prepared to conduct or be a part of a successful cross-cultural presentation means being aware of your own cultural values and those of the other participants: the importance of knowing that the Americans value logic, directness, competition, and equality; the Japanese value group harmony and information exchange; and Arabs value status and seniority. These customs are applied in the opening through the decision making and on to the closing. Without understanding and working with these contrasts in mind, success will remain elusive.

Cross-Cultural Written Communication

- *Why are business letters from Arab executives usually longer than those from other cultures?*
- *What is the proper way to introduce your company's product to a Japanese company?*
- *How do you establish contacts in an American company?*

When communicating in writing, it is important to be able to express yourself coherently. It is an additional burden when your writing has to conform to the guidelines of another culture. By learning to work within contrasting value systems, however, you have a definite advantage over those who don't work this way. As in other business functions, written communication (letters, faxes, memos, reports) reflects the writer's cultural background and values, as shown in Table 5. 5.

Cultural Objectives and Opening Business Communications. If written business communication is to conform to a different cultural style, it is vital to understand what each culture is trying to accomplish. This cultural objective and the purpose of the communication is related to the value system of each culture.

For example, the cultural objective of most written American communication is to provide information in order to seek a commitment from the other party and to put a plan in action. This process, again, is in line with the overall American value of being direct and action-oriented. In contrast to the American objective of providing information, Japanese business communication is to seek information, and to offer a proposal. The Arab form of written business communica-

Table 5.5
Cultural Contrasts in Written Business Communications

	American	Japanese	Arab
Cultural Objectives	Provide information; Seek commitments and action	Seek information; Offer proposal	Information exchange
Opening	Direct to objective	Offer thanks; Apologize	Personal greeting
Content	Factual; Plan of action	Specific questions; Solicit information	Background information; Indirect to subject
Persuasion Tools	Immediate gain or loss of opportunity	Waiting	Personal connection; Future opportunity
Nonverbal Communication	Urgency; Short sentences	Modesty; Minimize standing; Letterhead or marks	Lengthy; Elaborate expression; Many signatures
Closing	Affirmative; Specific requests	Maintain harmony; Future relationship	Future relationship; Personal greeting
Applied Cultural Values	Efficiency; Directness; Action	Politeness; Indirectness; Relationship	Status; Continuation; Acknowledgment; Wishes

tion is simply to exchange information on a particular subject, and to establish rapport, friendship, and trust.

Situation 20. Most American business letters state the purpose in

(a) The first paragraph.
(b) The second paragraph.
(c) A middle paragraph.
(d) The last paragraph.

Most American letters will explain the purpose within the first two paragraphs. This swift statement of purpose reflects the American values of time and directness.

Letters written by people from other cultures would most likely start with an extensive greeting and/or background information. The Japanese introduction, for example, usually offers an apology or thanks to the reader for previous efforts. An Arab letter starts with an extensive personal greeting and then gives background information before stating the purpose of the letter. Most Americans, however, will start with their conclusion, and then will support it with facts. If an American reader cannot spot the letter's objective quickly, the individual may lose interest and miss the subtle clues common to those cultures that communicate indirectly.

As a helpful guide to understanding cross-cultural written business communication, here are some introductions from actual letters. Try to find out from which culture each one comes:

Dear Farid:
   I am writing you a quick note to let you know that there is a marketing group here in . . . interested in scheduling the two-day "Global Strategy" workshop. I left a phone message one day last week; since I haven't heard a response from you, I thought I'd try another way.

Dear Dr. Elashmawi:
   Thank you for your faxes of the second and fifth of September. As always, I read your proposal with interest, but unfortunately, I must decline your offer. I wish to stress that this does not reflect on the quality of the program.

Dear Sirs:
   We would like to introduce ourselves to your esteemed company as one of the leading companies specialized in the field of foreign trade.
   We are working through local and offshore branches; whereas we have three branches in . . ., one in . . ., and another in . . ., as well as many well-equipped warehouses, with a storage capacity of 450,000 m/t of different products.

Can you figure out which letter is coming from a Japanese, an American, or an Arab? Each introduction has a different approach and mood to it. Use the explanations and examples throughout this section as guidelines to determine from where each came.

(*Answers: The first letter is by an American; the second one is by a Japanese; and the third letter is written by an Arab.*)

Content, Persuasion Tools, and Nonverbal Messages. After the introduction, the content of each form of written business communication follows the same cultural path. American business letters normally contain factual information to support their conclusions, to build toward developing a plan of action. The Japanese letter asks specific questions in order to solicit information they can use to make a decision. The Arab fills the letter with background information and comes to the objective by indirectly discussing the subject.

The main purpose of each letter is to convey some message to the other person; using certain persuasion techniques, each one can be designed to reach each culture's unique objective. Americans respond to time pressure and possibility for opportunity. Therefore, a letter to or from an American may have a statement of that nature to persuade the reader to act quickly. The Japanese usually write to seek information to be used for later decisions.

Situation 21. You are introducing your company products to an important Arab distributor. You should

(a) Enclose a letter of recommendation from the State Department.
(b) Send him or her a free sample of your product.
(c) Offer him or her a visit to your country if he or she meets sales quotas.
(d) Send him or her a copy of your credentials.

Arabs also have certain persuasive techniques they use in written business communication. This is where the proper techniques come into play. Since Arabs value status and the importance of good references, a letter of recommendation from the State Department and a copy of your educational credentials would be a persuasive device. Sending a sample of your product, rather than its description, will be good for persuasion too, because the sample will help the individual better understand your product. On the other hand, Americans would be satisfied with just a catalog of a product line. When communicating with the Japanese, it would be a good practice, again, to send a sample of your product. It would be even better, though, to send someone to demonstrate the product.

The Closing and Applied Cultural Values. When ending a piece of written business communication, it is important to follow the cultural guidelines of each individual. In closing a letter, Americans will clearly state the action or commitment they expect, and give a clear time frame for your response. Finally, they may sign using just their first name, emphasizing equality. Arabs will end a letter by reiterating their interest in maintaining a harmonious, long-term relationship. An Arab executive will sign correspondence with an indication of status, by using the title of "Doctor" or "President."

Situation 22. After a long communication process with a Japanese firm, you have received a letter stating, "We will keep your company name in our files, and if we need your collaboration in the future, we will contact you." You should

(a) Send a fax thanking them for the letter.
(b) Throw the letter in the trash because you won't get their business.
(c) Ask your go-between to see what is going on.
(d) Send a letter expressing your desire for future cooperation when they are ready.

The Japanese objective is to maintain harmony and future relationships. The response from a Japanese company will not be a direct "No," but an indication that they don't have the opportunity to do business with you at this time. You may want to send a fax or letter thanking them for their consideration and emphasizing your own commitment to a long-term relationship. This response would demonstrate your understanding of common values.

The closing of a business letter is also reliant on cultural values, and must follow the particular style of the reader. Here are some actual samples for you to guess which culture is being represented: Japanese, American, or Arab.

Please let me know when you might be able to schedule a trip to . . ., what the associated costs will be for this workshop, and how many people you can accommodate in one class.

I look forward to hearing from you soon.

Best regards.

Therefore, despite your earnest concern about introducing your program in . . . training, we regret that we must decline your kind proposal for the time being. Whenever we are in a position to have your program, we would like to let you know well in advance.

Thank you again for your kindness and we wish you the best for the coming year.

Sincerely yours.

We have been informed that you have useful experience in your market in many trading fields, so we did not hesitate in order to establish a good and cordial business relationship with you.

So, from this point of view, we wish to receive from you information on what kind of cooperation and business we can do together.

Wishing all the best for you and your staff.

Thank you, we remain your servant.

(Answers: The first letter is written by an American; the second by a Japanese; and the third by an Arab.)

To help better understand the process of written business communication, it is important to see how individual cultural values are applied. In the American culture, value is placed on efficiency, directness, and action. Any written business communication will and must reflect those values to be effective. In Arab culture, high value is placed on status, continuation of relationships, and hospitality. To work successfully within the Arab culture, you must reflect these values in writing.

Finally, the Japanese culture is one of modesty, politeness, and indirectness, and places importance on maintaining relationships. Your written communication with them must adhere to these strict guidelines, or may risk being ineffective and possibly damaging to future potential business dealings.

The following is another real business letter addressed to a mainland Chinese government manager by an American executive. Try to ascertain the cultural values as exhibited in the letter by the American writer:

Dear Mr. Chen:
1. Thank you for arranging the invitation.
2. Item 2 was done. Incidentally, payment delay was the fault of your office for not handling the document correctly.
3. Item 3 was also done. We sent an amendment copy earlier this week. I am very unhappy that our shipment of the letter of credit has not yet been made. These were to be shipped the end of July. On August 10 you advised me, because of serious floods, you could not ship goods to Hong Kong before the end of August. At that time, you asked for the delivery amendment, but at the same time, you also asked for other changes.

You have changed from FOB Hong Kong to CIF Chicago, which cost us additional dollars. It is very difficult to understand why you will hold up shipment when we have tried to explain we need this merchandise immediately. We have customers who have been promised delivery based on your original delivery information.

We care very much for our customers and we have always made every effort to take care of them. It seems to me that you should have the same attitude toward us. We are your customer. We have always tried to cooperate with you, but I am afraid you don't want to do business with us. Now I am in serious trouble with my customers because you are late in shipping. You must ship immediately.

I hope you understand what I am trying to tell you. Please let me have your answer, on all of the above, today.
Sincerely,
John Smith
Director

It is obvious the American executive has been influenced by American values of openness, directness, and action orientation.

Global Electronic Encounters

Today we have ever increasing options for electronic encounters with others beyond the telephone and facsimile transmission. Thanks to satellite technology in space, we can have both teleconferences and video conferences, as well as computers and modems that permit us to utilize the internet. With the latter, we can benefit quickly from information available from around the world, engage in rapid electronic-mail exchanges, or even enter an organization's homepage on the world wide web (http://www.) and join "chat corners." The e-mail capability is enhanced by an automated "list server" so that a group receives your message—that is, your e-mail letter is posted to a specific list of people who are interested in the same topic or business as you are. In effect, this is a private automated list that facilitates information exchange and gets ideas flowing. One company could use such a list to link representatives from its far flung subsidiaries; or a group of high-tech managers in one special field, such as biotechnology, could use this mechanism for professional development.

In electronic communications, one would hope that participants would utilize restraint and respect for each other; observe civil behavior and common courtesies; practice both business etiquette and ethics. For example, if you utilize some data obtained electronically, be sure to give credit to the author of that concept or insight.

However, there are cross-cultural perils inherent in using such telecommunications advances. Often, you have never met the people who you are exchanging with. Thus, you have little basis for forming personal impressions, or knowing their cultural backgrounds. Based on personal experiences in a group e-mail exchange on a specific subject, I know that too many people do not bother to compose their input off-line before transmitting. Instead, many people respond quickly, off the "top of their heads," sometimes to the detriment of another, which lessens the quality of the exchange. Thus, we offer these guidelines for electronic communication, especially with people you do not know well or have never met:

1) Exercise care and consideration in your transmissions.
2) Try to learn something of the receiver's culture; imagine who your receiver is and attempt to place yourself in that person's context.
3) Compose long e-mail letters carefully off-line, as you would an important business correspondence to be sent by regular post.
4) Restrain from using offensive or unclear words.
5) Set up an e-mail address book with accurate receiver addresses, or the master list sender or website master will return your electronic mail as undeliverable.

Much of the guidance we have provided about personal meetings and telephone usage, which helps you to move your brain instead of your body, applies equally to your participation in group teleconferences or video conferences.

Business Encounters with Asians

Answer the true or false questions to test your skills when interacting with Asians.

_____ 1. You must remind your Malaysian business partner three times to respond to your proposal.
_____ 2. The Chinese prefer white and black wrapping paper colors.
_____ 3. Most Koreans will involve status and authority in their negotiation process.
_____ 4. Indonesians regard your personal references more than your technical capabilities.
_____ 5. Upon the closing of a deal, all of the Indonesians involved expect to eat from the baked cake.
_____ 6. Touching the head of your Thai friend's child is a sign of caring, which Thais welcome.
_____ 7. The senior Thai always greets the junior Thai first.
_____ 8. Koreans most likely reduce your first offer by 50 percent.
_____ 9. Malaysians expect the boss to arrive and leave first in formal meetings.
_____ 10. Chinese indicate their anger or impatience with impatient nods and smiles.

(*Answer: 1-T, 2-F, 3-T, 4-T, 5-T, 6-F, 7-F, 8-T, 9-F, 10-T*)

My First Visit to Indonesia

In a first attempt to introduce my multicultural management and training seminars to Indonesians, I wrote directly to the editor of *Warta Ekonomi,* a local business magazine that hosts monthly events featuring international speakers. I waited for a response, but upon receiving none, I called one of my Indonesian friends in California, who immediately pointed out that I must contact the magazine's top person.

My friend found the publisher's phone number, and recommended I call him directly. I immediately phoned the publisher. Upon introducing myself, I presented my past achievements and accomplishments. To my surprise, he was more interested in the schools I had attended 25 years earlier and who I knew in Indonesia.

From this experience, I realized that Indonesians place a higher value on status and who are you affiliated with than on your past accomplishments, as most Americans do.

Later on, the publisher offered me the opportunity to speak at one of his magazine's monthly dinners. I took the opportunity, hoping that it would open the door for my programs in Indonesia. Because I was familiar with American and Japanese businesspersons, I began my pre-presentation conversations with either the typically American introduction: "What do you do, Mr. Ibrahim?" or the Japanese introduction: "What company are you with, Ms. Indrawati?"

I later realized that when most Indonesians introduce themselves they ask, "Where do you come from?" and then "Who do you know?" These questions are their ice-breakers. My inquiries were somewhat forward and offensive to them, and that is why I did not succeed in my first attempt at networking. Later on, I adopted the Indonesian style of introduction, and, not surprisingly, have found that my chances of success have greatly improved.

After my first seminar in Indonesia, I noticed that several of my student participants were eager to introduce me to their friends and other business executives. I had spent four days working with them and building close relationships, and they really wanted to show their thanks by offering me these connections!

One of the participants, Mr. Amir, introduced me to the managing director of a large car-manufacturing company. During our meeting, the managing director asked me for two copies of my book, one for himself and one for the president. He indicated that if the president showed an interest in the program, an introduction was almost assured.

After waiting three months, I phoned the managing director. He said he had not yet given the copy of my book to the president and therefore was unable to personally introduce me to the president. Considering three months too long of a time, I decided to try my luck with the company's training manager during my next visit.

After a three-hour presentation to the training manager and his staff, I received complimentary words and promises to get back to me. But several months passed without any progress. I later recalled my mentor's recommendation about being introduced to the highest person in an organization. I had not been patient enough—I should have waited for the introduction to the president.

The need of being introduced to the highest person possible is indicative of the Indonesian value system. I have found that Indonesians value relationships, cooperation, reputation, and group harmony. Communicating with high-ranking officials helps to reassure Indonesians that these values are being addressed. Contrasting these Indonesian values with the American priorities of equality, openness, risk-taking, and self-reliance, we can easily see there is great potential for friction.

Recognizing the importance of building relationships, I next recruited an Indonesian agent, Mr. Komuruddin, to market my programs in Indonesia. After six months of entertaining and visiting important clients, Mr. Komuruddin suggested I bring several copies of my book to potential clients.

The interpersonal marketing was rigorous. For example, we spent almost half a day with a prospective client, scheduling meetings with three of the company's important directors. Each meeting consisted of about forty minutes of waiting and five minutes of presentation, merely to hand each director a signed copy of my book.

I realized that Mr. Komuruddin was just planting seeds with the directors. Free samples, such as those of my book, were given to develop a relationship and spirit of cooperation that could eventually lead to the introduction of my programs.

Later, I found that this was part of a lengthy process that Indonesians follow to prepare the ground work for submitting official proposals. They must first guarantee that key people involved in the project are aware of it, will be satisfied with its outcome, and are ready to sign on.

Because I understand the Indonesian introduction and proposal process, I was easily able to reach Mr. Danang, director of a medium-sized advertising organization. My presentation went well, and I expected an immediate sale. However, Mr. Danang asked me if I would have dinner with him to further discuss my proposal and the training programs.

I happily accepted his invitation, and during our dinner we discussed our hobbies, our families, and world affairs. After dinner, Mr. Danang then referred me to his assistant, who was to handle final negotiations. To my disappointment, the negotiations with the assistant did not go well—the company could not afford my fees, a fact which the director could have told me directly. By referring me to the assistant, he was just passing the buck, and I ended up with a U.S. $200 dinner bill!

I have noticed that through my negotiations with Indonesians that they are not information seekers like the Japanese, or price negotiators like the Koreans, nor are they technology sensitive as the Americans are. They place more emphasis on maintaining harmony with their partners, and how the deal will benefit all participants involved.

This was ingrained in me when I asked some participants in my training programs to draw a picture of Indonesian culture. They simply drew a group of old and young Indonesians sitting down in a circle, ready to eat from the same meal! We have to share everything, the drawing conveyed. I then developed a negotiating stance that overtly emphasized group benefits. A win-win for everyone—both junior and senior staff members.

Thus, armed with my knowledge about communicating with Indonesian managers and proposing to Indonesian companies, I was able to make progress with a large telecommunications company. After a not uncommonly long process of introduction to the president and negotiation with team members, the manager in charge, Mr. Santoso, agreed on dates and prices for my program. I took this as a final confirmation.

To my surprise, after I faxed him the contract for his signature, Mr. Santoso replied that he needed approval from the vice president who was out of town for two weeks. I immediately realized that the deal was not complete yet! The deal eventually went through, but only after I learned I had to maintain continuous and patient communication with Indonesians in order to stay abreast of important developments.

To succeed with Indonesians, you have to recognize and work with four important characters: the person who can introduce you to the top person within the organization; the person within the organization who will lobby for your offer; the person who will orient the final selection toward your offer; and finally the person who will sign on the dotted line.

Communicating and working closely with Indonesians has taught me the lessons summarized in Table 5.6.

Table 5.6
Communicating and Working with Indonesians

- Greet Indonesians with a smile. Avoid highlighting your power, and don't act arrogant or self-centered.
- Show respect for the boss or senior person, and kindness toward his subordinates.
- Don't be misled by initial enthusiasm, as Indonesians will usually tell you what you want to hear.
- During discussions, invite Indonesians to participate. Otherwise they will be polite but silent.
- A deal is not a deal until the top person agrees to it and is assured that everyone will benefit.
- Relationships, reputation, group harmony, and cooperation are more important during negotiations than product prices or technological advancements.

Mr. Smith's Trip to Shanghai

Mr. John Smith, marketing manager for Global Mobile telephone company in the U.S., planned to enter his company's product into

Table 5.7
Tips for Personal Introductions—Southeast Asia

Korea	Indonesia	Malaysia	Thailand
Be humble and polite Make a good first impression Show your family status Don't mention counterpart's boss Avoid asking about family	Greet with a friendly smile Respect the boss Show kindness to subordinates Dont't highlight your power Don't use pressure tactics	Act conservative but friendly Mention your references Be compromising, harmonious Repeat lunch/dinner invitations twice	Greet with "Sawaddee" Younger persons greet elders Use polite words Avoid making physical contact Don't point your finger

Table 5.8
Tips for Conducting Meetings and Presentations—
Southeast Asia

Korea	Indonesia	Malaysia	Thailand
Arrange seating by seniority Allow everyone to present ideas Be aware that Koreans may exhibit initial aggressiveness Make decisions in meeting Avoid long prologues Don't interrupt or become angry	Create an informal atmosphere Provide breaks for long meetings Emphasize harmony Don't be emotional or confrontational Don't ask seniors direct questions	Expect the chairman to be tardy Allow the chairman to open the meeting Always serve refreshments Circulate an agenda beforehand Make meeting more ceremonial	Provide a leader, as Thais expect direction Establish trust and relationships Be aware that Thais are reluctant to express themselves Give them time to respond Give them a direct invitation to speak

mainland China. His experiences with exhibitions in Singapore and Taiwan were successful, so he decided to present the product at one of Shanghai's annual exhibitions. After one week at the show, he gave out 100 product samples and 5,000 brochures to exhibition visitors, and he was confident that he would receive a flood of orders upon his return. Six months later, he had received only five inquiries for technical information and no orders. He wondered what went wrong. This process had always produced orders in America, Singapore, Taiwan, Hong Kong, and other countries where he had made product introductions.

The reason for Mr. Smith's lack of success in China was his application of American cultural values and past experiences in other Chinese markets. As an American engaging in the development and marketing of new products, risk-taking, entrepreneurship, and taking advantage of new opportunities were strong motivations. He assumed that the very same things would be valued by his prospective Chinese buyers; he failed to recognize and understand China's business culture.

To achieve market entry in China, one must first verify if government policy allows a foreign company to introduce new products and services. For example, is it legal to invite a foreign supplier in a joint venture to sell mobile telephones? If the foreign businessman does not investigate relevant governmental policies, Chinese managers will only show a veneer of interest in the product, no matter how useful or marketable the product may be.

Once the businessperson has verified the existence of a compatible policy, and has learned its details, the Chinese partner will most likely insist on a joint venture. However, they will define it differently from westerners, who tend to construct joint ventures as a matching dollar-to-dollar and resource-to-resource endeavor. According to the Chinese concept of a joint endeavor, the foreign supplier will supply technology and capital, while the Chinese will match those contributions with land, labor, and a potential market. Westerners are frequently unaware of the Chinese expectation from joint ventures, which unnecessarily prolongs the negotiation.

Mr. Smith learned from his trip, the importance of establishing a formal relationship with Chinese government officials. He was advised by his Chinese friend from Hong Kong to meet with the mayor of Shanghai. Which of the following options should Mr. Smith choose to obtain a meeting with the mayor:

a. Find someone who is a good friend of the mayor and ask for an introduction.
b. Send a fax directly to the mayor's office asking for a meeting.
c. Have his secretary call the mayor's secretary for an appointment.

d. Send a formal letter to the Foreign Affairs Office of Shanghai requesting a meeting.

Based on his experience in Taiwan, he will probably choose the first option. In Singapore, when approaching a company or the government, the second option would be acceptable and in America, the third. But when dealing with Chinese government officials, you must adhere to a formal written communication protocol first, going through the channels to obtain a formal introduction. Then you may have to use a friend as a good reference.

You must adhere to formality. In his written communications with the Chinese, Mr. Smith learned some of their favorite, commonly used phrases such as "China is a big potential market," "We look forward to a mutually beneficial relationship," and "Let us stand together, hand in hand." Finally, after corresponding several times, Mr. Smith acquired his long-awaited meeting to discuss his joint venture with the mayor of Shanghai.

Mr. Smith then wondered how he could open the conversation. Which of the following topics should Mr. Smith discuss during his first encounter with the mayor:

a. The history of China.
b. Current developments in Shanghai and new investment policies.
c. Mr. Smith's company's accomplishments.
d. The mayor himself.

The opening subject of discussion with mainland Chinese is a very sensitive matter. The Chinese usually begin conversations by hinting about a mutually beneficial relationship in the future. This sets up a framework to begin negotiations. The process is initiated by getting agreement from their counterparts to agree on a general long-term goal that will benefit both parties. Once one has agreed to this general framework, the scene is set for both of you to compromise on any details involved in the general commitment.

Therefore, the proper answer is (b), which is to show interest in the long-term goals of the city, and in very broad terms, developing a business relationship. Talking about yourself and your company's accomplishments will probably be more impressive to your American counterparts. Asking the mayor to talk about himself will cause him and his Chinese colleagues embarrassment. Table 5.9 describes further cultural tips for conducting business meetings with the Chinese.

Table 5.9
Tips for Business Meetings with Chinese

- Arrive prepared and present yourself in a professional manner. Make your presentation formal and don't use humor.
- Conduct your presentation in English. Handouts and company brochures should also be in English.
- If language is a problem, use a professional interpreter; botched Chinese is unacceptable.
- A few weeks before your presentation, supply your clients with any complex technical data that you deem appropriate.
- Make your presentation free of technical jargon.
- The shorter the presentation the better. If you go over sixty minutes, you have gone on too long.
- Do not be secretive of your information. This will make the Chinese suspicious and reluctant to do business with you.
- Use graphics whenever you deem appropriate and provide copies of all your slides or graphics to the audience.

Summary Insights

In this chapter, we have presented many forms of communications across cultures. First, we discussed introductions, both business and personal. In some cultures, these two types of introductions work together to achieve winning sales or future business relationships. The exception is Americans, who may rarely continue a personal friendship once a deal has ended.

In addition, nonverbal communication plays an important role in business decisions. The problem with physical gestures is that each holds a different connotation for the various cultures. For example, the Japanese may smile to mask feelings of disappointment or confusion, while Americans use the smile as a friendly greeting. It is no wonder that cultural clashes occur: People don't understand each other's cultures well enough to resolve conflicts.

Telephone conversations are much like face-to-face confrontations. In some cultures, the telephone is used only to receive information. In other cultures, the telephone is used for telemarketing—the fast sell. To achieve a success, one must learn to use proper culturally-based phone etiquette. In this way, the person on the other end of the line will become happy with your business practices, and most likely will want to continue doing business with you.

Business meetings also have a range of different cultural styles. Each culture has a certain objective that, if observed, will help you attain business success. Americans are usually informal and confrontational in their meetings, whereas an Arab businessperson usually takes time to establish a relationship with the client before business is discussed in a meeting.

Presentations are also different in each culture. For example, the Japanese have a brief period of silence to think upon what was discussed in the meeting. Americans may ask questions when someone is speaking to ensure that they understand the material, or they may question any discrepancies. Arabs often rely upon religion (God's will) and friendship for the basis of the presentation.

In conclusion, communication in business differs with each culture. It is in your best interest to understand the culture of the people with whom you are dealing in order to achieve the ultimate business success—whether it be friendship, a sale, or a promise of future business opportunities.

Readers are urged to build upon insights gained from the three cultures discussed in this chapter to improve their cross-cultural encounters with businesspersons from other cultures.

CHAPTER 6

Managing Multicultural Human Resources

An Overview

- *What is the best way to teach an Arab technician how to repair a television set?*
- *What is the best way to motivate American workers to work overtime?*
- *What is the best way to conduct a performance review with a Japanese employee?*

Such questions reflect some of the dilemmas of managers currently involved in international joint ventures. Many organizations are now busy establishing plants and offices overseas, which will be staffed with local personnel with different technical and cultural backgrounds.

Settling in after the initial construction-to-production phase, expatriate managers are faced with how to train, motivate, and appraise their multicultural workforce. The same challenge occurs if your company is to utilize the facilities and employees of a foreign partner or subsidiary while providing expatriate management. Labor economics drive corporations to establish offshore plants in Taiwan, the Philippines, Mexico, or other newly industrialized countries. The problems of developing and managing local human resources naturally follow.

This chapter focuses on three important human resource development tasks related to the success of any international joint venture: training, motivation, and performance reviews.

For example, American managers face the problems of training Asian workers to use high-technology equipment, motivating them to produce high-quality products, and reviewing their work performance. Japanese companies face the same problems training workers in Asia and in managing American workers within U.S. plants.

Those managers without cross-cultural skills will generally apply their own cultural values when training, motivating, and reviewing the performance of local workers. This is inappropriate and ethnocentric. Applying the values of your own culture, when working with someone from another, will almost certainly result in culture clash.

This chapter presents a cultural contrast table and discussion using our three target cultures: American, Japanese, and Arab. Examples from these three cultures function to point out cultural differences, and to show the importance of adapting each process to the specific culture.

Each section is followed by situations that deal with each of the conceived key human resource development functions. These situations are designed to stimulate the reader's interest, and to challenge answers to his or her own cultural values.

Cultural Contrasts in Training

Your assignment is to prepare a training program for a new product for several overseas clients. What cultural factors do you need to consider in order to design and conduct an effective training program?

Table 6.1 shows the aspects of training design, and it compares the culturally related factors for our three distinct cultures: American, Japanese, and Arab. As you read further, keep your task in mind in order to apply the table's information to your target culture.

Group Composition

When planning training sessions, group composition is very important. Because of the Japanese emphasis on functional harmony and interaction, the size of the Japanese group is usually the smallest of the three cultures. Employees who perform similar functions, but at varying levels of seniority, feel comfortable in the same training group. Since the group will be sharing many experiences and doing actual training together, preestablished harmony must exist to maximize the learning skills.

Table 6.1
Cultural Contrasts in Training

	American	Japanese	Arab
Group Composition	Medium-sized; Mixed level OK	Smallest group; Grouped for functional harmony	Largest group; Very level conscious
Time	8–5 with breaks	9–6 with breaks; May go until 8 or continue informally after-hours	9/10–3 maximum; No lunch break
Preparation	Individual reading; Written homework	Group orientation	Not necessary or important
Getting Started	Self-introductions; random or by seating order	Introduction emphasizes company/ belonging; Senior goes last	Introductions by status; Senior goes first
Process	Emphasize "how to" and practical applications; Self-reliance; Specialization; More reading	Emphasis on doing/ discussing; Sharing experiences; Intragroup discussion; Role play; Rotation	Memorizing general skills; Coaching; Demonstration by leader; Minimal reading
Training Materials	Written; Self-explanatory	Visual with group discussion by doing	Visual; Coaching by team leader
Test of Knowledge	Direct questions to individual; Spontaneous, open questions	Group questions; Intragroup discussions; Directed questions	No direct, individual questions; Need preparation
Cultural Values	Self-reliance; Competition; Time conscious	Relationship; Group achievement; Group harmony	Seniority; Reputation; Individual achievement

Similarly, Americans tend to accept participating in the same group with others of different levels within the company, but for a different reason: The American culture values individuality and competition more than authority and seniority. American training groups tend to be larger than Japanese groups from different divisions. Each person comes to the training program with self-reliance and a competitive self-image.

The composition of Arab training groups reflects the cultural importance of level and status. Training groups must be homogeneous in terms of company hierarchy. Arab training groups can be the largest of the three cultures. You cannot set up a training program and invite the vice president of the company along with the company technicians. The vice president will be uncomfortable, and the technician will not challenge the vice president, especially if the program is participatory.

Time

The training schedule for Japanese, American, and Arab training programs follows the timetable of the normal working day. Americans value time and expect training sessions to begin and end promptly as scheduled. Americans will resist extended hours or weekend programs unless they receive compensation for their time. They may use breaks and lunch hours to network with other members of the training group, rather than to discuss the content of the training session or share personal experiences.

The Japanese, on the other hand, may extend the session into the evening, if the group is interested. The importance of group harmony often continues into after-hour drinking sessions that allow the group to process and share the training experience. The Japanese use the time for informal discussion; the training experience is enforced among team members and the instructors. The manager of the group and the instructor will generally give the signal to close the evening session.

Arab training sessions usually begin around nine o'clock in the morning and last until midafternoon with one coffee break. In most Arab countries, the main meal is served at home around three to four o'clock in the afternoon. After the meal, most working people take a one- to two-hour rest, or share this time with their families. To design or implement a western-style training schedule that goes from nine o'clock in the morning to six o'clock in the evening is culturally inappropriate. It is better to structure training over an extended period of two to four days, even if the same program could be accomplished in much less time in another culture.

Preparation

Americans, who value self-reliance, often send out pretraining materials to prepare participants in advance of the training session. These materials may contain reading or writing assignments that each individual is responsible for completing in advance of the group session. This reflects the cultural values of equality and preparedness. Each participant will want to begin the training session with the same background information as the others. Advance preparation also saves training *time*.

The Japanese may conduct a group orientation to build group harmony prior to the formal training session. During this group orientation, everyone has the chance to get acquainted and build team spirit. If participants receive pretraining materials, they may share time together to review and discuss it among themselves. If participants arrive early for the training session, they will spend the time building harmony by discovering what they have in common, such as home towns, schools, companies they've worked for, and so forth.

Arabs will not expect much preparation in advance of the formal training. Instead, they rely on the trainer to give them the information they need in the training session itself. Arabs learn by coaching and so they will wait until the trainer arrives to start the formal training process. Arabs may use any written training materials for further study during the training period in preparation for testing.

Getting Started

Americans reveal their individuality by introducing themselves, either randomly or by seating order. Most of them will give brief introductions that emphasize their responsibilities. They will avoid revealing personal information or background, except in a human-relations type of training. These introductions are usually brief and to the point, showing respect for everyone's time. Seniority, age, and position are not often taken into consideration in the introduction stage. Sometimes, a trainer will ask a new group to take five minutes to pair off and learn about another member. Then such individuals are asked to introduce the other person to the class, and vice versa.

Japanese programs begin with the most junior member and proceed to the most senior to reinforce the group relationship. Introductions stress company, department, and team identity, rather than the individual. Every member may reveal some personal and cultural background. Participants will not, however, highlight any major achievements or accomplishments as an American might. Japanese present themselves modestly, in harmony with the other team members.

At the beginning of the formal Arab training session, the senior person will begin by introducing himself. Introductions continue in descending order, reflecting the Arab cultural values of seniority and authority. The senior person will probably extend a warm welcome to the trainer and show the hospitality of the Arab culture. Individuals may reveal more of their personal and cultural background, social status, and position. This act will form the basis for the continuous interaction within the team, and forge the first links in establishing personal rapport with the instructor as coach.

Process

Americans expect training programs to focus on practical information that can be directly applied to a specific objective. They learn from self-reliance, which includes individual reading and the opportunity to tailor the information to individual or specialized needs. The training process must be very objective, and direct results should be measurable and achieved in the short-term. Multiple-choice testing is often used because it offers objective, tangible options and immediate and measurable results. At the end of the training program, Americans want to feel comfortable that they have achieved mastery of a specific skill that they can apply to other similar problems. An effective training program for an American audience should proceed from "what to do" to "how to do it."

The Japanese style of training emphasizes learning by doing, including ample opportunity for group discussion and sharing. Again, preestablished group harmony must exist to facilitate the sharing of experience and learning. Each person in the group must contribute to the learning environment and become part of the team. Team assignments are more effective than individual tasks. Role play and simulation present opportunities to watch and "feel" the situation. Visual and tactile materials, such as samples, are essential learning tools in Japanese culture.

By contrast, Arabs depend on repetition and are accustomed to more theoretical training programs to present materials that can be memorized. Memorization as a learning process has a long history in the Middle East. Presently, lack of sufficient equipment for trainees may be one reason why this practice continues. The trainer usually demonstrates general skills, which are then reinforced in one-on-one coaching. To be an effective coach, the trainer needs to establish rapport with the trainees from the beginning of the training session. Cooperation among team members is not as high as in Japanese groups.

The implication from this discussion is that cultural differences do exist in the way people learn, as well as in their group dynamics.

Training Materials

Americans do well with written, self-explanatory materials that are in tune with the American values of individuality and self-reliance. They prepare well for the training, take essential notes, and study afterwards. They appreciate an advance copy of the training materials. At the very least, Americans like to have the written materials in hand during the training session rather than at the end of the program. They place emphasis on visuals or other learning aids that illustrate the content.

For the Japanese, who have a highly nonverbal culture, visual material supports group learning and learning by doing. Prereading is not highly valued unless special time is allowed for group discussion of the material. Japanese participants expect materials to be handed out and explained at each stage of the program. Slides, videotapes, and other communication aids will be of interest, but not as a substitute for group participation.

Arabs also value visual training materials. They are more attuned to watching than participating. They may watch the group leader or the trainer demonstrate the equipment or procedure. They like to keep written material to read over, but not as a reference tool to replace the trainer. Many foreign companies complain that machine manuals are often thrown away, or not kept in good condition. The explanation for this problem is that once the information has been memorized, the manual is no longer of any use. If a problem comes up, the leader has the responsibility of knowing how to solve it. Remember in the Middle East, the culture favors aural learning.

Tests of Knowledge

Evaluating the results of training programs for American groups relies on the cultural importance of individuality, competition, self-reliance, and risk-taking. Americans do not hesitate to take individual responsibility for their answers in front of the group. The instructor may ask individuals at random to answer spontaneous questions. If the instructor asks the question to the group, someone will certainly volunteer. Multiple-choice questions are a very popular testing format. In the final feedback session, Americans expect the trainer to open the floor for discussion. Anyone who has something to contribute will do so, underscoring the American cultural values of openness, individuality, and competition.

The Japanese evaluate their training experience as members of a group. Competition is between groups, and group accomplishment is the goal. The group, not the individual, is tested. The instructor must carefully prepare the group for the question/answer period. Japanese trainees do not like to be put on the spot. Tests of practical skills, such as repairing a machine, are more valuable than written tests on the same material. The Japanese expect to be prepared for direct questions rather than the open-forum style that is comfortable for Americans.

Arabs, fearing loss of face, prefer private evaluations with plenty of preparation and study time. They prefer tests of overall knowledge that are segmented to minimize the memorization load. For Arab groups, the trainer must first solicit feedback from the member with the most seniority. Arabs usually reflect each others' opinions.

Cultural Values

Throughout the training process, from design to implementation, the consideration given to cultural values determines the success or failure of the program. In our examples, the most important American cultural values that affect the training function are competition, individual achievement, self-reliance, and time. Japanese cultural values that influence training are group harmony, achievement, and the importance of relationships. The most important Arab values include individual achievement, reputation, and seniority. Keeping cultural values in mind during the training process will enhance your training results. On the other hand, if you assume your own cultural values to be universal, culture clash will occur, and you will not achieve your training objectives.

A Test of Intercultural Training Skills

Following are several situations that managers may face during developing—or conducting—training across cultures. Try to identify the most appropriate answers. Keep in mind the cultural values presented earlier and base your answers on them. Consider your culture and others', and compare how your answer might differ.

Situation 1. You are sending new equipment to Japan. Which of the following is most important to send with the equipment?

(a) A detailed technical description in English.
(b) A detailed technical description in Japanese.
(c) Audio and video tapes in Japanese on how to use the machine.
(d) A technician to explain how to use the machine.

Most westerners rely on specific written instructions. The Japanese culture values learning by doing and sharing the experience within the group. In this case, a written, technical description in English and/or Japanese will not be adequate for the needs of the Japanese learning process. Sending an audio or video tape, while a better solution than a written technical manual, still represents a one-way information flow. The best answer (d) is to send someone to explain and demonstrate the machine. This solution allows the trainees to learn by *observing, doing, and sharing*—common Japanese values.

Situation 2. Betty Hu, in Taiwan, is new on the assembly line and she is still having difficulty putting the units together properly. You want to train her. You should

(a) Say, "Betty, you should pay closer attention to what you are doing."
(b) Shout across the room, "Betty, do you need help?"
(c) Tell her, "Betty Hu, you are learning very fast," and then show her exactly how the units are put together.
(d) Move her aside and show her how to put the units together.

Nonembarrassment, especially in front of peers, is an important value for most Asian cultures. Shouting at Betty, or telling her directly that she is not doing her job properly, will upset her and result in demotivating her. The best way to establish a close working relationship and to reinforce your position as her manager is to show her the proper way to assemble the unit. Words of encouragement, as in (c), help her maintain confidence and may lead her to come to you for help before she fails again.

Situation 3. You are planning a training session in an Arab factory on the latest modification to a piece of machinery. Who should you invite to the training session?

(a) The president of the division.
(b) Everyone using the machine.
(c) The section engineers.
(d) The section technician in charge of preparing the machine.

In Arab culture, status, position in society, and education are very highly valued. When you plan a meeting for any purpose, take a careful look at the level and status of the participants. If you invite a mixed group, the lower level people (in status, education, or even wealth) will not feel their comments are welcomed, even if their points are valid. The most appropriate answer is to conduct the training for the section engineers (c). The section engineers will, in turn, have the responsibility of training their technicians. If technicians attend the same training session as their managers, they will learn the same information as the managers, and the technicians will lose respect for the managers' authority. The chain of command is a reflection of the power of information and skills in the Arab culture.

Situation 4. You have just finished training a U.S. team on how to install a new product from Korea. At the close of the program, they expect you to tell them

(a) "Now you are on your own."
(b) "If you have any questions, talk to other members of the team."
(c) "Call me anytime if you need help."
(d) "Here is the reference manual."

When conducting training programs for American participants, keep in mind the important American cultural values of independence, self-reliance, and competition. Answers (b) and (c) would be appropriate for Arab or Japanese trainees, but not for Americans. The most appropriate response for American audiences is (d) because, again, it responds to the American value of self-reliance. Other cultures, like the Japanese, learn how to maintain group harmony.

Situation 5. After completing your training program for a Japanese operations team, you want to hear their views. You should

(a) Ask the senior person first.
(b) Ask for volunteers.
(c) Go around the room by seating order starting from the right.
(d) Ask the junior person first.

As in Situation 3, this example illustrates how age, seniority, level of education, and position in the company affect the success or failure of training programs. Respect for seniority is very important in Japanese culture. If you begin by asking the most senior (and probably the oldest) people for their comments, the younger and more junior people will withdraw from the senior members' comments. The most appropriate answer is (d). Contrast this scenario to western culture, where anyone is welcome to challenge the others' views in an open and direct way. Answer (a) would be most appropriate in Arab culture: The opinion of the senior member usually reflects the opinion of the group.

Situation 6. You have just received a new machine from Japan. You are disappointed by the lack of a detailed instruction manual. You conclude that

(a) The Japanese are not good at explaining themselves.
(b) They want you to depend on them for operation and maintenance.
(c) They expect you to learn by doing.
(d) You'll have to develop the manual for yourself.

When exporting equipment overseas, many companies are faced with the problem of developing an adequate manual for the equipment. Americans will feel comfortable reading the instruction manual and will follow it step by step until they can operate the equipment. Japanese industrial equipment often does not come with good operating instructions. Because this equipment was designed for a local culture that depends on group learning activities and shared experience, the most appropriate answer is (d). Most foreign buyers of Japanese equipment may have to develop their own operating instructions once they have mastered the operation of the machine.

In this section, we have presented important elements in the design of training programs across cultures. We have provided cultural contrasts for the three distinct cultures in several areas: group composition, starting and ending a program, participants' preparation, introductions, the training session, and testing. We have shown that each culture has its own values; each culture influences the training design and process.

A Training Design Challenge

Now consider that you have to design a training program for a Chinese or Russian team. You must start by identifying the cultural values that will affect each of the training segments discussed. Then you must analyze how these values will change the format and process of training you may be offering in your own culture, and develop your training program with cultural values in mind.

Many North American consultants develop training packages that they naively believe only require translation into a foreign language. At the very least, all instructional materials require a local editor to interpret the content, and determine its cultural appropriateness.

Presently, there is a demand for western management education in the Russian Commonwealth and its former satellite countries of East Europe. For almost fifty years, these new "trainees" have been culturally conditioned toward a centrally planned economy and management. Whether live, by teleconference, or through videos, American management trainers will have to do more than adapt their methodology and material. They will have to assist these "students of bureaucracy" to conceptualize many topics from the role of managers to entrepreneurs.

Those in management development sessions within transitional economies have much in common, whether in second-world countries such as Poland or Hungary, or third-world nations like Tanzania. The latter have been disabled by socialistic systems, and have to learn about free enterprise, management accountability, and other such subjects that westerners take for granted. However, these peoples in the former Soviet bloc or Africa also have unique strengths and resources for international trainees to build upon, such as an eagerness to learn new methods.

Cultural Contrasts in Motivation

In a multicultural work environment, not everyone is motivated by the same factors. Motivational processes, tools, and values reflect our culture, directly or indirectly. The motivation process—how it's controlled, who it appeals to, how to recognize it, and how to reward or punish employee behavior—directly relates to cultural values.

Table 6.2 shows the aspects of motivational tools and the cultural factors for our three distinct cultures: American, Japanese, and Arab. As you read, keep in mind your goals and own cultural values in order to apply the information in Table 6.2 to your target culture.

Management Style

Management styles are important and effective motivators in each culture. Americans react positively to a leadership style characterized by professionalism and friendliness. However, American managers separate personal and business matters. An employee who has a personal friendship with the manager may be surprised when the manager tells that same employee that he or she is not performing up to expectations on the job. Most American managers move up the corporate ladder by being self-motivated, willing to take risks, competitive, and success-oriented. Naturally, these managers use these similar values to lead and motivate others in career development.

Japanese managers also motivate employees through continuous counsel and persuasion. They maintain group harmony through involvement in the professional and personal lives of their staff. Employees look to their managers to develop their career paths, as

Table 6.2
Cultural Contrasts in Motivation

	American	Japanese	Arab
Management Style	Leadership; Friendliness	Persuasion; Functional group activities	Coaching; Personal attention; Parenthood
Control	Independence; Decision-making; Space; Time; Money	Group harmony	Of others/ parenthood
Emotional Appeal	Opportunity	Group participation; Company success	Religion; Nationalistic; Admiration
Recognition	Individual contribution	Group identity; Belonging to group	Individual status; Class/society; Promotion
Material Rewards	Salary; Commission; Profit-sharing	Annual bonus; Social services; Fringe benefits	Gifts self/family; Family affair; Salary increase
Threats	Loss of job	Out of group	Demotion; Reputation
Cultural Values	Competition; Risk-taking; Material possession; Freedom	Group harmony; Achievement; Belonging	Reputation; Family security; Religion; Social status

well as to guide them in major activities. Older or retired executives often assume a mentoring role with younger managers and become strong, motivational influences.

The Arab manager will be most effective in a parenting-type role that includes coaching and personal attention. The manager's status and authority level, and his ability to punish or reward the employee allow him to assume this role. At the same time, managers separate the working relationship from personal matters so as not to lose their authority and control over their employees.

Control

All people are motivated by the power of being in control of their own lives or work space. Americans feel good about being independent and in control of their own destinies—a direct reflection of American cultural values, which include control over decision-making, time, and money. Because Americans value privacy, self-reliance, and individualism, they are motivated to control their own decisions, even if this control involves considerable risk-taking.

On the other hand, Japanese motivation comes through group harmony and consensus. The individual feels in control when he or she is in harmony with the group; it is the greatest source of individual motivation. Similarly, maintaining harmony between different sections and departments is a very important task of upper level management. A top manager in Japan will not approve a decision unless all departments have agreed on its implementation. Of course, each department will have already gone through a similar internal consensus process with all of its members involved.

The Arab manager strives for control of others through a parenting relationship. Everyone tries to be in the position of the manager (parent) in order to gain respect and responsibility. Title and status play a major role in rewarding individual achievement. Contrast the Arab model with the Japanese model, in which age, seniority, and experience are all respected when making major decisions.

Emotional Appeal

Americans respond to available opportunity. Because the culture values risk-taking and is very time-conscious, Americans look at the configuration of resources at any given time as presenting unique opportunities. Americans often use the analogy of a "window of opportunity" —an opening to be used or lost. An American marketing manager will be motivated to open an overseas office if he or she believes a competitor is planning to enter that market. The motivation to take the risk in a new market comes from the desire to seize the opportunity. Likewise, American business is filled with sports analogies and terminology, like "win the game at all costs," or "you have to be a team player."

The Japanese are motivated by reputation and company success, which are allied with their cultural values of belonging and group achievement. A Japanese manager will feel he has to accept an overseas assignment in order to assure the company's success. Regardless of the disruption that such an assignment may cause to his personal life, the Japanese manager will not risk embarrassment by refusing the boss's request on behalf of the company's interest. The company's success and harmony within the group may take priority over the manager's immediate family requirements.

Arab motivation comes from an appeal to the sense of self within the authority structure. A manager will accept an overseas assignment if it results in personal gain in position, status, and money. Appealing to religious values may also be strong in times of crisis or celebration. Words of admiration and flattery for individual achievement are also motivational.

Recognition

Americans want to be directly recognized for their individual contributions and achievements. When a group project is successful, the group manager will expect recognition and reward for the achievement. This recognition may come in the form of a bonus, a salary increase, or a promotion to a position of higher responsibility. In turn, the manager will individually recognize the contributions of the team members during their performance appraisals.

Japanese recognition comes through identification with the group in ever-widening circles: family, working group/team, department, division, company, nation. Recognition for group achievement belongs to the group rather than to individuals.

Recognition in Arab cultures generally results from the individual's status in the hierarchy. When a department reaches its goal, the recognition will go to the department manager who will then recognize the next level under him. The ripple effect will continue until it reaches the lowest level employees.

Material Reward

The material rewards that are culturally appropriate reflect the values of the macroculture. Americans measure individual success more in material possessions than in social status or family/class membership. Monetary rewards motivate Americans. Increased salary, commission, or participation in a profit-sharing plan recognize individual efforts. Many American entrepreneurial technology companies motivate new employees by offering them company stock rather than high salaries. Rewards, like recognition, can take many forms: from a company car, to a promotion or a desirable transfer.

The Japanese are motivated by rewards shared among the group, such as bonuses, social services, and fringe benefits available to group members. Acknowledging the achievement of an individual member of the group is inappropriate. Recently, many Japanese companies have begun rewarding their employees with memberships to health or golf clubs for their efforts.

Arabs are motivated by gifts for the individual and family, which reflect admiration or appreciation for the individual's achievement. A one- or two-day salary bonus is a good motivator for Arab workers who, for example, exceed their normal efforts. Giving such bonuses to individuals is used as a motivational tool for others. In small business environments, an Arab business owner might send a good worker a gift in the form of household appliances that he or she can enjoy with his or her family.

Threats

The opposite of a reward is a punishment. The effectiveness of a punishment in the form of a threat as a motivational tool depends upon the cultural values of the individual. Since Americans' identities are often directly linked to their jobs, the threat of being fired is significant. However, since American society is highly mobile, Americans may react to the threat of being fired by quitting. Americans may not be as concerned as Japanese or Arabs who may lose their jobs in this situation.

To the Japanese, the greatest threat is formal or informal exclusion from the group. If an individual is not contributing to the group's functional output due to personal ideology that differs from the group's, the manager's task is to counsel that individual before he or she feels pressure from the group. Many Japanese complain that they cannot take full advantage of their vacation days. The Japanese feel that if they are away from the office for more than a few days, the other workers will treat them as if they had abandoned the group. Although a Japanese company rarely fires an employee, group pressure may force an individual to resign or ask for a transfer.

To the Arab, a demotion is a threat to one's reputation and status. If such action is necessary, it has to go through a lengthy review procedure to ensure that the action is justified and to give the employee ample time to correct his performance. Loss of a job is a deep embarrassment to the employee, his colleagues, and family, and will be difficult to remedy.

Important Cultural Values

As discussed, it is very clear that motivational tools and processes reflect each unique culture. In the American culture, competition, risk-taking, material possessions, self-reliance, and freedom are all motivational values. In contrast, group harmony, belonging, and achievement are important and valued tools in motivation of Japanese employees. The Arab workers value reputation, authority, and social status and respond to these values in their motivation process. Each organizational culture responds to appropriate and relevant motivational patterns within the larger culture's established values. What motivates you within your culture is not necessarily what motivates someone from another culture. Recognizing this simple fact is essential when working to motivate employees with diverse cultural backgrounds.

A Test of Intercultural Motivation Skills

The following are situations and examples you should consider when motivating people from different cultural backgrounds. Try to identify the most appropriate answer. Keep in mind the cultural values identified in earlier chapters and base your answers on them. Consider how your answers might change in different cultures.

Situation 7. You are working with an Arab colleague and want her to help you finish an assignment. You are most likely to get her cooperation if you say

(a) "In the name of God, please help me."
(b) "If you help me, I'll buy you dinner."
(c) "My friend, I need your help."
(d) "Let's be the first to finish this project."

An American might be motivated by statement (d), but an Arab values relationships more than direct competition. If she feels you are being competitive, she will probably exclude you from her network of friends. Religion is highly valued, but a reference to God will not be sufficient in this case. Trying to motivate your friend by offering to buy dinner as in statement (b) contradicts values of friendship and hospitality. The most appropriate answer is to appeal directly to your friendship. She will immediately volunteer to help you. However, she will also expect that you will reciprocate if she ever needs help.

Situation 8. You are a department manager in China. To motivate your production supervisor, you should tell him

(a) "If our department increases output by 10 percent, you'll get a 1 percent bonus."
(b) "I'm planning to reorganize the department, and I'm thinking of promoting you if production increases."
(c) "If your team doesn't meet the quotas, you're fired."
(d) "Why don't you put in some overtime to finish the quotas?"

Authority is important in Chinese culture. A manager may welcome a bonus, but the bonus won't change his position in the company. Threatening him with dismissal goes against his social values. He believes he is already working hard, and such a threat is not the norm. Giving him the option to work overtime will not motivate him either, since his success will depend on others in the system. The best motivational tool in this case is to link his performance to future promotion, answer (b). A promotion will give him higher status, position, salary, and authority that few people are able to achieve in Chinese society.

Situation 9. You are conducting an appraisal for one of your American subordinates. He will want you to recognize his

(a) Promptness.
(b) Creativity.
(c) Directness and openness.
(d) Accomplishments.

In American culture, promptness and being direct and open are the norm. To evaluate someone for that behavior will not motivate him. Likewise, unless creativity results in a finished product or tangible achievement, promptness is not rewarding in itself. Most Americans value success and accomplishment in their work and personal lives, so the best answer is (d). They expect to be measured by their accomplishments, and believe they should be rewarded for them. The first choice of a reward is a salary increase, followed by promotion.

Situation 10. Your Japanese team achieved its production quota last month. How should you acknowledge their achievement?

(a) Treat them to a sushi dinner where you give special recognition to the group leader.
(b) Don't mention it, because meeting quotas is their job.
(c) Call the oldest person aside and thank him.
(d) Thank the group at your next meeting and ask them to increase production even more.

The Japanese have a saying, "If the nail sticks up, hammer it down." They wear clothes without bright or distinguishing colors, reflecting the Japanese values of modesty and harmony. If you recognize only the group leader as in (a), the rest of the team may feel that you do not admire their team effort. Individual recognition does not reflect the Japanese values of group harmony and achievement. The most appropriate answer is (d). Acknowledge the group's achievement and stress that the group's continued efforts to improve production will enable the company to be more competitive.

Situation 11. You are supervising a factory operation in an Arab country. The group manager is not working up to expectation. How should you alert him to his performance?

(a) "Increase your group's productivity, or you're fired."

(b) "Do you need any help?"

(c) "You'd better take care of your group, or I'll replace you."

(d) "Why don't you hold a meeting with your group to find out what's wrong?"

In Arab culture, motivating an employee with the threat of firing is usually not appropriate, and goes against religious harmony. Such a threat is not a common tool because it directly affects family security, which is a concern even to the employer. Asking the employee if he needs help is appropriate if he is in a lower level position, and if he is approached with a coaching attitude. If the performer is in a management position, he will be motivated by the threat of being replaced or demoted, which would cause him to lose status with his peers and social group. In this case (c) is the most appropriate answer. If he held a meeting with his group, then he would expect to seek input from lower level personnel. This is not appropriate in Arab culture. Lower level personnel usually expect the manager to define the problem and guide them to a solution.

Situation 12. Mr. Hiro, from Japan, is working for you. He's probably motivated by

(a) Being part of a strong, leading international company.

(b) The promise of a good annual salary raise.

(c) A promotion to group leader and a better title.

(d) A trip to Hawaii for him and his wife after the project completion.

Seniority is important in Japanese culture, and most workers know that title and position come with age and experience. In a traditional Japanese organization, you cannot promote a young person directly to a leading position no matter how qualified or educated the person may be. Mr. Hiro knows that he will not be promoted beyond the level appropriate for his age and experience. With increasing affluence, leisure time has become important to many Japanese, especially the younger generation. A promise of a trip to Hawaii would be of interest to Mr. Hiro, if the reward is available to the whole group rather than to an individual. Salary increases and bonuses are usually equally divided among the employees based on responsibility. The most valuable motivation in this case is belonging to a successful international company that enjoys a reputation for good quality among its competitors (a). In Japanese companies, this kind of motivation is accomplished through a systematic indoctrination program that highlights company values.

Cultural Contrasts in Performance Reviews

Table 6.3 presents important differences in performance reviews across American, Japanese, and Arab cultures. Note how the objective, structure, interaction process, outcome, and closing of a review differ across these cultures. Keep in mind your cultural values and how they may differ from other target cultures.

Objective

The objective of the American performance appraisal system is normally to evaluate the employee's goals that have been preestablished between manager and employee. The employee usually has input into these goals, especially in the area of professional growth, and therefore takes on the responsibility for meeting his or her goals. Reward or punishment is then based on how the employee performed these goals given the opportunities and constraints of the situation.

The Japanese objective in performance reviews, on the other hand, is to ensure that the employee is functioning in harmony within the group. The core element in the Japanese system is the group's output, and every member of the group is evaluated on how the group performed, its contribution to other groups, and to the company in general.

For the Arab, the objective of the performance appraisal process is to reprimand and set back those employees whose performance does not meet the manager's expectations. The employee is constantly monitored and measured for individual performance. In contrast with the American system, which gives the employee opportunities and expects the response to be increased performance, the

Table 6.3
Cultural Contrasts in Performance Reviews

	American	Japanese	Arab
Objective	Periodic review based on preset goals; Identify personal strengths/ weaknesses	Find out why performance is not in harmony with group	Set employee on track; Reprimand for bad performance
Structure	Formal procedure; Every 6/12 months in manager's office	Informal, ad-hoc with employee; Frequent reporting to administration; In office, coffee shop, bar	Informal, ad-hoc; Recorded in manager's office
Interaction	Two-way, both sides present openly own point of view; Manager as leader/ advisor; Employee independent, self-motivated	Employee answers manager's concerns; Manager gives advice as parent, mentor, senior employee; Part of group/ family; Continuous feedback	One-way; Manager guides subordinate; Authority figure, mentor; Random feedback; Child in family
Evaluation	Success measured by performance to stated goal	Success measured by contribution to group harmony and output	Success measured by major personal contribution
Outcome	Promotion; Salary increase; Bonus; Commission; Salary freeze; Loss of title; Loss of power	Mainly affects amount of semi-annual bonus; Less important job; Job rotation; Dock bonus/salary	Bonus of ½-day salary; Promotion; Salary decrease
Closing	Stress agreement on expectation; Documented review	Performance continually forward to personnel department; Open door	Admiration or threat of punishment; One-way door
Cultural Values	Openness; Equality; Fairness	Group achievement; Relationship	Privacy; Authority; Parenthood

Arab system usually concentrates on keeping the employee at the same performance level.

Structure

The American appraisal procedure is formalized. Appraisals take place at regular intervals, usually every six or twelve months, in the manager's office. The interview is well documented, and must be signed by both the manager and the employee. This document is then reviewed by a higher level manager. Sometimes such evaluation meetings may be self or group appraisals.

Unlike the American system, Japanese appraisals are semiformal. The manager seeks to counsel an employee only if the employee's performance is not in harmony with the group, and if the manager sees that the individual's behavior is having a negative impact on the group's functional output. A Japanese manager may call a meeting with his employee if he is often late to work or argumentative with his group members. Most often, such a meeting will take place in an informal setting—a coffee shop, for example—to find out the reasons for the employee's dissatisfaction with the group. Many times the reason is personal. The Japanese manager will then take the employee's personal life into consideration when evaluating his or her job performance. This act is in contrast to the American system, which expects the employee to keep personal problems from having a negative impact on job performance.

The Arab manager will call an employee to his office if the employee is performing below expectation. The Arab manager will reprimand the employee in private, so as not to cause him public embarrassment. In this case, again, the Arab manager uses status and authority to signal to the employee that punishment will follow if performance does not improve.

Interaction

In an American performance appraisal, the manager acts as a leader, facilitating the discussion and encouraging the employee to present his or her own point of view. Communication flows in both directions. Both the manager and employee come prepared to discuss and defend their own interpretations of the employee's performance. In this situation, the employee acts as an independent, self-motivated individual. Both sides are ready to defend their positions openly and directly without major consideration for any personal relationship the employee and manager may have.

The Japanese scenario is very different. The manager acts as a senior family member to counsel and guide the employee. The employee, acting as a junior member, responds to the manager's concerns. Maintaining the relationship and harmony is very important during such sessions. This feeling of harmony comes from a previously established relationship of trust and respect for the manager. Personal and professional matters related to job performance may be openly discussed. Solutions are recommended by the manager.

In the Arab model, the communication flow is clearly one way. The manager is an authority figure and mentor whose role is to judge and punish, if necessary. The status and authoritative power of the manager must be maintained at all times. The employee's role is that of a reprimanded child. The American model of open communication and feedback is not appropriate here. If the Arab manager tries to apply the American model, he will lose status and respect from the employee. Likewise, if the manager is open and direct, he will be labeled rude and aggressive.

Evaluation

The evaluation of an American employee depends on how well that employee has performed the goals that were previously discussed and agreed upon by the manager and employee. These goals are the cornerstone of the evaluation process. Any problems or difficulties in achieving these goals will be openly discussed. A new set of goals and plans of action for achieving these goals in the next review period will be formulated. Personal problems are not considered a valid excuse for not meeting professional goals.

The success of the Japanese employee is measured by his or her contribution to the harmony and performance of the group. The manager is in charge of group goals and works hard to improve group performance. The manager has the responsibility to make sure each individual within the group is making a contribution to the group's output. In an auto assembly line, for example, the Japanese manager watches that everyone is following the correct sequence for the general success of the company. The next group in the assembly line is considered to be the client. All employees are measured by efficiency and the quality of the product.

The Arab employee's performance is evaluated on major personal contribution. Group members must excel individually to prove to the manager that they have performed up to expectation. Each employee will be aware of his achievement at each step by the manager's continuous admiration or criticism.

Outcome

What are the outcomes of the performance appraisal process? The American employee who receives a positive evaluation can expect a promotion with a salary increase or a bonus. A negative evaluation may lead to a freeze in salary or position, a lateral transfer to a less powerful position, or even a demotion. He or she expects a tangible reward in the short-term, and will defend this expectation directly to the manager. Employees who are not satisfied may ask for a transfer, or even leave the company.

For the Japanese, the main tangible reward is the traditional semi-annual bonus. A failure to meet the group norm could result in less important job rotations or perhaps a decrease in pay. The amount of bonus usually reflects the employee's contribution to the group's output, harmony, contribution to the department, the department's contribution to the company, and the company's overall performance. In this culture, every member counts and is measured on his contribution to the overall performance and output.

Positive outcomes for Arab employees include a bonus representing one or two days of monthly salary, or a promotion that automatically includes an increase in salary. Punishment for poor performance usually comes in the form of a decrease in pay or a demotion. The system rewards individual excellence rather than overall performance as in the Japanese culture.

Closure

Americans strive to end performance appraisal interviews on a positive note. The manager and employee directly work out any conflict or disagreement before the meeting ends. Any unresolved conflicts will be referred to a higher manager or the personnel department. At the close of the interview, the results of the evaluation are written up and signed by both parties; the document then becomes part of the employee's file.

In the Japanese appraisal system, the manager will frequently send information to the personnel department on how well the employee is working within the group. This information serves as input to calculate the employee's bonuses and salary increase. It is also used to review the employee's job rotation assignment, and to identify any special skills that could contribute to the growth of the group and the company.

In Arab culture, the manager will congratulate the employee on his performance, and offer him a reward in the form of a promotion, which will involve a salary increase, or the manager will threaten him with punishment if he is not on track with the manager's expectations. The employee may be honored in a special ceremony if his contribution resulted in increased value to the company; for example, a new patent, major cost savings, or a big order.

Cultural Values

The American appraisal process emphasizes open communication between managers and employees. Ideally, both parties enter into the process as individuals who are equals. Americans see the formal system of conducting periodic appraisals with written results signed by both manager and employee as reinforcing their values. In contrast, the Japanese system reflects the cultural values of group harmony and relationship. The individual's role as a functional part of the group is most important, and his performance is measured according to group norms. Conversely, the Arab model emphasizes the cultural values of authority and seniority.

A Test of Intercultural Performance Review Skills

Following are examples and options to be considered when conducting performance reviews with personnel from different cultural backgrounds. Try to identify the most appropriate answers. Keep in mind the cultural values identified in earlier chapters. Consider other cultures and compare how your answers might differ and why.

Situation 13. Most Japanese managers conduct formal performance reviews of their subordinates

(a) Once a year.
(b) Twice a year.
(c) Never.
(d) Whenever required.

In most Japanese organizations, performance is a continuous, measurable process between the employee, his group, and his managers. If employee performance declines, the group will immediately notice and respond. The only appropriate answer here is (d). Formal feedback is a review sheet that the Japanese manager submits to Human Resources as input for the employee's bonus and salary adjustment.

Situation 14. Most Japanese companies offer their employees a bonus twice a year. Each employee's bonus is based on

(a) Individual creativity and achievement.
(b) The overall performance of the company.
(c) His or her manager's review and recommendation.
(d) A combination of individual, section, department, and company performance.

In Japanese companies, individual creativity is important to the extent that it contributes to the group. Contrast this ideal with the role of individual creativity in American organizations, where individuals receive direct rewards for the results of their creativity. Although the Japanese manager's reviews and recommendations are important inputs into the employee's bonus, there is a better answer. The semiannual bonus, a significant part of the Japanese reward system, is based on the employee's ability and efforts as a team member, the team's contribution to the organization, and finally on the company's overall performance. Answer (d) is the most appropriate.

Situation 15. During a performance appraisal with a manager, an American employee would probably

(a) Agree with the manager because he is the boss.
(b) Point out how the company stock is rising and demand a share.
(c) Openly discuss any issue and defend his point of view.
(d) Point out his good relationship with other employees.

The performance review in most American organizations measures individual achievement against preestablished goals. In many Asian countries, when such reviews are formally conducted, they are ceremonial; the employee does not challenge the manager. The manager acts not only as the boss, but also plays the role of mentor and parent figure. In American culture, personal relationships are separate from business. The employee stands ready to justify his actions and expects acknowledgement and reward for personal achievement, regardless of the performance of the group or company as a whole. Interpersonal relationships and group harmony on the job, while important, are much less significant than individual performance.

Situation 16. You are an American employed in an American company. After six months, your manager has still not discussed your yearly goals with you. What should you do?

(a) Nothing.
(b) Call this to the attention of your manager's boss.
(c) Write down your goals and ask your manager for his signature.
(d) Openly discuss it with him and insist on writing down your agreement.

In American culture, decisions are based on the analysis of facts, numbers, and logic. This analysis is usually open for discussion. If your manager has not approached you to set your yearly goals, you should not go over your manager to his boss. Your manager expects you to communicate directly and openly with him (d). In developing your goals with your manager, you should prepare your own input for the discussion and be ready to defend it. Once you and your manager have agreed, you should ask to put it in writing. In Arab culture, you may do nothing and assume that the boss will take care of you at the end of the year.

Situation 17. You are conducting a performance appraisal with a Vietnamese member of your group. You ask, "Where would you like to be in two years?" He looks at you in surprise. The reason may be

(a) He expects you, as the manager, to know the answer to that question.
(b) He thinks you are suggesting that he will leave the company.
(c) He thinks you want him to change jobs within the company.
(d) He thinks you are not giving him a good evaluation.

In most Asian cultures, the manager acts as the parent for the employees. Not only does the manager see that they perform their jobs, but the manager should also be aware of their family life and personal problems that may affect their job performance. The manager's role is also to develop the employee's professional skills. In American culture, employees are responsible for defining their own goals and showing their own initiative. The Vietnamese worker will be surprised at the manager's question because the worker expects that the manager will already know the answer (a). If the manager is American, the non-American worker may interpret the question as a suggestion that he look for another job, or that his job performance is not satisfactory.

Situation 18. In most Arab organizations, a performance review is not important because

(a) The relationship between the manager and his staff is already well-established.
(b) Once employees are hired they cannot be fired.
(c) The reward system, or salary increase, is set by the general manager.
(d) Arabs avoid personal loss of face.

The formal appraisal system in most Arab organizations is not as developed as in other western countries. Salary increases are mostly based on the overall salary structure and employee's level within the structure. However, such an established situation does not preclude the implementation of a formal review system. Rather than expecting a reward for a good performance, an employee can expect punishment for poor performance that caused a major setback. Firing an employee is a major step, because it involves consideration not only for the individual, but for his or her family and local status within the community. The most appropriate answer is (c). In general, the reward system depends on the condition of the organization and established criteria for salary increase.

Training and Motivating Southeast Asians

True or False

Answer true or false to the following to assess your understanding of Asian business culture.

1. ____ Indonesian trainees expect snacks during coffee breaks.
2. ____ It is acceptable to reprimand a Malaysian worker in front of his or her peers.
3. ____ Thai trainees do not mind working overtime.
4. ____ To motivate Malaysian workers you must allow them independence.
5. ____ You can mix management levels during Korean training sessions.
6. ____ If a Malaysian worker comes with a problem, you may just point out the answer in the manual.
7. ____ When training Indonesians, provide one-way instruction rather than class dialogues.
8. ____ When training Thais, use local examples and case studies.
9. ____ Koreans prefer a well-documented training manual for post-training study.
10. ____ Many Korean workers will prefer a salary increase rather than a title.

Answers (1-T,2-F,3-F,4-F,5-F,6-F,7-T,8-T,9-T,10-F)

Supervising Southeast Asian Workers

Fong Chang, a Chinese immigrant with a degree in computer science from Stanford University, has worked for Surge Semiconductor in California's Silicon Valley for just over a year. Mr. Russell, his American boss, has decided to review his past year's performance.

"Well," the boss says, "I must say that we've been quite happy with your work. Your input on the Phase Two project really opened some doors for us. We have no complaints about your work." Fong thanks Mr. Russell and says that the year he has worked for Surge has been very rewarding. Mr. Russell then says, "Well, tell me, then, where do you want to be one year from now. Let me know what your ambitions are while working for Surge."

Embarrassed, Fong blushes and smiles sheepishly. He does not tell Mr. Russell how he would like to move up within the ranks of Surge Semiconductor. To the surprise of his boss, within a week he quit his job at Surge.

Fong quit his enjoyable and promising job because he misunderstood his boss's inquiries. Mr. Russell offered Fong an opportunity to sell himself. He liked his work and wanted to learn about his long-term goals with Surge Semiconductor. But Fong interpreted Mr. Russell's inquiries as a sign of abandonment. Because of his Chinese cultural background, he expected his boss to be more of a patriarch who expresses concern about his workers and directs them appropriately.

Ignorance of the American value of direct and open communication cost Fong a great job. He may lose more jobs if he doesn't learn about the differences between American and Chinese cultures.

An extremely important American value is independence. Nho Dahn, who has recently been hired by an American laser manufacturing company, learns this in our next example. He has lived in America for three months, and this is the first job he has had that pays well. He wants to save enough money to send his wife and daughter in Vietnam to America.

After two days on the job, Nho encounters difficulties with the equipment he is using. He asks his supervisor how to fix the problem. The supervisor gives the technical manual to Nho and tells him to fix the problem himself. Two hours later, Nho finishes repairing the machine. But a few days later, another problem occurs with the machine. Again, he goes to his supervisor, who tells him to fix the problem himself.

The supervisor becomes angry when this happens a third time. He notes in his personnel file that Nho has very little initiative. He also expresses his anger to Nho directly. "This is not the way we do things in America. You can't come to me with every little problem you have. You must learn to solve your problems alone."

This concerns Nho. He realizes that he must try to work independently and go to his supervisor only when all other options have been exhausted. He worries that these incidents may jeopardize his employment when his performance is reviewed at the end of the year. Keeping his job is Nho's main concern. He fears he may never be able to send his wife and daughter to America if he is forced to find a lower paying job.

Contrasts in Training Southeast Asian Workers

Tables 6.4 and **6.5** present cultural contrasts in training and motivating Asian workers. Note again the reflection of Asian cultural

Table 6.4
Tips for Training Asians

Koreans	Thais	Malaysians
Don't mix the levels of managers. Apply strict rules and intense activities, as Koreans expect this. Allow breaks every hour. Provide a well-documented training manual.	Coordinate training schedule so it does not exceed daily working hours. Use local examples and case studies. Question individuals directly to check their understanding. Use an off-site training facility.	Follow a coaching style. Recognize individual achievement. Give positive reinforcement. Provide ongoing rapport. Allow the boss to open and close training sessions.

Table 6.5
Tips for Motivating Southeast Asians

Koreans	Thais	Malaysians
Be a mentor. Promise promotion with title. Provide overseas training. Recognize that Korean workers have closer relationships with those in authority.	Give them recognition. Organize training courses. Give them authority. Offer bonus plans. Praise workers who perform well.	Show respect and exhibit positive values. Be aware that formality is important in business. Emphasize the position of the person and not the company.

values in each of these activities. Status and strict orders, for example, are important for Koreans. So when dealing with Koreans you will be more successful if you follow a semi-military style. Most Koreans will do their utmost to please their boss, and in return, expect a mentoring relationship.

We note a less structured and more relaxed culture among Thais. Thais will not welcome working or training overtime. Trainers must learn to overcome Thais' initial resistance to participate and ask direct questions. Trainers can usually do this by forming small teams with assigned leaders and group tasks. Ongoing praise, recognition, and off-site training will guarantee the best results from Thai workers.

In Malaysia, a coaching style with positive feedback and public recognition of individual achievements will work best. Trainers should coach in a formal and ceremonial manner. Senior management should present certificates of completion, which will be highly appreciated by participants. Management should open and close the training session to indicate to the participants the importance and value of the training.

Contrasts in Training Among Indonesians

Table 6.6 presents contrasts in conducting training within one country—Indonesia. Indonesia is a multicultural society, and one

Table 6.6
Tips for Training & Motivating Indonesians

	Javanese	North Sumatran
Reviewing Performance	Maintain group harmony. Be formal. Be a mentor. Describe outcome: promotion.	Be open and frank. Be informal. Designate a leader/advisor. Describe outcome: bonus. Focus on target.
Motivating	Give clear instructions. Use polite language. Control emotions. Use a parental style. Don't publicly reprimand.	Give clear instructions. Use common language. Provide material and treats. Use a coaching style. Direct reprimand OK
Training	Use visual aids. Speak clearly, politely. Allow time for breaks. Allow intense group discussions. Provide one-way instruction.	Use plenty of visual aids. Speak clearly and loudly. Allow less time for breaks. Limit group discussions. Allow open dialogue.

must be aware of its cultural diversity. Table 6.6 presents two of the most diverse cultures in the country, Javanese and North Sumatran.

Summary Insights

In this chapter, we again pointed out the importance of recognizing and adhering to the cultural values of the individual, group, and country in developing human resources.

Whatever the task—training, motivation, or performance review—its success depends on the manager's recognition, understanding, and adaptation of tasks to each individual's cultural values.

In our emerging multicultural society, many of us will be faced with the task of developing organizational human resources. In this chapter, we have provided important cultural contrasts and elements to be considered in designing and implementing such tasks.

Recognizing your own set of cultural values and how they differ from others', you should be able to develop and contract an effective and adaptable human resources development program.

In the next chapter, we will discuss how cultural values influence the success or failure of business negotiations.

CHAPTER 7

Managing Intercultural Business Negotiations

An Overview

- *Is it time to negotiate?*
- *Who is the decision-maker—the technical manager? the older person? the group?*
- *I gave them all the price concessions they wanted; why didn't I get the contract?*

In international business negotiations, successful deals often depend on the intercultural skills of the negotiator. Although technology and money may be a factor in the negotiation process in our fast-growing world, the cultural competence of the negotiator will give a company the competitive edge.

This chapter will introduce us to the process and contrast in negotiations across cultures. We will again focus on the three targeted cultures—American, Japanese, and Arab. Of course, the situations presented should be applicable to your culture as well. Elements of negotiation include negotiating group composition and number, importance of time and space orientation, establishing rapport, and persuasion tools used across cultures. The concepts presented will be supplemented by several mini-situations that many managers face, abstracted from business cases to reinforce the skills presented.

Cultural Clashes During Negotiations

- *What are we negotiating for? Price? Relationship? Delivery . . .?*
- *Why haven't they responded to the price proposal I gave them last week?*
- *Why is he asking me to sit beside him?*
- *We have only two people on our team; why did they bring seven?*

Let's explore the following cultural clashes that occur during negotiations. How people respond may influence the success or failure of the outcome.

Situation 1. Your company has decided to sell its product line in Japan through a joint venture with a local distributor. To identify a good local distributor, you should first

(a) Participate in an open exhibition in Tokyo.
(b) Look in the Japanese Yellow Pages for a local distributor.
(c) Place an advertisement in *Tokyo Business Today* highlighting your product's low price.
(d) Ask your Japanese friend to introduce you to several local distributors.

Most western companies would probably commit themselves to participating in a large exhibition, (a). They would base that decision on the assumption that an exhibition gives wide exposure to their product's high technology or low price. They may expect several orders as a result. The Japanese would be happy to visit the exhibit to gather information. However, the results of participating in such an exhibition would not produce the relationship that Japanese companies look for with their partners. The most suitable answer is (d). The proper introduction is very important and valuable to initiate a relationship. The Japanese must build a relationship first, then they will consider your product or services.

Situation 2. Your company has just received confirmation that a high-level delegation from the People's Republic of China will visit your office. Since the Chinese have already received a sample of your products, the purpose of their visit is probably to

(a) Sign an agreement to act as your local distributor in China.
(b) Establish a firm relationship with the company management.
(c) Learn more about your company's technological advancements.
(d) Visit your country as a reward for their hard work at home.

Here, as in Situation 1, the Chinese delegation is visiting your company to establish rapport and gain more information before committing themselves to a long-term relationship. You should not expect any immediate agreement as a result of the visit. Technical know-how and information exchanges are usually left to second-line managers. The most appropriate answer is (b). Such delegations may also include some members who are sent as a reward for their hard work, not because they are key decision-makers.

Situation 3. For the past six months, you have been discussing a joint venture with an Arab government agency. During your last visit, your Arab counterpart invited you to visit a local historical site for the day. While you were touring the site, he started talking price. This was his way of

(a) Strengthening his personal rapport with you.
(b) Showing his pride in his country's historical tradition.
(c) Persuading you to cut prices.
(d) Obligating you to invite him to your country.

After six months, your Arab counterpart has already established a personal rapport with you and has gathered information about your product. He is now in the persuasion stage. He has created this opportunity to persuade you to offer a price concession. The most appropriate answer is (c).

Situation 4. You are negotiating a price with an American supplier who has just told you, "If you don't accept my offer right now, there may not be another chance." She is using these tough words to

(a) Scare you.
(b) Make you feel that you are missing an opportunity.
(c) Show you Americans believe in straight talk.
(d) Get out of the deal.

Many Americans use the prospect of loss of opportunity to persuade buyers. Since Americans negotiate on the basis of equality, the American supplier is not trying to scare you, nor is she interested in establishing personal rapport. Her main interest is in closing the deal immediately. In American culture, opportunity is a powerful motivator. She is using this as a persuasive factor to motivate you to accept her offer. Other cultures might look at this statement as threatening or insulting, and may break off negotiations as a result.

Situation 5. In successful negotiation with South Americans, you should start by

(a) Making concessions to the other party to show good faith.
(b) Presenting information about your business.
(c) Persuading them to accept your first offer.
(d) Establishing personal rapport.

The most appropriate answer in South American culture is to spend time establishing personal rapport, (d). Getting directly into business might not lead to a successful outcome, for personal rapport comes into play a great deal during the concession stages.

Intercultural Negotiations

Intercultural negotiation consists of three major processes:

- Establishing rapport
- Exchanging information
- Persuading

Our cultural values influence all aspects of our behavior in business matters. Throughout this section, we will focus on the process of intercultural (not necessarily international) negotiations. We will identify the general process that people and companies go through in establishing a relationship or negotiating an exchange of products/services.

While negotiating with others, keep in mind your own cultural values and those of other cultures that have been discussed throughout the book. In recognizing how such cultural values influence everyone's behavior, you will be more sensitive to their needs, and will negotiate with understanding.

Table 7.1 presents important components and cultural contrasts in the negotiation processes among Americans, Japanese, and Arabs. Important elements include group compositions, the number of people involved, space orientations, and other elements as shown in the table.

Table 7.1
Contrasts in Intercultural Negotiations

	American	Japanese	Arab
Group Composition	Marketing oriented	Function oriented	Committee of specialists
Number Involved	2–3	4–7	4–6
Space Orientation	Confrontational; Competitive	Display harmonious relationship	Status
Establishing Rapport	Short period; Direct to task	Longer period; Until harmony is established	Long period; Until trusted
Exchange of Information	Documented; Step-by-step; Multimedia	Extensive; Concentrate on receiving side	Less emphasis on technology, more on relationship
Persuasion Tools	Time pressure; Loss of opportunity; Saving/making money	Maintain relationship references; Intergroup connections	Go-between; Hospitality
Use of Language	Open/direct; Sense of urgency	Indirect; Appreciative; Cooperative	Flattery; Emotional; Religious
First Offer	Fair +/– 5 to 10%	+/– 10 to 20%	+/– 20 to 50%
Second Offer	Add to package; Sweeten the deal	–5%	–10%
Final Offer	Total package	Makes no further concessions	–25%
Decision-making Process	Top management team	Collective	Team makes recommendation
Decision Maker	Top management team	Middle line with team consensus	Senior manager
Risk-taking	Calculated; Personal; Responsibility	Low group responsibility	Religion-based

Many of us are involved in intercultural negotiations in one form or another. It is important to keep the following points in mind during this process:

First, what are we negotiating? Is it price, a relationship, a product/service, or a delivery time? Each culture has its own timetable in the negotiating process. Many cultures, such as the Japanese and Arab, may start the negotiating process by building a relationship before moving into serious business discussions. On the other hand, most Americans and westerners will move directly into the product/price negotiation process and worry about establishing a relationship later, if at all.

During intercultural negotiation, you should address subjects in a culturally appropriate order. For example, most westerners have a shorter time reference than Asians and Arabs, hence westerners move faster in their negotiation process. Non-western cultures may look on a fast sell as a high-pressure tactic, however, and may withdraw from the negotiating process altogether.

Nonverbal messages certainly influence the outcome of the negotiation process. Among these are the use of space during meetings, the way presentations are given, seating arrangements, and interpersonal dealings. Dress codes may give very important clues to the negotiation environment and status. Formal dress may convey rigidity. In contrast, the practical, action-oriented, informal dress of Americans may connote a willingness to give concessions.

The number of participants, their status and age, and the skills of team members might also give direct clues to the stage of negotiation and its importance in the negotiating process. Westerners may bring a minimum number of participants to a negotiating session to avoid the possibility of an internal conflict. The Japanese may have more team members than the other side. The membership of the Japanese team often rotates during the negotiating process, depending on the responsibilities of the team members. Arab negotiating teams, on the other hand, may present the most senior person first and leave the details to more junior members or the technical staff. At the final stage, the senior person may come back to close the deal in order to demonstrate his or her powerful position on the team.

Establishing Rapport

- *Why does he keep asking me what I do for a living? I hardly know him.*
- *Why does she keep asking me about my family? She has never met them.*
- *Why do they keep sending us these faxes about prices? We have only recently met.*

These are some of the reactions businesspeople can encounter when they negotiate with other cultures. In many cultures, establishing rapport is considered an important preliminary step for business; other cultures may find it of only minimal importance. Let's now look at the process of establishing rapport and its value in each of our three sample cultures.

Table 7.2 presents the main contrasts in establishing rapport among the American, Japanese, and Arab cultures.

American Values

Most Americans value directness and are action- and task- oriented. In most of their business encounters they will give less emphasis to personal relationships, and focus directly on the task. In negotiating with other cultures, Americans do not give priority to a personal relationship. Many Americans will say, in essence, "Let's do business, and then if we have time, we'll be friends." In contrast, other cultures may say, "Let's be friends and then we'll do business."

To most Americans, establishing rapport does not go beyond exchanging business cards. Once an American has your card, you become part of his or her network of business contacts. Many Americans like to do business over the telephone, and are not really interested in meeting their clients face to face. In many other cultures, a face-to-face meeting is important in order to build the personal rapport essential to establishing a business relationship.

An American meeting you for the first time will probably ask, "What do you do?," meaning "What is your profession?" Americans

Table 7.2
Establishing Rapport

American	Japanese	Arab
Short-time/task orientation	Considerable time spent in negotiation	Longer negotiation period than American and Japanese
Personal relationships not as important	Group consensus and harmony	Established trust through references and personal relationships

make a business call to focus on the sale, not on the person. This is completely appropriate and acceptable within the American culture.

For other cultures to deal successfully with Americans, they must then adhere to the American time frame. If you set up a business meeting for nine o'clock, Americans expect to begin the meeting at nine o'clock and start business.

In the negotiation process, many Americans quickly focus on negotiating price. In other cultures, the future relationship may be the bottom line; any business agreements would come after the personal relationship is well established.

Americans tend to look at negotiation as a separate and distinct task in the business process. They present their product, negotiate price and delivery time, deliver the product, get paid, and go on to the next deal. For many other cultures, negotiation is a process with overlapping segments. After the relationship is established, it is followed with agreement on the exchange of products and delivery. When it comes to negotiating prices, all elements are available for compromise and concession.

Establishing rapport in American culture is generally limited to exchanging names, business cards, and initial small talk such as "Hi, how are you?" From there, Americans go directly to business. Therefore, Americans exhibit their cultural values of directness, openness, informality, action orientation, and time.

Japanese Values

- *Why do I have to repeat my presentation to the new manager? I have already explained everything to the last manager. Aren't they working for the same company?*
- *I have no time for small talk. Let us get down to business and finish up!*
- *Our product speaks for itself. Why are they asking for all these references?*

The Japanese time frame is usually longer than that of the westerner, and they may use it to establish the sincerity of the other side towards building the business relationship.

Most Japanese spend considerable time cultivating this phase of the negotiation process. This phase usually starts with an introduction from a reference. Next comes the process of verifying the other side's cultural values to determine if they are in touch with Japanese values: A friendly relationship is a prerequisite for any business negotiation or deal. Many westerners may fail to understand this step; they approach the Japanese market with their product once they learn that a demand exists. In their introduction, Americans stress product features, technology, or even competitive prices. The Japanese may recognize all of these from the first meeting, but cannot deal with the foreigner until they have built a relationship.

However, the Japanese workplace is not just for social interaction. Socializing and exchanging information after work is a vehicle for harmonizing and building social and group relationships. Many westerners who host Japanese businessmen may leave them on their own over the weekend when, in fact, the Japanese may welcome the idea of being together after work or on the weekend. They are looking to establish an interpersonal relationship with their foreign counterpart.

You may find that you have to meet with every member of the Japanese team with whom you will be negotiating. Every member must feel comfortable with you. Even during formal negotiations, foreign businesspeople may have to give their entire presentation to a new Japanese manager—not for the technical portion—but to establish a personal rapport and relationship with the new manager.

When meeting Japanese businesspeople for the first time, exchanging cards is very important. They may look at your card and note your company, department, position, and name. They will probably engage in small talk about your trip and your interest in their country and company.

Several tips can be used to enhance rapport during negotiations with the Japanese. Refer to all the work that you have done with Japanese organizations to show you are trusted by their culture. Join them for dinner or drinks after work. Keep in touch with them by making telephone calls whenever you are in Japan or even overseas. During national holidays, exchange greeting cards and gifts to show your interest in a long-term relationship. Show your willingness to compromise on small issues such as meeting times, where to eat dinner, or required documents.

Situation 6. A Japanese company has accepted your proposal to visit and present your product line, including a technical presentation and a discussion of price. One month after the presentation, you have not heard from them. It is your impression that they were impressed with your product. What should you do?

   (a) Forget it. If they were interested they would have contacted you by now.
   (b) Call them to find out what is going on.
   (c) Send them a letter.
   (d) Make another trip.

In general, after a presentation by a foreign company, the Japanese team will study the proposal for its technical merit. If the team is interested, they will probably send you a letter within one to two months expressing an interest to exchange further information. The Japanese will use this time to observe your cultural values. One to two months is a reasonable time to expect feedback from the Japanese. If they are not interested, you will probably not hear from them, or you will receive a letter thanking you for your visit. Calling will not help unless you have managed to establish a personal rapport with someone within the group. Making another trip might be a sound idea if it is combined with another, related task.

It is important to remember that relationships and group harmony are very important in the Japanese value system. These factors are vital at any time, in any business, and should be considered before getting into more detailed negotiation. In order to discuss any serious business details, you must first be within the context of the Japanese value system. Once you are in, you will not easily be separated.

Arab Values

The Arab view is that establishing rapport is even more important than it is for the Japanese. However, business is primarily done on a personal level, in contrast to the Japanese who identify with the company through its representative group. The Arab time frame is longer because their information gathering system is much less extensive than that of the Japanese team. In general, a personal relationship is usually established between the foreign partner and one Arab team member.

The success of your negotiations will largely depend upon the number and quality of previous contacts you have made. It is vital that you spend extensive time with the person in charge of the negotiating team, until the person feels you can be trusted to discuss matters related to business.

You can achieve personal rapport through communication during evening dinners with various business acquaintances, which must be reciprocated in your home country. Gift giving and special favors, such as assisting a relative or friend overseas, may show the desired degree of mutual trust.

Let us highlight some of the previous ideas through the following situations:

Situation 7. You are visiting Saudi Arabia to present your company proposal for a joint venture. You want to discuss this deal with the president of the company. You should plan this meeting

(a) At the company president's office the day after your arrival.
(b) During dinner after a visit to his office.
(c) At the president's house.
(d) During an open seminar to the company managers on the first day.

If you are negotiating with an American firm, (a) or (d) would be culturally appropriate because there is no need to strengthen your personal relationship with the president. In Arab culture, it is not appropriate to discuss the details of business matters at the first meeting. It takes several sessions before such discussion is acceptable. Thus, the best choice would be (b).

It is more acceptable to open the subjects of long-range interest and the possibility of joint ventures after dinner, when the president will be attuned to discussing business. Discussing this matter during an open session with all managers will not give the opportunity to establish a one-to-one relationship with the key person. At the president's house, it may not be appropriate to discuss business unless the host initiates the subject.

Situation 8. You are now aware that establishing personal rapport is very important in Arab cultures. You have been informed that a key negotiator is visiting your company office and you want to establish such a relationship. Will you

(a) Invite him to your house to meet your family?
(b) Ask him if you can help him shop for his family at the department store?
(c) Order two tickets to the movie that he mentioned he would like to see?
(d) Ask him if he can join you for dinner after your presentation?

It may be too early to ask him to visit your house and family since he does not know you well. Taking him to the movie would be nice, but would not provide an opportunity for dialogue. However, it would be nice to treat him to the movie as a weekend activity. Offering to join him shopping is also friendly, but will intrude on his freedom to buy personal and family belongings he may not want to share with you. The best answer is to ask him to join you for a quiet dinner (d) where you can exchange personal information and get acquainted before the business meeting the next day.

Situation 9. You are on a vacation in an historic Arab city. You admire one of the antiques and ask the street seller how much he wants for it. The Arab salesman replies, "How much do you want to pay?" He is asking this to

(a) Find out how much money you have.
(b) Find out your bottom offer.
(c) Establish rapport with you.
(d) Find out if you are serious about buying.

This is a typical strategy for an Arab street seller in most tourist sites. He may start by asking you, "Where do you come from?" or "Are you happy with your visit?" He may surprise you with a few words from your language. All these factors lead him to a personal rapport with the buyer (c). After that, he will enter the stage of negotiating price/commodity exchanges.

In summary, the Arab value of personal relationships is reflected in many of their negotiation and decision-making processes. Most Arabs prefer doing business with people they know and are comfortable with, or individuals who have been referred by someone they know and respect. The Arabs may give a foreign visitor the benefit of the doubt and forget one or two cultural mistakes, but will not conduct business with you if you choose to remain unfamiliar with their values and attempt to start business with them before establishing a personal rapport.

Exchanging Information

The second most important stage in intercultural negotiation is task-related information exchange. In this section, we will look into how the three cultures exchange information during the negotiation process, and again mention the basic cultural values that motivate behaviors.

Table 7.3 presents the different forms of information exchange among the three described cultures.

American Values

Most Americans come well-prepared to exchange information in order to close a deal. In the American context, information is given briefly and directly toward achieving the deal's objective.

Table 7.3
Information Exchange

American	Japanese	Arab
Brief and direct	Most important step	Least important step
Step-by-step approach, Learns from actions	Seeks more information than given	Personal trust base as a contingency for final decisions
Facts first, justification second	In-depth explanation, clarification, justification, and evaluation	Technical personnel involved

For example, in making a presentation while negotiating a joint venture, most Americans will present their project in a concise format. They will structure their presentation formally, using several different media tools such as overhead projectors, charts, and videos. The presenter will leave some technical and marketing information for the other party as tangible documentation of what was presented.

Following their presentation, most Americans will put forward their terms. In their approach, they usually present the minimum package that their clients would consider satisfactory, but it may not meet all of their clients' terms. In such negotiations, Americans often will add options and other items once the other party is "sold" on the basic package.

Consider the following situation of American cultural values during the information exchange stage:

Situation 10. You are making a presentation to a group of American managers on your project. One of them disagrees with the data you are presenting. Will you

(a) Ignore his remarks and proceed?
(b) Ask him why and then justify your point?
(c) Tell him you can discuss the point with him after the meeting?
(d) Remind him that you do not accept questions during presentations?

The American, of course, feels free to ask such direct questions during negotiation. If you ignore the manager and proceed, he may be offended. If you tell him to talk after the presentation, he may believe that you want to cut an indirect deal with him. The appropriate answer is to answer him openly and justify your point (b). Clearly, the answer would be completely different if you were making your presentation to an Asian team. Most likely, if Asians disagree with your point, they will not openly state it, but will discuss it with you after the meeting or in a group discussion.

Situation 11. You are making a presentation to American company executives who are considering appointing you leader of their negotiating team. To impress them, you should emphasize your

(a) Harvard Ph.D. and Stanford MBA.
(b) Managerial style as a motivating leader.
(c) Past accomplishments.
(d) Family background.

If you are making the presentation to Arab executives, (a) and (d) might impress them. However, most American executives will give greater value to what you have accomplished than your family background. Answer (c) would be correct. This is in complete contrast to the Japanese value of harmony and the process of negotiation: Both are more important than the result. In Japan, which road you take is more important than where you are going.

As we have said, not all communication is based on the spoken word—nonverbal communication can differ between cultures as well. The seating arrangement in a meeting provides a good example of nonverbal communication, as it may dictate the tone of the information exchange and negotiation. In a typical arrangement, Americans are seated on the opposite side of the table from the other negotiating team. The Japanese and most Asian teams prefer a circular seating arrangement, while Arabs use a side-by-side arrangement.

Before a negotiation session, Americans will give the other party the information the Americans plan to present. They expect that their counterparts will review it in detail (do their homework) and be prepared to ask questions openly and directly. During the process of information exchange, Americans will take a more active role in asking questions than will people from most other cultures. However, if Americans proceed in that direction, they might find themselves losing the other party in the discussion by concentrating too hard on the bottom line.

In summary, Americans come to the information exchange stage ready to deal. Their objective is to present their side directly for open discussion. During this process, the American negotiator expects the other side to be open and direct—ready to exchange fair information. In short, they want to find out what it will take to make the sale NOW!

Japanese Values

Situation 12. After exchanging letters for several months with a Japanese company, they have agreed to a meeting in Tokyo. They are offering this meeting to

(a) Negotiate the terms and conditions of your proposal.
(b) Seek more information on your product.
(c) Exchange more information with you on their company.
(d) Present you with their proposal.

Setting up meetings with Japanese firms is not an easy task for most non-Japanese business people. Many Japanese companies will not even respond to your requests until they have achieved a more significant level of information exchange and trust. The purpose of the initial meeting is to collect information for another round of internal discussions about your proposal (b). Many westerners travel to Japan believing that they will negotiate the terms and conditions of their proposals (d).

In Japanese business culture, the information stage is the most important phase of negotiation with foreigners. If you succeed with the first stage, they will probably exchange information about their company. However, the Japanese will need more information. If you have given them 100 percent, they'll want 120 percent before they can make a decision. To understand this seemingly insatiable appetite for information, you must remember that Japanese firms operate through the consensus and group decision-making process. Each phase of the internal discussion process may generate more questions that must be forwarded to their foreign counterparts for a response. To deal successfully with the Japanese, you may not want to provide all your information at one lump time. Instead, respond to their requests step-by-step, in the expectation that they will seek more information. In this way, you will be in harmony with their internal processes and avoid appearing as if you are withholding information they desire.

Although establishing good rapport is important, a deeper level of dialogue is necessary to advance the negotiation process. This level of information exchange usually takes place in an informal setting. Within the Japanese culture, interpersonal communication is usually achieved through an informal discussion with others involved in the negotiation. The Japanese team usually works in groups that support each other. They will not present themselves or their products formally, the way most Americans do, but rather in a more modest fashion. The Japanese may use a lot of visual images such as pictures or samples, or propose an on-site visit to further communicate their messages.

Situation 13. After your meeting with a Japanese company in Tokyo last month, you received a letter asking for more information on one of your company's products. Will you

(a) Send them your full catalog?
(b) Send a fax asking them why?
(c) Telephone them for more information about what they need?
(d) Send your sales representative with the information in the hope that he or she will close the sale?

During the evaluation process, the Japanese generate questions and always seek more information before they come to a decision. Sending your salesperson (d) would not be necessary since they just need information. They probably already have your general brochure and now are looking for more specific information. Sending them a fax (b) is not a bad idea, but will slow down their process since responding to you would require another round of internal meetings to prepare a response. The best answer (c) is to call your counterpart and ask them for more information about their request. Follow up the phone call with a letter giving them the information they seek. In this way, you are building your relationship and cooperation within the harmonious environment the Japanese value regarding information gathering.

Situation 14. You have been in contact with a member of a local Japanese company, but your relationship is not as strong as you'd like it to be. You are visiting Tokyo, and want to arrange another meeting with him. Will you call

(a) To offer a sushi with sake lunch?
(b) To ask for more information on the company's new product?

(c) To suggest a meeting time to give new information you have?
(d) To meet after work for a drink?

Answer (b) will not open the door since the Japanese will not give you any direct information. Offering to meet him for lunch or dinner may not be received in good faith since your relationship with him is not yet at that working level; you are still in the introductory stage. The best answer is (c), to indicate to him that you have new information for the company and are ready to come and discuss the information. In this way, you are appealing to the Japanese information-seeking process to justify the next steps of the working relationship.

Situation 15. You have been negotiating with Mr. Yamamoto of Nihhon Metal Company for a year. Having established good rapport with him, you hope that you are close to a contract. However, for three months, you haven't heard anything from him, and after calling, you find out that he has been transferred. What should you do?

(a) Nothing, since you already have good relations with someone in the company.
(b) Find his new telephone number and ask him to introduce you to the new manager.
(c) Make a quick visit to his company and ask to meet with the new manager.
(d) Consider your past effort wasted because you did not have a contract with your old friend before he left.

This dilemma represents a typical problem for foreigners negotiating with the Japanese: After putting out all the effort to establish rapport with a key manager, that manager moves into a new position. Due to the Japanese rotation system, a manager will typically only hold a position for a two- or three-year period. The incoming manager is now in charge and must also be convinced of your values. In fact, he will not even talk to you unless he has received a recommendation from your old contact. Following your introduction, the new manager will again expect you to proceed toward further discussion. The most appropriate answer in this case is (b). In Arab culture, answer (d) would probably be true, since business relationships are based even more on personal relationships, and the rotation system is not as fast as it is in Japanese companies.

In summary, information exchange during negotiation within the Japanese context is mainly one-sided. You may find yourself giving more than you are receiving. You have to recognize this stage and play it slowly, responding to their need for further information to satisfy the group consensus process. Be patient and maintain an open communication channel with continuous contacts by telephone, fax, letters, and personal visits. As we will see, the Arab culture also has a particular process of information exchange that differs from both the American and Japanese methods.

Arab Values

Most Arabs move into this stage without ever realizing it, for it is a natural extension of their business rapport. Unlike the Japanese and Americans, who tend to move in steps, the Arab information exchange process overlaps other stages of negotiation. Information is exchanged indirectly and may even be through a third party.

Situation 16. After several contacts with your Arab counterpart, you arrive to present your company's offer for a joint venture. You should plan to

(a) Book a conference room at a hotel for your presentation.
(b) Make an hour-long presentation at his office the first day of your arrival.
(c) Discuss your plan with him when he visits you after dinner.
(d) Give him your offer to read overnight.

Given Arab cultural norms, you should not hand your potential business partner something (d) without following up with an immediate discussion. If you fail to do this, he will probably turn it over to others, and you will miss his opinion on the matter. Discussion of detailed business matters in the first stages of negotiation have to be in a quiet environment, far from the daily business interruptions that often occur in most Arab offices. The best way is to open the subject after dinner, having built on previously established personal rapport during the meal (c). Having a room at the hotel for a presentation will be too formal for the Arab businessperson, and will not lead to the frank and open feedback the American is seeking. This approach may be acceptable, however, for technical presentations where second-line managers are involved.

Since decisions in Arab businesses are often made by the most senior person, detailed information is usually handled by more technically oriented personnel. Technical and financial matters are left to committees to review and develop a recommendation for management. After that, it is up to the senior manager of the company to make the final decision. Political or personal matters, in addition to the committee recommendations, may influence his decision.

Situation 17. You are invited to make a presentation of your project to an Arab government agency. To convince your audience, the meeting should include

(a) A video of your facility and production lines.
(b) A description on how your product was invented and a technical evaluation.
(c) A host dinner after the presentation for informal discussion.
(d) A one-hour question-and-answer period after your presentation.

While it may make an interesting story, background information on your invention would not be of significant value to the review committee. A video would be a nice way to explain your company, but the most appropriate answer is (c). Here, you will have a chance to build rapport with members of the review committee attending your presentation, as well as to give them a chance to indirectly inquire about your products. Do not attempt an hour-long question-and-answer period, since they may not be in a position to ask many questions but only to challenge your presentation.

Situation 18. After your presentation, you feel that the members of the committee do not yet comprehend your product's features. Will you

(a) Make a videotape of your product and mail it to the company president to review?
(b) Offer the technical manager a month-long trip to your factory to observe your operation?

(c) Invite the president of the company, with his technical and financial managers, to visit you at your expense?

(d) Send a letter letting them know they are welcome to stop by to visit your facility when they can?

If you are negotiating a potential project, answer (c) is the most appropriate response, given the Arab cultural value of hospitality. While they are visiting, you will be able to strengthen your personal rapport and answer any questions or concerns from the technical or financial managers. Inviting the committee at their expense would not be received very favorably, as it does not show the level of hospitality they would expect. Sending a videotape is a purely technical strategy and would work only in western-oriented cultures. Offering the technical manager a one-month trip would be accepted, but might not result in a contract: the president and the financial manager are still key players in the decision-making process. This special trip may be included in the proposal for the deal, however.

In summary, Arabs first like to strengthen personal rapport; they will then be inclined to complete the negotiation process and proceed to the next stage of the process—persuasion of the other side to accept your terms and conditions. This concept is discussed further in the next section.

The Persuasion Process

The third phase of negotiation is "persuasion." During this stage, you attempt to gain acceptance of your offer as close to your original terms as possible. Let's look again at how each of the three cultures—American, Japanese, and Arab—move into this stage. As we go further into the process, we will attempt to show how each culture's values play an important role in this process. To begin, consider this simple situation:

One of your employees approaches you and says she is not happy with her job and is planning to accept a position at another company. She has been doing a good job, and her experience is valuable. How would managers from various cultures try to persuade her to stay?

Most American firms would probably ask her how much extra money she would be making at the new job and then give her a raise to keep her at their company. In France, the manager would be likely to say, "I am very happy for you. Good luck!" A Japanese manager would suggest that they go to the coffee shop or meet after work and discuss the situation. He could probably talk the disgruntled employee into an internal transfer. In the Arab culture, the division manager might inform the general manager, who would then ask the employee to his office and try to convince her to stay. The manager would probably persuade her to stay by using the parent/child relationship common between Arab managers and their employees. Table 7.4 presents how Americans, Japanese, and Arabs use the persuasion process.

American Values

This stage in negotiation is the most important step. To reach it, Americans move quickly through the rapport process, exchange information formally, and inquire what is needed to close the deal. Now they are ready to persuade you to accept their offer. Have you ever seen or heard these phrases while visiting an American city? "This sale won't last," "Act now; call for free information," "Last chance, two-for-one sale." These business sound bites are indicative of the American style of business persuasion.

Table 7.4
Persuasion

American	Japanese	Arab
Most important stage	Persuasion behind the scenes	Most important stage
Decision changing at the negotiation stage	Sense of others' feelings	Bargaining attitude
Opportunist: loss or gain of deals	Mutual agreement	Language/emotion used for responses and decisions
Directness and openness	Long-term interest	Long-range profits
Time pressures		Use of mediator
Space orientation		Use of intuition and religion
		Administration and status

Americans come to the persuasion stage prepared to make changes during negotiations. They may ask, "What will it take to close the deal?" or "What is an acceptable price?" Their method is direct, and they expect an open and direct response.

During this process, many Americans are persuaded by the opportunity to make a good deal. Since the short-term goal of closing the deal is most important, the tone will be one of urgency and strong persuasion techniques will be used.

During negotiations, time pressure is often applied by the use of a deadline. To force a decision, Americans may offer a price concession, valid only for a limited time. The American time frame is much tighter than it is in other cultures. What an American expects to accomplish in one hour, other cultures may expect to take a full day.

American companies frequently rely on the advanced technology or brand name of their product as a means of leverage without fully considering other cultural negotiating factors.

Situation 19. You are in a negotiating session with an American company. They present you with their price list. You might expect them to say

(a) "How many units would you like to order?"
(b) "We are offering you a very special price."
(c) "Our price is firm for one week."
(d) Any of the above.

Americans may use any one of these statements (d) to pressure you to order, making you feel as if this is a golden opportunity. What do you think the answer to the same question would be if a Japanese firm presented this offer? What would they say after presenting their price list?

(a) "We hope that you will accept our offer."
(b) "We are looking forward to a long-term relationship."
(c) "We expect you to respond favorably."
(d) Any of the above.

Again, the answer is any of the above (d). The Japanese have a completely different persuasion technique than do Americans.

Situation 20. You are negotiating a joint venture agreement with an American firm. You want to persuade them to cut the price by 15 percent. Will you

(a) Offer the firm a ten-year contract rather than their proposed eight years?
(b) Invite the negotiating manager to your lovely summer home for a week?
(c) Tell them to come back when they can accept your offer?
(d) Inform them of the ongoing negotiations between you and two of their competitors?

You must know by now the most appropriate answer is (d). Nowhere is the American value of time clearer than during the persuasion stage. Here, they appeal to the urgency of a potential loss of opportunity. Unlike other cultures, which highly value the establishment of rapport in a business deal, the American negotiator seeks mainly a direct response or a material gain. Thus, their approach is direct, cutting straight to the heart of the matter. Success is defined by their ability to close a deal quickly with the highest return—not necessarily on the establishment of a lasting relationship.

Japanese Values

Persuasion in the Japanese context is a part of the overall process of negotiation. In general, the Japanese do not negotiate as the Americans do. The Japanese use persuasion to compromise on certain conditions so that the two sides can close a deal. Consider the following situation in a Japanese business:

Situation 21. A Japanese firm has established a strong relationship with one of its potential suppliers and is working toward closing their first contract. The firm wants to buy 100 sets of widgets from the supplier at $1,000 per set. The supplier offered $1,200 per set. How will the supplier respond to the buyer's offer of $1,000? By

(a) Sending a fax, insisting on $1,200 but offering a shorter delivery time and reminding them of the price deadline.
(b) Calling the person in charge to attempt to negotiate a price with him over the telephone to discover his bottom-line.

(c) Proposing a dinner meeting with the top manager to open the subject.

(d) Proposing a meeting with the group in charge, presenting them with a new price of $1,100.

In the Japanese context, negotiating prices over the telephone will not succeed because the final price was based on group consensus. Sending a fax reminding them of the deadline might be looked upon as breaking the harmony that has been developing between the supplier and buyer. Offering a shorter delivery time is not a reliable tactic, as the Japanese firm may have already scheduled their production based on your initial delivery plan. Meeting with the top manager is a good idea, but he or she would have to persuade the other team members and secure their agreement. The most appropriate answer is to make a compromise, present it to the group, and discuss it with your clients (d). For many Japanese firms, it is difficult to turn down an offer of compromise. How would this have been answered if the company was American?

Several factors of Japanese culture must be considered to successfully negotiate through the persuasion stage. Among these are the importance of maintaining harmony, avoiding loss of face, and gaining the agreement of all involved. In this regard, most decisions are discussed informally, behind the scenes. This factor is really a continuation of the process of establishing rapport.

Situation 22. It has been almost one year since you traveled to Japan to introduce your product to a potential joint-venture partner. You have not yet received an offer from them. What should you do?

(a) Openly ask them if they are still interested.

(b) Make a brief visit and discuss the partnership.

(c) Find out the name of the manager and talk with him on the telephone.

(d) Invite the middle manager to your country to visit your facility.

These answers are all good possibilities. However, if you insist on a direct "yes" or "no" answer, you will probably get neither. Your potential clients will probably respond that they are still discussing the proposal. Making a direct telephone call to the manager (c) will be viewed as out of line, and will probably achieve the same response as in the first situation. Inviting the top manager to your office (d) will enhance your relationship, but he will probably not accept the offer since a recommendation did not come from his line management. The best persuasion tactic in this case is to maintain open communication and find every reason to visit (b), and to share more information or discuss other related topics during your visit.

In general, whatever offer a foreign company makes to the Japanese will be used as further input into their internal discussion, and they will weigh it along with all the related factors. If the consensus is to work with you, they will come up with their own proposal, which they will submit to you. Many foreign companies make the mistake of trying to negotiate with the Japanese even further. These companies do not recognize the efforts that the Japanese have gone through to come up with that offer. It is generally wise to accept their first offer, provided the offer is in line with your expectations. Your acceptance shows you are ready to cooperate, and opens the door for further inside opportunities: Your goal is to be an insider.

Situation 23. You have finally received an offer from your potential Japanese client to supply 5,000 units of your product at $1,000 each. You quoted $1,200/unit. Will you

(a) Send a fax, stating that you still want $1,200?
(b) Accept their offer?
(c) Accept $1,000 if they order 6,000 units?
(d) Counter their offer with $1,100?

Answer (c) will probably not receive a good response from the Japanese, as they have already decided on the number of units. Insisting on $1,200 may make you lose an opportunity. Remember, your client took a long time to come up with his proposal. If you can make some profit (or gain market share) you should accept his offer. Accepting his offer immediately changes the way he views you, and is the first step toward being part of the team.

Arab Values

This stage of negotiation is the most important in Arab culture. It differs completely from the American style of direct and forceful pressure, and relies even more than the Japanese on the value of personal rapport.

Arabs will continue to maintain their indirect approach to business, calling upon the personal rapport that they have built in the first stage of the negotiation process. Indeed, rapport is so integral to this stage of negotiation that the lines between business and personal discussion are often confused. Arabs will switch unconsciously between the two "worlds" while displaying the richness of their language through flattery and admiration. During these discussions, Arabs will hint at future personal and business relationships, proceeding slowly, waiting for just the right time and place to discuss the terms of the final agreement.

The following situations show how the Arab persuasion process differs from that of other cultures:

Situation 24. You have been considering a local distributor in one of the Arab countries. Before making a final decision, you visit your potential distributor. She may try to persuade you by

(a) Inviting you to meet the Minister of International Trade.
(b) Mentioning that she can now accept a 5 percent commission rather than the 10 percent she previously requested.
(c) Inviting you to her office to meet her technical staff.
(d) Preparing market research data on the market potential of her product.

The Arab distributor will certainly maintain her request for a 10 percent commission. You may be interested in meeting her technical staff and reviewing her market research. However, your potential Arab partner is more interested in introducing you to the top people she knows as a way of persuading you, answer (a). She will display the extent of her local connections in an attempt to gain your respect and trust.

Situation 25. You are representing your company in an important joint venture with an Arab company. You are to meet with the vice president of the Ministry of Communication. When you arrive at his office to present your proposal, he will probably

(a) Use authority to persuade you to cut your price.
(b) Use technical expertise to challenge your proposal.
(c) Flatter you and extend a warm welcome to his country.
(d) Promise a long-term relationship of mutual interest.

All but one of these are likely to occur in your meeting with the vice president. Meeting a high-level official is part of the persuasion process that most Arabs would use. This reflects their cultural values of age, seniority, and parenthood. If you show that you have a good relationship with the top ("the father"), you are in a good negotiating position. In addition, the vice president hopes that you will reciprocate with a price discount. He will then also hint at a possible long-term relationship. A detailed technical discussion, on the other hand, would not be appropriate. Such matters would be referred to the technical team for review.

Situation 26. You have received a letter from an Arab partner. Before reading it, you notice it is one full page. Most letters you receive from American companies are shorter. This is probably because he is

(a) Putting in a large order.
(b) Evaluating your proposal at length.
(c) Apologizing for a late response.
(d) Starting with a flowery greeting and ending with a promise to meet with you in a quest for a long-term relationship.

When comparing notes and letters from different cultures, you will notice that most Arab letters start with personal greetings and wishes for peace and harmony. After discussing the main subject, they will close with a wish to meet with you soon, again, a reflection of the Arabs' tendency to switch back and forth during the persuasion process.

How do the different cultures we have been studying make final concessions and reach an agreement? In the American culture, concession and agreement are made through a sequential win-win approach. They use a step-by-step, action-oriented approach, learning through trial and error. Calculated risks are often taken in accepting or refusing a deal.

Japanese concession is made through group consensus. Once the group has reached a decision, it is difficult to ask for further concessions because this offer represents what they believe to be a fair price or deal for both parties involved. After this deal, they expect to work well together since they made concessions only to those they view as being part of the team.

Arabs' final decisions depend largely upon the feelings and intuition of the senior employee. A decision is generally based on the opinions of the top three people. Members of the group merely receive the order to implement what the managers have agreed upon. By having decisions made only by the top-level managers, Arabs attempt to create a trust-based relationship, which, if not established, makes it difficult to conduct business.

Testing Your Intercultural Negotiation Skills

The following are more situations from different cultures. See if you can determine the most appropriate responses (answers are at the end of the box).

1. You are invited to give a training seminar in South America.* They ask you to quote your fee and terms. Will you
   (a) Ask them about the number of participants and how much they usually pay?
   (b) Quote your nominal fee but insist on first class air travel?
   (c) Double your fee to allow for tough negotiation?
   (d) Ask them how much they are prepared to pay?

2. The Chinese government has invited your company to submit a quote for 10,000 personal computers. Each unit costs you $500, and you plan to offer the computers to them at $1,000/ unit. They ask you first for a sample of 100 units. Your per-unit offer for the sample units should be
   (a) $500.
   (b) Free.
   (c) $1,000.
   (d) $1,200.

*For more information on South America, see Appendix A.

3. Your agent in Indonesia is late with a $20,000 payment. He pleads he has short-term cash problems, and asks you for another $10,000 shipment to help him out. Will you
   (a) Terminate your relationship and consider it a tax write-off?
   (b) Visit him to discuss the matter?
   (c) Ask your lawyer to immediately send him a threatening letter?
   (d) Tell him that if he pays $10,000 now, you'll send him another order?

4. You have been stopped by a policeman in Morocco who accuses you of parking your car in the wrong place. He demands ten dollars in cash, or he will have your car towed away. Do you
   (a) Tell him you cannot pay cash?
   (b) Tell him you will report him to his superior?
   (c) Ask him if he has change for twenty dollars and offer him five dollars?
   (d) Tell him to tow your car and take a taxi home?

The most appropriate answers are: 1-d, 2-c, 3-d, 4-c.

Negotiating With The Chinese

Test your knowledge of Chinese culture by answering true or false to the following.

____ 1. Laughing is one way the Chinese show nervousness or social discomfort.

____ 2. Discussion about one's income is taboo.

____ 3. For the Chinese a contract is a complete and binding set of specifications.

____ 4. Chinese negotiators have no authority to make final commitments.

_____ 5. If a Chinese negotiator encounters opposition, he or she will simply restate the original argument.

_____ 6. In China, harmony is promoted by de-emphasizing individual needs and desires.

_____ 7. The Chinese find close business relationships of great value.

_____ 8. Chinese tend to be good at compromising during business negotiations.

_____ 9. Most Chinese people are alike.

_____ 10. The overseas Chinese are likely to be different than mainland Chinese.

(Answers: 1-T, 2-F, 3-F, 4-T, 5-T, 6-T, 7-T, 8-F, 9-F, 10-T)

Mr. Smith Meets the Mayor of Shanghai

Mr. Smith has been trying to sell telecommunication infrastructure-improvement projects to the Chinese government for several months. After finally attracting the interest of the mayor of Shanghai, he is referred to the mayor's staff for a detailed discussion. Once the staff has determined that the project fits within city plans and policies, Mr. Smith is asked to visit Shanghai and to present his project. Now he wonders where the presentation should be held. Should it be in the mayor's conference room? Mr. Smith's local agent office? The Sheraton Hotel conference room? A restaurant during dinner?

Smith decided to do as he had in Singapore and hold his presentation in the mayor's conference room. However, he was sorely disappointed when he received a reply from the mayor's office staff saying they were not available for a meeting with him. He immediately picked up on a hint given to him about the best place to hold his meeting. It was more appropriate to invite the Chinese negotiation team members to the Sheraton meeting room, where there was room to meet with 15 members of the mayor's staff.

Mr. Smith was now ready for his presentation. Which of the following should Mr. Smith mention first:

a. His last trip to China and how many friends he made.

b. New developments he has noticed each time he has visited.

c. Improved U.S. policy toward China.

d. His interest in a long-range mutual and beneficial relationship.

Mr. Smith first brought up his own past accomplishment of achieving U.S. $1 million in sales last year in Hong Kong, as well as his keen interest in moving fast with the current project in China. He also went on to indicate that U.S. policy toward China is passing through a difficult time, but assumes the outcome will lead to further cooperation. He noticed more interest from his audience when starting with the second option (b), followed by the last (d).

Smith believed it would be appropriate to have dinner with his Chinese partners since they had to leave early. Would he insult his Chinese hosts if he were to invite them to dinner on his expense account? He recalled his trip to Taiwan, where he was invited, along with his team, for dinner by his Taiwanese hosts; therefore, he decided that the best approach would be to wait for their invitation. However, just to test the alternate possibility, he invited the mayor's staff for dinner as his guests. To his surprise, the Chinese delegation had been expecting it and eagerly accepted. Later, he was surprised again when the Chinese insisted that on the last day, they act as hosts for the formal dinner together as a farewell to him and his team. Now Mr. Smith is obligated to return to Shanghai to pay them back.

In China, the foreign businessperson that presents a product or service is initially expected to host the Chinese. You are expected to approach them in a formal and respectful manner. When they host you on the last day, they feel you are obligated to come back and reciprocate the honor for future business dealings. They expect you to be their host on the first day, and insist that they entertain you on the last day. On the other hand, in Singapore, equality is highly esteemed, and entertainment expenses are shared.

Mr. Smith pondered what to talk about during dinner. Should he talk about his own work and family, the number of cars he owns, the size of his house, his travel experiences, current inflation in China, or perhaps the move toward democracy in Hong Kong? After trying to converse about all of the above, he finally discovered that they were most interested in his work and family. The other subjects were just received with a polite smile. At this stage of the relationship, it is appropriate to talk more personally and informally; whereas, formality is essential at the beginning.

After spending almost U.S. $300 making the Chinese delegation happy during dinner, he was confident that his presentation the next day would bring him a spectacular order. Finally, Mr. Smith had to close the sale and discuss the price. Which of the following approaches should Mr. Smith have chosen:

a. Present his price and offer them three days to accept it.
b. Present testimonials from his clients in Singapore, Taiwan, and Hong Kong to demonstrate customer satisfaction with his product.
c. Ask the group leader to state his view of the offer.
d. Finish his presentation with a statement that stresses their long-term, mutually beneficial relationship.

To his surprise, none of these were good options. The group leader, Mr. Chen, immediately asked him for a 30 percent discount to guarantee long-term success. To Mr. Smith, this was a hint that the Chinese were really interested in his product. Since he was authorized by his Board of Directors to give a maximum discount of 10 percent, he immediately made a counteroffer of 10 percent, which the Chinese received with appreciation, but without firm commitment. They asked him to reconvene with them the next Tuesday for further negotiations. Mr. Smith was confident and immediately faxed his boss in California with the good news of the large order.

Mr. Smith spent the weekend beside the Sheraton Hotel swimming pool, drinking and celebrating the order, which he expected the following week. On Tuesday morning, Mr. Smith met with the Chinese. To his surprise, half of the team had been replaced by older, more senior managers. When he began to discuss the order, the new senior negotiator informed him that they could not accept the given discount on the order, and would need another 10 percent discount to take his offer to Beijing. "What about my agreement with Mr. Chen?" Mr. Smith asked. The Chinese negotiator explained that Mr. Chen was only the junior negotiator; whereas, he, the senior member of the team, would be the one to take the offer to Beijing. Without any further authority to discount, Mr. Smith had no option but to remain silent. He recognized that he had failed to identify the levels of authority of the negotiation team.

Mr. Smith had given up everything he could discount. The client, Mr. Lee, offered him more tea. (Mainland Chinese businessmen signal that a meeting has concluded by offering more tea, thanking you for coming, or summarizing what has been discussed.) Mr. Smith went back to the Sheraton wondering how he could justify his U.S. $5,000 entertainment charges during his one-week stay at the Sheraton in Shanghai and the loss of the big order he had promised.

When negotiating with mainland Chinese, keep several factors in mind. The group composition of the negotiators will be middle to high managers, depending on the stage of the negotiations. Negotiators will receive instructions from superiors throughout the negotiations, and will demonstrate a formal style. They will establish rapport by hinting at the long-range, mutual benefits, and will try to persuade you to meet their terms by stressing benefits over the long term and how large their market is. The decision process will involve their seeking formal approval from the department head.

To respond effectively to their negotiating style, it is crucial that you identify the level of the negotiators at each stage. Ultimately, it is the top-level manager who finally decides. When the Chinese hint about long-term benefits, reciprocate and show that you share their vision, but focus on results, step by step. In response to their suggestion that you will gain a large market and plenty of business connections, stress their gains in technology, capital investments, and exportability. Focus on their point of view and economic needs. If there is an opportunity, influence lobbyists. Allow for their need to reach consensus and obtain approval. Be patient and ready to compromise, but never indicate your lowest price.

Another way of understanding the unique mainland Chinese negotiation style is to contrast it with that of other Pacific Rim groups. In terms of persuasion tools, as mentioned, the Chinese hint about long-range benefits and their large market. In contrast, other groups reflect other dominant themes and values in their own negotiations. Indonesians, by contrast, stress future business opportunities, but emphasize the large profit margin to be earned as well as the personal gain of each participant. Japanese feel consensus to be essential; a recommendation from a "sponsor" will be approved by the top manager. Koreans will integrate you into their own interpersonal process through ceremonies such as visits to shrines, etc., while Americans press for immediate decisions or the loss of the opportunity.

The decision-making process is also handled differently in the business cultures of various Pacific Rim trading partners. The Chinese seek formal approval from the department head, who adheres

Table 7.5
Tips for Doing Business with the Chinese

Remember there are as many significant value differences and perspectives among those of Chinese origin who live in Singapore, Taiwan, and Hong Kong, as among those of the same heritage who live in British Columbia, San Francisco, or New York.

Be aware that decisions are made through a process of consensus involving several layers of management.

Apply the basic principals of Confucian philosophy to your interactions with Chinese.

Watch for these signs of discomfort: silence, periodic looks at a watch or clock, avoidance of eye-contact, impatient nods and smiles, hand-waving in front of face.

Table 7.6
Different Approaches of the Chinese when They Negotiate with Foreigners

	Mainland	Singapore	Taiwan	Hong Kong
Group Composition	Middle/high managers	Middle manager takes charge	Junior managers	Middle and senior managers
Establishing Rapport	Long-range benefits	Relationships and references	Credibility and reputation	Semi-formal relationships
Information Exchange	Capital and technology	Immediate mutual benefits	Cautious and slow	Fast and pressured
Persuasion Tools	Capital and export potential	Afraid to lose— "Kazo"	Price-conscious	Immediate benefits
Decision Process	Adhere to policy	Fast but low-risk	A top-down process	Fast-based and low-risk
Decision-makers	Top management	Middle management	Top management	Top management

to strict policy. On the other hand, Indonesians engage in a three-stage process in which a spokesman initially recommends you, then an influential person within the company sponsors you, and finally, a decision-maker, whom you may never meet, will approve your transaction. Koreans engage in a bargaining process until compromise is reached. Japanese, who feel consensus to be essential, will make recommendations, which will be submitted by a sponsor for approval from a top manager. Americans, by contrast, ensure that facts back up the business arrangements discussed before making a formal commitment. Tables 7.5 and 7.6 present further cultural tips for dealing with the Chinese.

Summary Insights

As noted in Chapter 6, our cultural values and how well we understand other's cultural values influence the success or failure of our business ventures. Negotiations are also influenced by these values.

When negotiating, the number of people involved, seating arrangements, time of arrival, and style of conversation can all give you an indication of important cultural values that you can build on to achieve successful negotiations.

The importance of establishing personal rapport varies across cultures. Americans tend to downplay such rapport, while the Japanese and Arabs consider it a prerequisite for most deals.

During the negotiation process, the format and ways of exchanging information are also strongly affected by different cultural values. Finally, to close a sale you must keep in mind culturally-based persuasion processes such as the threat of a loss or gain of opportunities, long-range business prospects, and use of a third party or mediator. It is very important to keep in mind all of the cultural values of the country, company, or person with whom you are negotiating.

As you embark on negotiating your next deal, from the moment you shake someone's hand—and throughout the negotiation process—you should be able to pick up and give the cultural clues that assure successful negotiation outcomes.

CHAPTER 8

Globalization and Technology Transfer Management

An Overview

As the 20th century draws to a close, the globalization of the market and business is progressing rapidly, impacting multicultural management. Our final chapter discusses why and how this is happening, particularly in terms of expansion strategies and the exchange of information technology. Although the trend has been toward the creation of multinational or world corporations, most companies today are national rather than international. However, the opportunity to grow out of a localized market and into a global one remains exciting as well as challenging. There are many reasons for becoming globally oriented. In this chapter, we will discuss the forces driving globalization.

This chapter covers new developments in information technology and its resulting influence on the new political and trade order. The influence of such technology on the new world citizen and consumer will be described from the cultural perspective.

We also present the strategic stages of going global, the influence of such expansion on organizational management, and product marketing. Finally, we will discuss the cultural factors inherent in technology transfer, to better negotiate and manage the transfer process.

A Test of Globalization Strategy

The following are ten introductory questions pertaining to globalization. We then answer 24 related key questions throughout this chapter.

True or False

Test your knowledge of globalization strategy by answering true or false to the following.

____ 1. New information technology has created a new world consumer.

____ 2. Global consumers will demand products that are produced only locally.

____ 3. Global products will be the ones that can be produced at the lowest price.

____ 4. Management of a global company must think globally about acquiring technology and finance.

____ 5. Global companies need not take into account different cultures when creating advertisements.

____ 6. A country that succeeds in the global market must provide a local environment for entrepreneurial and financial services.

____ 7. A current challenge to globalization efforts is the unavailability of skilled workers.

____ 8. The management of the global company should look at the world as one expanding market.

____ 9. The future success of global companies will depend on government regulations for market entry.

____ 10. Future headquarters of global organizations must be located close to their manufacturing sites to ensure product quality.

(Answers: 1-T, 2-F, 3-F, 4-T, 5-F, 6-T, 7-F, 8-T, 9-F, 10-F)

Going Global—Why?

New Information Technology

Question 1. Most companies are interested in going global because

(a) Local competition is increasing due to free trade.
(b) Most products can be produced more cheaply overseas.
(c) Regional trade barriers have been formed.
(d) New information technology is creating globally-aware consumers.

Many executives, responsible for their company's expanded activities, may be responding to current free trade and open market policies by establishing facilities overseas to take advantage of special tax incentives or cheap labor. Other executives may be fearing regional trade barriers and local market protection, such as those currently being sought in the European community, and are therefore going global to secure an overseas presence before restrictions are imposed. Many companies have also gone overseas during the last decade to take advantage of a less expensive workforce in developing countries, especially in Asia.

All of these answers may be valid reasons for seeking expansion into the global marketplace. However, the current and future driving forces in globalization are the swiftly developing advances in information exchange technology (d). This technology has produced many products that directly or indirectly reach new global consumers.

Technological advances have allowed cable television programs to be broadcast worldwide, via satellite. Mobile telephones are increasingly accessible throughout the world, augmenting the already well-established use of pagers, allowing executives and managers to be in continuous contact with their counterparts worldwide. The fax machine has undergone several advances, from black and white to color, and from bulky to portable, making the exchange of information and business communication through this medium extremely accessible worldwide.

Another example is the establishment of video conferences for meetings and training activities. All of these communication technology advances and the resulting products have enabled executives to conduct global business at a much faster pace than in the past. This new mobility permits managers to readily move their workload overseas, and not necessarily their "bodies." Networking can now be done electronically as well as personally. The internet, with its capabilities for electronic mail, websites, and chat corners, as well as for ordering products and money exchange, opens new vistas for global communications. Miniaturization from chips to laptop computers, digital and imaging developments, along with voice recognition equipment, also expedite this process of planetary interchange, even from remote areas. Furthermore, there are now software systems that provide simultaneous translations of text from one language to another.

New information technology has also contributed to the recent globalized liberalization in financial services management, without the previous bureaucracy and constraints on international lending. Today, companies and investors can easily shop across borders for money at the best possible interest rates, which also helps support companies worldwide. However, this brings new risks, as was seen by the global scandal of the Bank of Commerce and Credit International. The regulatory world and financial institutions have not kept pace with this information revolution, and they are finding it difficult to manage and regulate international financial transactions.

Advances in information exchange have also contributed to the advertising media—television, billboards, newspapers, and magazines. Through computer-aided graphics, an advertiser may develop his ad and circulate it worldwide within a very short period of time. Such information and product advertising can be launched throughout the world almost instantaneously.

In addition to the advances mentioned, specialized delivery services such as Federal Express, United Parcel Service, and DHL have aided this new expansion in global communication. Overnight document delivery can be guaranteed across borders, which is a very powerful tool for global business.

Advances in technology are moving so swiftly that by the next century, we can expect the global consumer to have access to virtually any company in the world.

Consider the following:

Question 2. A global company must maintain

(a) Extensive worldwide distribution channels.
(b) Its own corporate culture worldwide.
(c) Worldwide advertising.
(d) Access to worldwide technology and financial capital.

In going global, organizations may depend on extensive distribution channels to reach consumers worldwide. Others may try to impose their corporate culture onto overseas subsidiaries. Large organizations may also depend on extensive worldwide advertising for global acceptance. All of these are classic strategies for internationalization. However, the most successful global company must develop and maintain a globally-oriented leadership and access to worldwide technology as well as financial capital resources (d).

Question 3. IBM may be considered a global company because

(a) It adapts its products to local consumer requirements.
(b) It can produce products in the market where demand exists.
(c) It has influenced subsidiaries by its corporate culture.
(d) It has strong worldwide access to technology and finance capabilities.

Of course, IBM possesses and depends on all of these criteria for global success, but the main factor that defines IBM as a global company is its access to global technology and finance (d). However, even IBM is in transition responding to new consumer demand in products and services.

The New Global Consumer

As mentioned, new information technology has created what may be described as a "global consumer." Such consumers are becoming aware of almost every major product available worldwide. Not only has this created a new consumer, but a new type of world citizen as well. Political events, such as the student democracy movement in China and the free-enterprise developments in eastern Europe and the Russian Commonwealth, occurred in large part because of increasing access to information worldwide, heightening consumer demands.

The new global consumers will certainly desire products that enrich their lifestyle, making life easier and more rewarding. International customers will care more about product quality, price, design, value, and appeal and less about the product's origin. Yet, these buyers are not satisfied with products simply because they have been exported to their country. These buyers insist on a product that is sensitive to their culture in all respects, from design to utilization. Consumers will also expect quick services that respond to their swiftly changing needs.

An example of a consumer group driven by such information is young Japanese women, aged 24–40. The advances in information technology target this demographic group, exposing them to a variety of products that they find attractive. This group is also very like-ly to travel overseas, where they encounter unique products that they begin to demand, directly or indirectly, at home. In response, local manufacturers or distributors import or acquire local manufac-turing licenses for these products.

In part because of this, many foreign countries are putting strong pressure on the Japanese government to adopt more liberal trading policies, allowing foreign companies to market their products to the Japanese consumer. This political pressure has traditionally been resisted by the Japanese government. Eventually, however, this problem will be overcome; not because of political pressure but by consumer pressure, driven by the information now available to them. Constant consumer demand around the globe is forcing the alteration of obsolete trade practices and political systems. These phenomena of the global consumer will be the main incentive for most companies to go global.

Question 4. Industries that have recently gained strong revenue from globalization include

(a) Car manufacturing.
(b) Public utilities.
(c) Financial services.
(d) Consumer electronics.

It is now obvious that because of the technological advances in advertising and its ability to reach the global consumer, major elec-tronic manufacturers such as Sony, Phillips, Panasonic, and others have been able to branch out and gain global acceptance (d). Other industries have been able to expand as well, but not as globally as the consumer electronics industry.

Question 5. The new global consumer, motivated by the advances in information exchange, will most likely demand products that

(a) Are produced locally.
(b) Have a global image.
(c) Are of high quality and low price.
(d) Are adaptable to local cultures.

The new consumer will eventually purchase products without regard to whether they were produced locally. A customer will have the option of choosing many different products from many different sources. Of course, the buyer will insist on high quality and low prices, so competitiveness among global suppliers will be based on who is able to best adapt their products to the local consumers' culture (d).

Question 6. The pressure on major companies to go global will be driven by

(a) The need to diversify to protect shareholders' investments.
(b) Increased local competition due to their home government's commitment to an open-market policy.
(c) Free trade among regional countries.
(d) The changing needs and preferences of global consumers.

All four reasons have been and continue to be strong motivations for companies to go global. However, as discussed, the driving force to become an international company will be the needs and changing preferences of the consumer, inspired by their access to worldwide product information (d).

In our fast-moving information society, our multicultural environment will eventually put another constraint on global strategy. In many areas of the world (California, Singapore, Canada, etc.), we already find multicultural communities. This quickly expanding transcultural demographic will create new challenges for global companies, who must additionally respond to cultural diversity within a single market. The ability to customize for such multicultural sensitivities will be the factor that gives certain companies a crucial marketing edge.

New Political and Trade Order

As mentioned, the developments in information technology that have driven consumers to demand more products have also created global citizens. These global citizens, through access to this technology, have created a new catchword in the political structure: interdependence. This word is demonstrated by the recent development of political and economic cooperation between former adversaries. The current relationships between the U.S. and the Russian Commonwealth and Germany, and regional cooperative efforts among Asian countries, have resulted from citizen/consumer pressures on governing officials. In contrast to the traditional protectionism of nations, the trend is toward regional trade agreements and cooperation, as seen in the European Union, the North American Free Trade Agreement (NAFTA), and Mercado Comun Del Sur (MERCOSUR), which is a kind of South American common market (see Appendix A). However, there is still a need for emerging regional markets, as we will discuss next.

Let's take the United States as an example of an economic system. The U.S., with its 50 states, is a microcosm of the future global economy. There are no political trade barriers between the states. Any company may seek financial resources within any state, as well as have full access to American consumers throughout the nation. The consumer may choose from products produced in any of the states and, by showing their preferences, dictate just what products will be available. American companies design, market, and distribute their products by appealing to the American consumer's desires. This is the same structure that the world is headed toward in the emerging global economy.

In the decades to come, the primary global economic competition among companies will be driven by specific regions, such as:

- The European Union (EU)
- The Pacific Rim countries, including Japan
- North America including Mexico.

Of course, all of the countries in these regions will participate in global competition to some degree, but the real driving force will be global companies that are able to respond to the global consumer. Sony, Coca-Cola, and Nestle are prime examples of such companies.

Many CEOs of major American companies see the number one benefit from globalization as increased revenue. Many organizations have gone overseas to lower their production costs. Other groups have expanded globally to diversify into new markets by acquiring new companies to augment their distribution systems or technology.

This move toward globalization is the direct result of current political changes. Companies are responding to the new consumers, who essentially require that companies globalize to survive. Lower production costs, better distribution, and the acquisition of new technological advances are only some of the fringe benefits of a change driven mainly by consumers and their product demands.

In previous decades, companies made these decisions themselves, based on their success in local markets. Following local success, the natural progression was to begin exporting to foreign markets. This resulted in partnerships with independent overseas agents who would establish foreign-based trading companies for exporting and importing. Likewise, many companies were expanding overseas in response to lower production costs because of cheap labor. Others licensed their technology and production facilities, leading to joint ventures in research and the development of new products.

The increasing influence of the global consumer has made such activities more of a necessity than a luxury today. Many companies, finding it necessary to quickly establish a presence overseas, are using global financing to establish alliances through mergers and acquisitions. During the 1990s, major companies no longer have just the option of going global; the new consumer has made it a requirement.

Globalization, in general, is not for every product, company, or industry. However, for those that must, it is important to view the world as one market. Global managers must make internationally-minded decisions on strategic questions concerning technology and capital. However, these managers must also make decisions on tactical questions concerning packaging, marketing, advertising, and especially management. These decisions must consider to a great extent local consumer cultural values and their impact on business. Eventually, natural boundaries and local regulations will be irrelevant in the move toward global businesses.

Strategies for Going Global

In the last section, we explained our views on the multiple forces behind globalization. We emphasized that the information age and technological advances have created a global citizen/consumer who is pushing companies toward globalization. In response to this, we have seen many new developments in the world's political and trade order.

In the following section, we will focus on specific strategies for executives seeking to take their company/product to the global consumer.

Strategic Stages

Stage One. Any company embarking on a global activity must first establish a base of operations for its products and/or services. This gives the company the test market, both technologically and culturally, to determine its position, initially against local competitors. Once the local market has reached its capacity, the organization will take the first step in introducing its product globally.

Stage Two. The next stage is to test your product through an established export channel, in a specifically defined regional market with potential growth. This stage will give the company a good insight on the potential for adaptation of your product to the local market. Many companies then embark on acquiring local distribution channels to gain a higher market share in that region.

Stage Three. The third stage, if consumer response is positive and your product is valued equally against any competitor's, is to establish overseas assembly/manufacturing facilities. It is important at this stage to support the facilities with technological know-how and to secure financial backing.

Once operations are in place, one of the most important ingredients in global success is to allow local management enough freedom to make local and strategic decisions on issues such as operations, marketing, and distribution. Indigenous personnel are the best resource for locally-based decision-making, for they possess the necessary cultural sensitivities to the local consumer.

Stage Four. Following these steps, your organization must be in a position to reduce its exports to the region and rely more heavily on local production, adapted to the local consumer, to satisfy the demand in the new market. At this fourth stage of globalization, your headquarters will only have to support local facilities through global sharing of technology and financial resources.

Question 7. In a global strategy, products sold in any given market must eventually come from

(a) Wherever they can be produced for the lowest price.
(b) The country in which the company headquarters is located.
(c) The closest central production region.
(d) Local market.

Many executives and organizations have emphasized the first three options. However, sustained global success will eventually come from the local market supported by product adaptation and regional advertising (d).

Question 8. The management of an emerging global company may look at the world market as

(a) A few emerging regional markets.
(b) An expanding free-trade market.
(c) Many countries, each with their own particular market demands.

As the economic barriers between nations continue to fall, it will become more and more difficult to think globally in any other sense but as a single expanding market (b).

In going global, managers must have a global vision: to see what locals, from their limited perspective, are unable to see. This mind-set usually develops from managers who have the sensitivity and awareness of the differences of many cultures.

Organizational Management

Question 9. The best location for a global organization's headquarters is

(a) Close to financial and technological resources.
(b) Close to major manufacturing facilities.
(c) Close to major distribution centers.
(d) Anywhere in the world.

Most organizations were originally established near their main manufacturing or distribution centers, and are still located there. However, the current emphasis and focus of major organizations has been on the development of technology and financial resources. Thus, many headquarters have moved near these resources. Eventually, a successful global organization's headquarters could be located anywhere in the world, supported with the technological advances in communications that have given rise to the global/ mobile executive. This also brings the manager closer to the global consumer.

Global organizations must create a new international culture and value system for their global subsidiaries and employees. This set of values cannot contradict or devalue local cultural values. If the headquarters attempts to push cultural imperialism, the resulting conflict will impede the success of the venture. Domestic interaction must be separated from the responsibility of the headquarters, and be entrusted to local management.

Headquarters must view each part of the operation as a collective whole, and must not separate any one section from the rest. Headquarters' executives must establish a global vision for what the local company does not see in new product markets and technology development opportunities.

A successful global organization will probably end up being neither a monopoly, a cartel, nor a collaborative, but a "globomonopoly."

Question 10. The management of many global companies think globally in terms of

(a) Packaging.
(b) Advertising.
(c) Finance.
(d) Technology.

Certainly, in the new emerging worldwide market, managers must take advantage of global technology sources, as well as global financial resources. However, they must be extremely sensitive to the culture of the local consumer in the areas of product packaging and advertising, as these influence consumer buying and utilization patterns. Successful handling of these factors will position the organization in a better competitive position among other local or global competitors.

This emerging global manager must possess strong technical, interpersonal, and intercultural communication skills.

Currently, most successful managers at home possess both technical and interpersonal skills. The higher the manager moves up the ladder, the more his or her interpersonal interaction and technical skills will be valued and supported. However, for this manager to cross the cultural barrier and succeed in managing globally, on the road or at home, he or she must develop and master the intercultural communication skills as well.

Question 11. Management's commitment to future global activity must now focus on

(a) Its stockholders.
(b) Research and development.
(c) Local government regulations.
(d) The global consumer's needs and preferences.

Again, all of the above answers have been and will continue to be important elements for any local business. However, to expand globally, successful managers must give their full attention to the global consumer's needs and preferences (d).

Question 12. Companies may fail in their globalization efforts because of

(a) A lack of financial resources.
(b) Government regulations.
(c) Consumer demand for low-cost products.
(d) A lack of multicultural management expertise.

The current management of many local and even some globalized organizations has focused heavily on seeking financial resources, fighting government regulations, or producing products at a lower cost. However, the most demanding task in global expansion is the expertise required to manage a multicultural workforce. In their efforts to manage globally, managers must be trained to think globally (d).

Organizations are putting new emphasis on developing globally-minded employees at their headquarters. This idea is a good start, but an equal emphasis must be placed on cultivating *local* management to think globally as well. Some companies place foreign employees from the country in which they are venturing onto their board of directors and into senior positions to facilitate this global style of thinking.

Companies should use local expertise not only technically, but in the field of communications, with local institutions and public relations organizations establishing a good local reputation for the newly established global organization. A strong emphasis must be placed on identifying the new corporate culture, which should not be just the main office's view. Many organizations try to force their parent company's culture onto the local culture, which eventually fails and results in managerial and cultural conflicts.

The local manager in a global corporation has to operate as an insider in his market, and has to feed information regarding local cultures to his company, so that products can be adapted to local cultural values. Global designers have to be trained to think in terms of the various markets where their products will be sold: Asia, Europe, America, and so on. To complete this task successfully, the designer must be armed with useful information regarding the customs and habits of the local culture.

Product Marketing

Question 13. To execute a successful marketing strategy, a global company must eventually

(a) Distribute its product from centralized locations worldwide.
(b) Produce and sell/export its product from its home base.
(c) Produce and sell its product from the cheapest production base.
(d) Produce and sell its product where the market demands it.

The first three options have been used in one form or another by international organizations. However, global organizations must plan to produce and sell their products to local markets from local production facilities. The success of this strategy is illustrated by the many Japanese companies that have entered into joint-venture arrangements for the production of cars, televisions, and so forth in local markets in Europe and the U.S.

Question 14. In establishing overseas subsidiaries and production facilities, emphasis should be placed on

(a) Seeking local capital financing.
(b) Lobbying for government protection.
(c) Developing new technology locally.
(d) Adapting product design and packaging to local markets.

Global companies with offices in local countries must seek local capital financing, lobby to secure favorable government policies, and develop technology important to the local economy. However, as mentioned, the strongest emphasis must be placed on designing, packaging, and promoting products manufactured to local consumer preferences (d).

Global organizations must eventually move from simply exporting products to true global joint ventures, which should include all phases of design, production, marketing, and distribution. In going global, companies must identify regional companies that can penetrate other regional markets. This strategy should help build important local and regional facilities and, most importantly, help improve management skills in the global arena.

Effective global operations also require that global managers respond to each client, regardless of geographic location, with equal speed and concern. This has been made easier by advanced telecommunications systems, such as mobile telephones, fax machines, and teleconferences. The efficiency and ease of air travel has also made managing global ventures easier.

Question 15. A company should plan to think about entering the global market as soon as

(a) It feels local markets have been saturated.
(b) Competitors start moving into the local market.
(c) It has completed a prototype of the product.
(d) It senses a demand from global clients.

Many managers do not think globally because they have been experiencing great success at home and do not anticipate that competition may reduce their market share. The company must also act as a responsible local citizen. Others may try to expand globally as soon as they produce their first prototype, without determining consumer demand. However, the successful company will be the one that is attuned to the demands of global consumers and takes advantage of this demand to introduce their product globally (d).

Further, to establish a good local presence in the global market, the company must also act as a responsible local citizen. Local global organizations must contribute to the social well-being of the local citizens. Many global companies just provide jobs for local workers in an assembly-line format. However, these companies eventually contribute to increases in the export of locally manufactured products, which in turn provide a source of hard currency for the local population. Therefore, plans must be made to utilize locally produced materials in any product the company is manufacturing. In addition, part of the profit must be channeled through established foundations to contribute to the social, cultural, and educational well-being of the local citizens. Showing respect for the local consumer, by responding to their needs and concerns, will eventually expand a company's acceptance locally.

Sensitivity to the local environment must also be highly valued. A company must not simply utilize natural resources as if they are inexhaustible and release dangerous waste into the local environment. To do so will exploit the local economy and cause a loss of goodwill in the local area. Global companies must reinvest wealth, employ and train local workers, and pay taxes as local citizens, which positions the competitive local organization as a world citizen, despite their origin.

Global Technology Transfer

In this section, we will focus on the transfer of technology, particularly across cultures, barriers to such transfers, and management techniques needed to complete the process successfully.

The transfer of technology is becoming part of the globalization strategy. Joint venture partners must include, in some manner, the transfer of knowledge. In the past, many overseas projects have been labeled "turnkey"—the project is complete as soon as the host turns the key to start production. This process is not acceptable in today's global market environment, where companies have to share their technology to succeed.

Consider the following:

Question 16. The most important role of governments in encouraging the transfer of technology may be to

(a) Send as many students overseas as possible.
(b) Invest in local research centers.
(c) Provide financial resources to local entrepreneurs.
(d) Continuously hire overseas consultants to conduct public lectures.

Governments have a major responsibility to enhance the transfer of technology. Most developing countries, for example, send students overseas to acquire new knowledge. Many also place scientists in research centers to develop new technology. However, making financial resources available to help and encourage local entrepreneurs in the private sector is the most practical way to encourage technology transfer (c).

An example of such a process can be identified in the entrepreneurial companies of California's Silicon Valley. These companies would not have been able to proceed further than the garage, where some actually began, without the availability of additional financial resources.

Question 17. The successful transfer of technology must start by

(a) Preconditioning the environment to develop new technology.
(b) Trading technology with another company.
(c) Adapting the technology to the needs of the local market.
(d) Absorbing the technology as part of the "norm."

Many countries buy or are involved in the development and transfer of technology without preparing for it properly. "Preconditioning" is the process of preparing the environment, both physically and socially for the new technology. This means that the government must provide energy, roads, water, and buildings for newly established factories. People must be trained to make the products. These steps must be planned and implemented long before any technology is imported, so the correct answer is (a), then (b), (c), and finally (d).

"Technology trade" is the actual transaction between the supplier and the recipient of a proposed technology. This trade includes sales of equipment, industrial rights, technical services, personnel training, plans, and documentation. Following the actual technology trade, "technology adaptation" occurs. This requires that the technology be adapted to the local environment, including how it is used and applied. If both the preconditioning and adaptation processes are successful, "technology absorption" should result. This process is reflected in the degree to which the recipient has been able to successfully look upon the transferred technology as part of the local economy.

The Technology Transfer Process

Let us now focus on the specifics of the technology transfer process. There are four basic elements: the supplier of the technology, the receiver of technology, the technology itself, and, most importantly, the channel through which the technology is transferred.

The process has several steps. First, an organization must find the technology it desires to improve its product or service. Second, the company must negotiate with the supplier of the technology to set the terms and conditions of the transfer. Naturally, this transaction must not be completed before an assessment of the local infrastructure and available workforce is made to ensure that the technology transfer will be effective.

The following are some of the major barriers to global transfer of technology:

- Political obstacles
- Technological gaps
- Financial resources
- Cultural differences

On the political level, international relations between, for example, the U.S. and the Russian Commonwealth, play a significant role when a transfer of technology takes place. The existence of a technological gap between supplier and receiver, in terms of existing infrastructure support, and manpower, imposes a gap on the success of the transfer process as well. For local entrepreneurs, the availability of financial resources plays a leading role in enhancing the transfer process. Finally, the various cultural differences provide the last barrier to success of the process.

The practical steps that any company or country would follow to transfer its new technology are as follows:

Phase 1. Import products, but do not introduce technology.
Phase 2. Import products, and introduce the technology at a nominal fee.
Phase 3. Import the technology, but not products.
Phase 4. Acquire technological capability and international competitiveness; begin exporting products.
Phase 5. Gain technological independence; develop new technology and export products, but not the new technology.
Phase 6. Export technology, but not products.
Phase 7. Produce products overseas using the imported technology.

These phases demonstrate the process that many successful companies and countries have followed to introduce, adapt, absorb, and finally sell technology. Without these steps and adequate preconditions, any technological transfer will not be successful.

Technology Transfer and Culture

Let's now focus on the cultural aspects of what happens when technology is exchanged between two major countries. Table 8.1 shows the process for both American and Japanese companies that have transferred technology successfully.

Table 8.1
Innovations and Applications of New Technology

American	Japanese
Radical innovations	Process innovations
Basic research	Applied research
Individual skills	Managerial skills
Creation/innovation	Adaptation/absorption
Short production stage	Mass production
New ideas	Repetition

As indicated, most innovations that have come from the American laboratory have been based on research and radical innovations, while those of the Japanese have come from applied research and process innovations. This factor is naturally reflected through a basic cultural difference—American individuality versus Japanese group cohesiveness and loyalty.

Most American scientists, who value individual achievement, have been innovative and creative in their development of technology. Their Japanese counterparts, on the other hand, have simply absorbed and adapted existing technology. Furthermore, American manufacturing has had a reputation for an initial short production stage, while the Japanese move from the development stage quickly into mass production.

These differences in development may be a result of the educational systems in the two countries. In America, students are often rewarded for original thinking and interpretation, while in Japan memorization is more often the key to success. Likewise, a young American scientist who demonstrates remarkable ability and creativity may be promoted quickly in spite of age or experience. In Japan, seniority and position are well connected with age; it would be difficult for a young person to hold a senior position.

Question 18. You are offered a chance to buy a specific new technology. What factor would be most important in your decision?

(a) The price.
(b) Its potential to develop new products.
(c) The export potential from its application.
(d) Its lifecycle.

This is a very important question to answer when considering the transfer of technology. Many companies will immediately engage in a transaction that may be based on price, product, and export potential—important factors in the 1980s. However, in today's environment of almost constant innovation and technological advancement, the life expectancy of a given technology must be closely evaluated. If not, one may find a competitor developing a new technology before your product is even introduced (d).

Question 19. Traditionally, suppliers of new technology consider the transfer process complete when they

(a) Receive the final payment.
(b) Release the design codes.
(c) Train the staff to operate the facility.
(d) Give the plant operation key to the manager.

In the past, many joint venture projects were considered complete when operations were ready. However, this solution may not have represented a complete transfer of technology. The suppliers may have lacked, as we have mentioned, preconditioning, adaptation, or absorption of the new technology. In that case, the suppliers' lack of knowledge of the technology means that the transfer is nothing more than a sale of equipment. Some vendors may consider the technology transfer complete when they train the plant's staff. However, in general, this process does not give the new owner the ability to modify or significantly upgrade his facility. The process can be considered complete when the new personnel have a chance to learn more details about the design process from the supplier (c).

Question 20. Whether or not technology was successfully transferred to a country can be measured by

(a) The level of technology absorption.
(b) The level of technology adaptation.
(c) The new product produced, based on this technology.
(d) The increase in the country's exports of products and technology.

Any successful technology transfer process, as we have discussed, must eventually achieve Phase 7, the ability to export products based on the newly imported technology, followed by the second phase—the export of the technology itself (d).

Technology Transfer Negotiations

In the previous section, we outlined the elements for a successful transfer of technology and the process a company or country must follow to successfully absorb new technology. Now we will discuss specific issues that are important during the negotiation process.

Let's start with the following example:

Question 21. You are negotiating to buy a refinery from a supplier. The supplier said that they will train ten members of your staff how to operate the plant, which implies that

(a) Your organization can now conduct any operational maintenance.
(b) You will be able to increase the plant's operational capacity by 15 percent.
(c) They will transfer the plant's operational technology.
(d) They will train your personnel how to operate the plant.

In this case, the supplier will only commit to train your staff to operate the plant (d). In a real sense, no technology will be transferred. During the negotiation stage, many buyers of facilities fail to stress that they want the transfer of technology for further plant design and/or modification. But only the supplier will have the ability to further modify or improve the capacity or change any plant parameters, of course, at an extra charge.

Many suppliers and buyers of equipment consider training a transfer of technology, but this is only a part of the process. Here is another example:

Question 22. You are involved in negotiating the purchase of a power plant, which includes the transfer of technology. You should prepare your staff to be involved with the supplier

(a) At the design stage.
(b) Only when construction starts.
(c) During the initial testing of operations.
(d) When the training program begins.

In contract negotiations, many suppliers will try to involve the buyer only at the training stage. However, to achieve a complete and successful transfer of technology, the buyer's staff should be involved from the creation of the design specifications through the construction, initial testing, and up to full operation. If the buyer's staff is involved at an early stage, they will be able to acquire, comprehend, and apply their new knowledge.

Several forms of transactions exist in the transfer of technology. Some buyers prefer to pay for specific information as a direct sale, gaining full possession and the freedom to determine its use. Other suppliers will only license their technology for a specific application. The buyer in such an arrangement will pay a lump sum for the rights to use the technology and agree not to transfer it to a third party.

A simple example of technology transfer is found in many computer software programs (Lotus, Word/Windows, etc.). The developer of the programs agrees to license his product to the buyer for unrestricted use, except that the buyer is not allowed to let other people copy the software for their own use. Global corporations producing software, such as Microsoft, dominate the world computer market and create, in effect, international business systems. Other forms of licensing give the right to the seller to receive royalties from any product that is developed by the buyer using the software.

Technology transfer agreements in general include:

- Loyalty to the supplier
- Securing the design codes
- Future design modification
- Training personnel

All these terms must be discussed during the negotiation stage. As stated, many suppliers will focus solely on personnel training. Most buyers will not give enough attention to the design codes or future modifications. Both sides may spend more time on the amount of royalties and the initial cost of the equipment or technology than other equally important points of negotiation.

The channel through which the technology will be transferred introduces another important term of negotiation. How would the transfer occur? When and by whom? There are several ways to transfer the new information. For example, the buyer can be given a manual that explains the equipment. Even in this method, cultural adaptations should be considered. To illustrate, consider the example of a piece of equipment that is being sold to a Japanese company.

Question 23. With this equipment, the buyer will prefer to receive

(a) An instructional video tape.
(b) An audio tape in Japanese.
(c) A manual in Japanese or English.
(d) A technician to demonstrate how to operate the machine.

As you may have recognized by now, the ideal transfer would include a technician to demonstrate the equipment (d).

Many equipment buyers will send some of their staff to be trained by the supplying organization. How you prepare the staff and how they will act while at the supplier's facility is crucial to their training. Many suppliers will offer to train a number of the buyer's staff, but will not take the necessary effort to adequately prepare and adapt the training program to their facility, especially in a foreign environment, so the buyer needs to coach the staff beforehand.

Question 24. You have been hired by the government ministry of foreign affairs to measure the degree of the country's technology trade. Which is the most important parameter you will evaluate?

(a) The dollar amount of the machinery imported.
(b) Technical services and consultant hours supplied.
(c) Technological licensing contracts.
(d) Amount of royalty paid by locals to technology supplier.

All of these are important criteria for measuring the degree of local activities toward technology transfer; no one item alone can measure the true success of the transfer process. As stated, the export capability of a country may give some indication of the success of transferring technology. Many developing countries usually assign a free trade zone within their own boundaries as an incentive to foreign investors. This zone, in return, attracts many overseas investors to build and operate local facilities, resulting in increased employment opportunities for local workers. However, technology transfer in this free zone does not tend to mature. New technology in this case will only provide new skills to local workers and perhaps increase local managers' management skills.

A natural step in the negotiation to purchase technology is the ability to market it for resale. An important consideration is the technology's life cycle.

Tables 8.2 and 8.3 provide a synopsis of our main points regarding the world trend toward globalization of organizations and markets.

Multicultural Team Building

Indonesian Case Study

Indonesian organizations have implemented multiple joint ventures with foreign partners. These partners bring capital, technology, and management expertise, while Indonesians provide local support, marketing, clients, and expected profits.

The following case study presents an example of cultural clashes that develop among multicultural individuals and organizations in joint-venture partnerships. The company we studied is a leader in the Indonesian telecommunications industry. American experts joined the local Indonesian managers in forming this new partnership.

Table 8.2

Going Global—Why?
1. Products have shorter life cycles.
2. National boundaries and regulations are becoming less important.
3. States and companies are moving from controlled to market-driven economies.
4. Local governments offer overseas investors better tax incentives.
5. Infrastructures for regional expansion are continually improving.
6. Consumers demand quality products, showing less concern for prices.
7. Consumers are becoming exposed to a wider variety of products.
8. Consumers can see for themselves the tastes and preferences of other countries.
9. Advanced communication systems lower the cost of advertising, package delivery, and information flow.
10. Advances in air transportation make international travel faster and easier.

Table 8.3

Going Global—Strategies
1. Look at the world as one market.
2. Make global-minded decisions on strategic questions about technology, product, and capital.
3. Make local-minded market decisions on tactical questions concerning packaging, marketing, advertising, and management.
4. Give local management more freedom for marketing and human resources.
5. Maximize utilization of local resources through marketing and manpower; support it from regional headquarters with technology, major capital, and strategy.
6. Develop new multicultural skills to respond to new or changing workforces and consumers.
7. Establish rapport between local managers, employees, venders, distributors, and customers.
8. Identify new corporate cultures and establish reward systems to enhance new values.
9. Fine-tune corporate cultures to the realities of the local office.
10. Create a new culture and value system that emphasize a global vision.

Americans and Indonesians each came to the venture carrying personal, cultural baggage. After just a few months into the joint venture, they realized that cultural differences had drastically reduced the productivity of the individual teams: management, operations, marketing, sales, and production. In response to their needs, they invited us to develop and implement training programs, that were designed to:

- Increase employees' awareness of the cultural differences that impact their daily business activities.
- Develop participants' competency for conducting multicultural meetings, presentations, problem-solving sessions, training, and motivation sessions.
- Provide a forum for team-building among cross-cultural and multidisciplinary staff members, and define current and future corporate cultures.

Before the program, we surveyed both American and Indonesian staff members on their concerns working together. Table 8.4 summarizes their input.

Language problems, of course, came as no surprise to company management. Indonesians complained that Americans often spoke too fast and used unfamiliar slang terms. Americans were confused about the nonverbal communication of their Indonesian partners (nodding, smiling, and hand and body movements). In addition, Indonesian employees thought the Americans sometimes underestimated the Indonesians' capabilities. The root of this problem was in the logistics of the joint venture: Since the Americans were the group transferring the technology, they understood the equipment and procedures best. But their technical mastery was useless until they successfully transferred the technology to the Indonesian culture.

Another problem the company faced was a lack of trust among new employees and departments. Americans complained that many Indonesians came to meetings late without being fully prepared. As

Table 8.4

Multicultural Problems
1. Indonesians often indulge in side conversations and interruptions.
2. Expatriates (Americans) frequently speak too fast and use unfamiliar slang terms.
3. Many Indonesians come to meetings late and unprepared; meetings exceed their time limits and rarely remain focused.
4. Different corporate organizations are slow in sharing data.
5. Americans sometimes underestimate the capabilities of Indonesians.
6. Deployment schedules for construction projects are always changing.
7. Suppliers cannot deliver data on time and often deliver data in the wrong format.
8. The corporation suffers from a lack of new ideas and feedback.
9. The company suffers from a lack of trust among employees and departments.
10. Employees often receive unrealistic and unachievable goals.

the focus and agenda of the meetings were lost. Side conversations and interruptions were commonplace. In addition, nobody appointed decision-makers. Employees also stated that the corporation suffered from a lack of active involvement concerning new ideas and feedback—this problem could not be remedied until meetings were designed to meet the expectations of multicultural employees.

Other areas of concern for the joint-venture corporation included the logistics of day-to-day operations among diverse employees. Employees often claimed that different corporate organizations were slow in sharing data. It goes almost without saying that this can paralyze a corporation. When data includes customer feedback, projected sales growth, employee concerns, production levels, and research information, it must be channeled to the appropriate persons and groups in a timely manner.

Employees also stated that deployment schedules for construction projects were forever changing, and action plans weren't always implemented. Needless to say, multicultural conflict has had a paralyzing effect on the operations of this multinational corporation.

To remedy this corporation's multicultural problems, we designed a two-day intervention program to stimulate the creation of newer, more flexible corporate cultures. Brainstorming activities included brief lectures and interactive group discussions, both of which lead to a clarification of current and future corporate objectives. We used role-play and simulation activities, so participants could experience potential situations that arise during the implementation of new corporate values. We also employed case studies and video presentations in the two-day program.

We covered topics similar to those we have already discussed. Thus, this case study synthesizes the many concepts presented in this book (see Table 8.5).

The personal differences in values (see Table 8.6) have influenced multiple business activities. American values include self-reliance, competition, personal success, directness, and risk-taking. These values contrast the Indonesian values of group harmony, consensus, respect for seniority, and cooperation. As these are important values for survival and co-existence in each of these cultures, new cultures among members of the company or team must be developed.

Table 8.5

Intervention Topics		
1. Cultural Diversity (Determine what is inside each other's cultural baggage.)	**2. Corporate Cultures** (Define each other's organizational culture.)	**3. Business Encounters** (Learn how to communicate with various cultures.)
4. Training and Motivating (Understand how to train and motivate those of different cultures.)	**5. Negotiations** (Realize the proper way to negotiate with those of other cultures.)	**6. Technology Transfers** (Acquire the skills needed to successfully transfer technology across cultures.)

Table 8.6

Values Americans vs. Indonesians	
Americans	**Indonesians**
Individuality	Consensus
Competition	Loyalty
Freedom	Religion
Personal success	Harmony
Family	Family
Materialism	Relationships
Openness	Respect
Equality	Seniority
Time	Cooperation
Risk-taking	Wealth

Tables 8.7 and 8.8 present the cultural contrast between American and Indonesians in conducting meetings, presentations, and decision-making.

Table 8.7

Conducting Meetings and Presentations
American Style
Everyone attending, especially decision-makers and leaders, participates. Meetings stay on time, and have clearly defined purposes and agendas. Formal introductions and ice-breaking sessions are short. The audience asks many questions, and leaders expect open dialogue among participants. Before the meeting is adjourned, a list of actions is drawn up, accountability and responsibility are assigned, and the next meeting is scheduled.
Indonesian Style
Senior person usually opens and leads the meeting, and announces conclusions. Successful meetings maintain harmony, formality, consensus, and ceremony. Meetings consist of formal openings and closings. Senior persons invite participants, although many participants attend as backups. Meetings focus on complete analysis of history, facts, and data.

After brainstorming and team-building, participants came up with their own multicultural plan for conducting meetings and presentations. Central to their plan were two overarching requirements: First, appropriate persons must attend and participate. Second, meetings should start and end on time and must include refreshment and prayer breaks.

Participants also believed that leaders should enforce the meeting's agenda, as well as publish its minutes, purpose, agenda, and length. Questions and discussions were identified as key elements to the problem-solving process, and the group suggested that the meeting secretary keep a list of action items consisting of task assignments, dates, and responsibilities. Finally, before any meeting ends, the leader should establish the date, time, and location of the next meeting. The final suggestion participants made may be the most important: Stay focused on the meeting's objectives and goals.

Table 8.8

Problem-Solving and Decision-Making
American Style
Consider situation strengths, weaknesses, and opportunities. Collect, analyze, and present data on the problem.
Discuss several alternative solutions to the problem, while keeping profits and other business implications in mind.
Find the root cause of the problem and quantify the cost of the solution.
Get management's approval to implement solutions.
Take risks and change bad decisions.
Indonesian Style
Form special teams to discuss problems, create solutions, and make decisions.
The group prepares the recommendations, which are approved by the boss.
Base implementation schedule on action priorities.
Base problem-solving on cooperation and togetherness.
Top management officials must sign letters on decisions.

Participants then developed their own suggestions for improving cross-cultural decision-making, which falls into two basic categories: problem analysis and group dynamics.

Of utmost importance to the group is the ability to make detailed and accurate definitions of the problem using reliable data. Once the definition has been developed, the company must provide clear, specific solutions to the problem. Data owners and decision-makers should work together to identify several alternative solutions based on the data.

Alternatives should be selected based on group and management consensus as well. Extra efforts should be made to achieve group consensus. In addition, costs, profits, and human factors must be kept in mind. Especially important to Indonesian participants was maintaining cooperation and togetherness at all levels of brainstorming, problem-solving, and decision-making.

Due to the technological nature of the joint venture, it so happened that part of the American team's responsibility was to transfer complex technological machinery and operating procedures to the Indonesians. Tables 8.9 and 8.10 summarize the appropriate training and motivating guidelines when transferring technology to Indonesians.

Table 8.9

Training Indonesians
Survey pre-training needs.
Do not mix management levels.
Use a mentor approach and recognize individual achievements.
Use training tools such as videos, case studies, role plays, and group discussions.
Speak English clearly and loudly—avoid using slang or speaking too fast.
Do not assume the audience is inexperienced.
Develop a rapport with the audience during breaks. Give breaks every one to two hours.

Table 8.10

Motivation Tips
Recognize and reward both group and individual achievement.
Build a trusting and friendly atmosphere, including a comfortable workplace in a good location.
Reward the best players, but do not ignore the team.
Provide written appraisals and appreciation.
Offer good salaries, career planning, bonuses, and awards.
Maintain two-way communication, which is a key to keeping employees aware and enthused.
Allow employee participation in decision-making that affects them personally or as a group.

Tables 8.11 and 8.12 summarize important points to remember when encountering Americans and Indonesians in business situations.

As the result of team-building activities, which rested in a better understanding of cultural differences and working toward common goals, participants came up with the following mottoes:

- Together Everybody Achieves More (**TEAM**)
- Technology Excellence Advancement Money (**TEAM**)

As the result of the intervention with multicultural management training, both American and Indonesian participants were able to recognize their cultural differences and understand how their values influence daily business activities. The program resulted in stronger

Table 8.11

Working with Americans
Describe the present market situation, your business opportunity, and your opportunity's benefits.   Point out the seriousness of your venture.   Compare your product or service with the competition.   Emphasize long-term growth, partnership, and cost-savings.   Lay out the total costs and discounts.   Focus on the business at hand.

Table 8.12

Working with Indonesians
Identify key players and their supporting staff.   Don't ignore social factors—talk about hobbies, family, business success, etc.   Define who, when, and where—send formal invitations to the meeting.   Reach an agreement and document it accordingly.   Permit them to demonstrate their products.   Relax and socialize when negotiations have ended or have been suspended.   Always end with a polite thank you gesture.

multicultural teams and the formation of a new culture based on respect and admiration for each other's values.

Summary Insights

New information technology is becoming the driving force toward a new world order. This advance has influenced political changes occurring around the world. Products introduced and based on new technology have created new world citizens and consumers that companies can't ignore.

Successful globalization strategies must consider these driving forces and respond with cultural sensitivity to the new consumer. Product design, marketing, manufacturing, and sales promotion all must consider the local consumer culture to gain a competitive global edge.

In order to ensure domestic and foreign tranquility within the same company, cultural synergy must be created. The Indonesian company from the previous case study is doing that through a form of team building. But cultural synergy must also be extended to one's region, whether in terms of economic or environmental cooperation. The problem is illustrated by the farmers in Indonesia who burned forests to cultivate more land without consideration of the environmental impact on the entire East Asia region. Because of El Niño weather conditions and droughts in the area, severe pollution, or a type of "smog," blanketed many countries and jeopardized the health and welfare of millions across the region. The message this sends is that the country, company, and people who have cultural competency and practice cultural synergy will eventually prosper in the global marketplace.

Epilogue

So what? After all this detailed information, what does it all mean?

We hope that by now you have acquired a process by which you will be able to interact successfully in our fast-growing multicultural environment, both locally and globally. Here is a summary of the main steps in this suggested new process that we have inherently incorporated throughout the chapters of this book:

1. Keep in mind the new definition of culture: the norms that a group of people have agreed upon to survive or coexist. Be aware that many of these norms may vary over time and certainly by group.
2. Cultural dimensions include any and all of the following: language, nonverbal communication, religion, art, food, space and time orientation, and so forth.
3. Culture is itself culturally defined based on one's life experiences and the group with which one is associated.
4. Identify your own set of values and its priorities. This will be adapted over time and reflects your group norms (family, work, country) as well.
5. Be aware that your daily behaviors are being influenced by that set of values.
6. Watch the behaviors of the others with whom you interact—their verbal and nonverbal messages.
7. Identify values and priorities as exhibited in others' behaviors.
8. In interacting with others, first search for common values and be aware of differences. By the time a decision is made to form a group (friends, family, business partnership), new cultural values will emerge that all must agree upon to coexist.
9. Make an effort to enhance your physical senses: listening, watching, and, most important, feeling when communicating with others, especially in cross-cultural encounters.
10. Finally, create an agreed-upon new cultural value with whomever you wish to form a partnership (wife/husband, businessperson, or just a friend) for successful multicultural encounters.

Throughout this book, we have focused on three specific important and distinct cultures: American, Asian, and Arab. No book, in fact, can teach about every culture. Our goal was to help you, our readers, recognize your important set of values and how it influences your daily cross-cultural interactions. It is hoped that by identifying these values, you can now develop a greater sensitivity to whomever you will interact with from any culture. The more you know about yourself, the more you will strengthen your own cultural roots, and the more you will be sensitive to others. You can now recognize one side, at least, of the cultural differences, or what others call "the cultural clash." You may then, as the expert, help others recognize their values and how they are different and respect yours as well.

By now you should be able to identify several of your own cultural values that have shaped you since childhood. We have provided a sample of cross-cultural encounter cases to help you see how your set of values will interact with those from other cultures. What are several of these values and their priorities? Why are they different from several of your direct acquaintances or other foreign businesspersons you have been dealing with? You may now recognize that most of your daily behaviors are a reflection of your personal set of values.

If not, you may start with the suggested 20 values we used to identify several of the unique values of the American, Japanese, and Arab cultures in Chapter 3. Which are the most important three or five from the list for you? Ask your wife, husband, or a friend to select five from this list that are most important to them. If differences exist, as they most probably will, discuss with them the reasons for the differences. It is often because they have been cultured in a different environment than you, one that rewarded values different from yours.

From the time of birth, our mothers and fathers have given us our first set of cultural values. In school, our teachers gave us the second set of values. Our local community provides us with the next set of cultural values, and as we engage in business, our company dictates to us a set of business values. So, we are continuously being shaped with both traditional and new sets of values.

Let us take the example of a marriage. Why does success or failure occur? First, a man admires his prospective wife and vice versa.

Respect then builds and results in a marriage, love, children: a family. In fact, both sides come to the marriage with a different set of values: some are similar; some are common, but with different priorities. Why do some marriages succeed and others fail? If both husband and wife fail to recognize each other's values, and never agree which values must be maintained and which can be adapted, many clashes will occur. However, differences can be adapted to create new cultures in order to survive as a family. If admiration and respect for each exists, the process of adaptation and reaction of this new value set accelerates. However, if admiration or respect no longer exist, creation of a new common value for the family to survive fails, and divorce may occur.

Watch other people when they approach you. Try to identify several of their important values during their interactions with you verbally, behaviorally, or in writing. An American, for example, will not tell you he values openness and is action oriented, nor will a Japanese tell you that he values group harmony and consensus, nor will the Arab tell you he has a high value for religion. These are all reflected in each one's culturally common daily behaviors. They have been rewarded since childhood for these values by their parents, teachers, bosses, and country.

As you interact with others, in business or social life, you must make an effort to identify the important values of the other person. From how you shake hands to how you say goodbye, you must be able to identify these values that can help you synergize with that person and avoid cultural clash. In order to achieve such synergy, you must also strengthen your own set of values and respect both, not only your own.

Cultural clash often occurs because we are not fully aware of our own values and their influence on our behaviors. It occurs also because we are not aware of others' values and how they are shaping their behaviors. No one can force his values on others. Only the shared, agreed-upon values remain; it is a new culture.

Search for a common value between you and other cultures. Share values you have in common. Work on being accepted in that new culture. Then, finally, introduce your own set of values. If it fits in with the new environment shared by the new group and all agree upon it, it will become a norm of the group.

We close with statements from some of the business managers we have interacted with throughout the development of this book. These managers were exposed to the major part of the material during multicultural management training workshops we conducted. Their reflections after receiving this training may be similar to yours after reading this book.

"It is impressive that rediscovering my cultural values will help me understand other cultures."

"It is important to think of the process, rather than just to know the culture dos and don'ts."

"There is no right or wrong culture, just different."

"First of all, we should discover ourselves."

"It is not a matter of who is right or wrong; it just depends on how you were taught."

"It is important to understand the differences."

"It makes me realize the bare fact that each culture has its values and should be respected."

"Heightens my awareness of the differences in behaviors of people in business due to the cultural differences."

"Recognizing the importance of being perceptive and adaptive in contacts with my local counterpart."

"I was able to learn more about myself, and this will help me appreciate and respect other people's feelings."

"Everyone in the world has a biased viewpoint. We have to overcome such viewpoints."

"How we Japanese are looked upon by foreigners is quite different from how we look at ourselves."

"There are differences between our generation and elder generations."

"Business styles should not always be the American way."

"'What is culture?' is the most impressive question to me."

"Every group shares some common cultural values on which to build a relationship."

"Cultures are different. Cultural awareness is critical. Stereotypes are dangerous and self-defeating."

> "Recognizing our own cultural values and how they are different from other countries provides explanations to misconceptions that often arise when dealing with foreign counterparts."
>
> "Culture does not come from the top but emerges from within the organization."
>
> "To be successful in negotiation is first to learn our partners' cultures."

We close the book by noting that self-discovery—the answer to the questions of who and where we are—is what we, as human beings, are always seeking. We hope that we have managed to help you answer part of the first question: "Who are we?"

MEXICO

ATLANTIC
OCEAN

HONDURAS

NICARAGUA

GUATEMALA

PANAMA

EL SALVADOR

CENTRAL
AMERICA

GUYANA

VENEZUELA

SURINAME

FR. GUIANA

COSTA RICA

COLOMBIA

ECUADOR

PERU

BRAZIL

PACIFIC
OCEAN

BOLIVIA

PARAGUAY

CHILE

SOUTH AMERICA

ARGENTINA

URUGUAY

MERCOSUR COUNTRIES

1. ARGENTINA
2. BRAZIL
3. PARAGUAY
4. URUGUAY
5. CHILE (ASSOCIATE MEMBER)

ATLANTIC

OCEAN

ANDEAN GROUP

1. VENEZUELA
2. COLOMBIA
3. ECUADOR
4. PERU
5. BOLIVIA

Profile of Latin America—
The Hispanic Challenge

Throughout *Multicultural Management 2000,* we have targeted three specific cultures: Arabian, American, and Asian. Now we will focus on a fourth cultural grouping: Hispanic, or *Latino.* We provide this profile because, in the words of Dr. Rangel-Sostmann, there is a "need to comprehend our divergent cultures if we are to work together effectively for mutual benefit." Vincent Crapanzano, a professor at the City University of New York, suggests that engaging another culture is like learning another language—you enrich your own cultural understanding as you come to know the other culture. That is what we hope you will experience as you become aware of myriad nationalities and people who might be classified under the heading "Latin American" or "Hispanic."

Managers from around the world and from a variety of fields increasingly do business in Latin American cultures or with people from that cultural background. Case in point are joint ventures, particularly maquiladoras (production-sharing enterprises) between foreign companies and those operating in Mexico, Central, or South America. There are more than 1,500 such endeavors along the Mexico/U.S. border where commercial representatives from the U.S., Canada, Germany, Japan, South Korea, Taiwan, and other countries utilize local personnel, facilities, and materials to assemble their products, which are then shipped duty-free to North American markets or elsewhere. The Mexicans benefit from investment, job creation, and technology transfer. It can be mutually advantageous when expatriate management is sensitive to the local customs, environment, and ecology. One example of this synergistic relationship in border utilization occurs along what is known in Texas as the Rio Grande and in Mexico as the Rio Bravo del Norte—a river that flows 1,200 miles, both separating and uniting two nations. The river supports twin cities in both countries as well as a farm-factory culture extending to the Gulf of Mexico. In the pursuit of work, commerce, or pleasure, millions of people from both countries engage daily in a transcultural exchange, too often without awareness or appreciation of the other's cultural differences and opportunities. On this frontier, both First and Third World economies mingle and engage in free trade, lured by the provisions of NAFTA. In the "Tex-Mex" area alone, 47 maquiladora plants employ almost 22,000 Mexicans, while a new mass culture emerges.

In the multicultural cauldron of the Americas, some 772 million people living between the Canadian Arctic and Tierra del Fuego are undergoing a regional transformation. This is fueled by the north-south capital flow and consumerism, as well as by south-north human resource flow and contributions. Since the end of the Cold War, this hemisphere has featured growing economic integration, free markets, and democratic institutions. Today, in a booming economy, the Pan American "ruling class" manifests intellect, urbanity, and optimism, while the poor and homeless grow in destitution and desperation. The more open borders have also fostered transcontinental problems, such as increasing crime, especially drug trafficking and addiction.

For the 21st century, the multicultural societies throughout Latin America hold both promise and challenge. Since it is impossible for this profile to cover all of Latin America's countries and peoples, we will deal with two representative nations of this cultural grouping—namely Mexico and Argentina. You should realize that due to the influence of Spanish explorers and traders, the Hispanic culture extends across the Pacific Rim to such places as Guam and the Philippines.

An Overview of Latin America

In the global marketplace of the 21st century, emerging business opportunities will be found within Latin America. In the 1990s, two strong indicators for this are NAFTA (North American Free Trade Agreement), which links Canada and the U.S. in an economic union with Mexico, and MERCOSUR (Mercado Comun Del Sur), a South American common market of Argentina, Brazil, Paraguay, and Uruguay. The former involves an open market of some 373 million people, while the latter aims to do something comparable for some 240 million citizens living in the area from Brazil's northeast coast to the

Pacific Coast, where Chile is already an associate member of the partnership. Add to that the revival of the older Andean Group made up of Venezuela, Colombia, Ecuador, Peru, and Bolivia. The Andean Group and MERCOSUR are negotiating to collaborate in common economic trade policies that are market friendly, and to reduce protectionism.

Geographically, Latin America encompasses that area of the world beginning with Mexico at the southern border of the U.S., and extending downward throughout the nations of Central and South America.

Latin America Profile

Land Mass: 8,755,985 square miles
Population: 468 million +
Nations: 24 apart from the Commonwealth of Puerto Rico and the 12 island countries of the West Indies.

Major Cultural Inputs

- Native Americans misnamed as "Indians"[descended from the aboriginal "Clovis" peoples thought to be mainly of Asian origin who seemingly migrated from Siberia across the then Bering land bridge southward less than 12,000 years ago. However, the latest archeological evidence demonstrates a more ancient human presence in Monte Verde, Chile, at least 1,000 years before that (some stones there may have been flaked by human hands 33,000 years ago)].
- European—principally Spanish throughout most of the countries with lesser influences of Germans (Brazil, Venezuela, Paraguay), Italians (Brazil), English ("British" Guyana) and French (French Guiana) except in Brazil where dominant influence is Portuguese.
- African (Brazil).
- Asian—principally Japanese (Brazil, Mexico).

Religious Cultural Inputs

- Ancient belief systems and rituals of "Indian" (Aztec, Mayan) or African (voodooism, spiritualism) origin often disguised in "Christian" saints, holidays, and rituals.

- Roman Catholic belief systems, feast days, and rituals (diminishing influence).
- Protestant Christianity from the traditional, mainstream sects to the ever growing Evangelicals (Adventists, Pentecostals).

Socio-Political Developments

- European colonialists, primarily conquerors from Spain and Portugal, imposed feudalistic societies on developed Indian civilizations, causing cultural lag. Small, elite privileged class maintains economic/political control over the majority who live in poverty and abjuration, often peasants of Indian or African origin.
- Centuries-old political institutions often dominated by military coups and dictatorships lead to totalitarianism and social instability caused by numerous revolutions and growth of guerrilla and terrorist movements. In Mexico, this lead to overthrowing French/Austrian dominance, yet Napoleonic Code of Law largely prevails.
- Family oriented with authority centered in the father and often extended to the "father of the nation," the national leader.
- In the last quarter of the 20th century, there has been strong affirmation of democracy, free enterprise, and interdependence in most Latin societies, except Cuba.
- International investment and development facilitates modernization and expansion of industry and finance. Reorganization of production and economies expands the middle class and consumerism, although some individual and traditional countries lag behind these trends.

Education

- The upper classes in Latin America often send their offspring abroad for higher education in Europe or the U.S. Many attend Ivy League universities, especially Harvard, Yale, or M.I.T., and the University of Chicago for finance and economics. Typically, these Latin American students obtain graduate degrees and frequently end up as government ministers and legislators or corporate executives and consultants. These mostly sophisticated males become bright, young members of the technocratic elite who are reshaping their countries in the direction of a more democratic, free-market enterprise. They speak several languages and are linked to prominent members of the New World's "old boys'" network. Their own "Latino" leadership network of academicians, industrialists, and policy makers communicates daily across borders by the latest in telecommunications technology. They have access to current global knowledge and information, especially relative to macroeconomics. Latin America's new ruling class includes people of intellect, urbanity, and optimism, which is in sharp contrast to a growing underclass disillusioned with poverty and lack of education and employment.

These are only a few key dimensions of Latin American culture which have roots in a variety of distinct national cultures. Even though most Hispanics share a common linguistic heritage of Spanish, their specific cultures reflect a unique history and context.

Social Customs

- The *abrazo* (embrace) is still common among males. A handshake or little bow is also accepted.
- Latin Americans place importance on courtesies and pleasantries, especially at the beginning of a business relationship.
- They observe formalities (e.g., written invitations, thank you notes, flowers in appreciation) and formally use titles and last names, calling others by first names only when they are invited to do so. University graduates are often given the honorific title of "Doctor," and engineers include "Ing." before their full name. A mother's maiden name or initial is often attached to the surname (e.g., Dr. Jose Dominguez de Ragoza, or, Dominguez R).
- Business relationships tend to be long-term commitments and deals are normally concluded in person. Building trust is essential in developing international partnerships. Written documentation,

often in triplicate, is essential for meeting the demands of both civil and bureaucratic codes.

- Latin Americans are generally less time-driven, and work to live, not vice versa. Their sense of time is historical—the past is very much part of the present. Time is relative, and Latin Americans do not rigidly adhere to schedules. They allocate time on the basis of relationships and priorities. Since they do not value time-management and efficiency, this can cause friction in international business dealings. Modernization and industrialization are changing this time-orientation, and locals are in a hurry to catch up, which sometimes results in a short-term view of planning. The traditional *siesta* (two-hour lunch/rest period) is giving way, though many businesses still close at 6 P.M. and dinner continues to begin at 8 P.M. The Latin sense of space is closeness among individuals, hence the tendency to embrace relatives and friends.

Themes

In all cultures there are themes—basic orientations shared by many or most persons within it. These are the beginning points for understanding and sometimes for forming a pattern of behavior. These themes and patterns may differ somewhat in different locales, depending on how traditional or conservative, cosmopolitan or progressive, the local inhabitants may be.

- **Familia.** Latin Americans cherish family life, which extends to god-fathers/godmothers. Males are very protective of wives, female relatives, and children. Mothers supply care, affection, strength, and security. Traditionally, the female is the nurturer, and Latin Americans expect females to have an escort or chaperone when outside the home, especially the unmarried; demeanor and dress are to be modest. Harmless flattering or flirting by males with a foreigner's wife is considered acceptable. It is not uncommon for the male to have both a legal wife (for children) and a "private" wife (a mistress for comfort) if he can afford such a relationship. The role of women in this culture is slowly changing, particularly because of higher education, career pursuits, and economic realities.
- **Personalismo.** Concern for one's personal family, friends, activities, or self. For the male, everything is personalized—his wife, children, *compadres,* team, organization, town, country, and above all, his pride in himself.

- **Machismo.** Respect for one's maleness. A macho *hombre* (male) manifests virility, zest for action, daringness, competitiveness, and the will to conquer. Thus, in business, a man must demonstrate self-confidence, forcefulness, courage, and leadership with flourish or in the exercise of power. Latin American women refer to machismo as the male's sexual attractiveness and prowess as a lover. This cultural proclivity is implanted early in life in both genders, but in reality, the female may control the home, children, and husband.
- **Civility/dignity.** Latin Americans consider good manners important. They take care not to lower one's dignity, as directly related to one's social class and occupation. Traditionally, where aristocratic values dominate, this is a stratified (not egalitarian) society, in which each has his or her place, depending on whether one is "high" or "low" born. Increasing industrialization, mass education, and a growing middle class undermine this approach in more economically advanced Latin societies.
- **Authoritarianism.** Authoritarianism traditionally does not allow for questioning and is manifested in the authority of the father in the family, the manager in the plant or office, and the military or political leader of the country. In the past, the *caudillo* (owner-manager) was a strongman, master of his own domain, although his power and authority were subject to someone stronger who could influence his decisions. In such a hierarchical order, whether in the religious or civil sphere, decision-making is a top-down procedure. The *patron* is a man of power or wealth who sustains loyalty from those of lesser statuses who are dependent upon his authority; he is all-knowing and those of a lesser status have to be respectfully subservient. As Latin America undergoes a social revolution that moves beyond the traditional agricultural society toward modernization, industrialization, and democracy, authoritarianism is transforming into the authority of competence and knowledge, regardless of one's origin, gender, race, social class, or inheritance.
- **Get rich quick/fatalism.** A boom/bust mentality. Because of the instability in many Latin American economies, this characteristic is prevalent. The desire to "get rich quick" leads some to speculation, manipulation, and gambling. There is an attitude of wealth coming and going—rich today and poor tomorrow. This leads to a fatalistic view that outside forces govern one's life, so there is a chance to

let chance guide destiny, resigning to the inevitable and "taking what comes." This is in marked contrast to the North American attitude of the self-made person who can influence the future.

Hispanic North America

Throughout Pan America, the Hispanic market grows rapidly and is marked by cultural diversity (Spanish, Indian, African, and others). Apart from Mexico, which is geographically located within North America, Latino culture has permeated many areas of both the U.S. and Canada. The Latin or Hispanic heritage within the present U.S. extends more than 250 years before the nation was founded—when the Spanish colonized not only Florida and California, but the entire Southwest. This is principally evident from Florida on the Atlantic Ocean across the Southwest to the Pacific Ocean. Spanish has become the second "unofficial" language of the U.S., spoken by a Hispanic population that is expected to rise to 30 million or more by the year 2000—that is estimated to be about 15 percent of the U.S. population! In the last decade alone, Hispanics within the U.S. have grown by 60 percent, representing a growing political party. Latin culture not only dominates the Commonwealth of Puerto Rico, but many U.S. urban areas as well—Los Angeles, CA, for example, is said to have the largest Mexican population outside of Mexico City, while Miami has the second largest Cuban population outside of Havana. In *The Emerging Latino Class,* based on 1990 census data, Pepperdine University researcher, Gregory Rodriguez, found that within the five-county Los Angeles area, half of the households headed by U.S.-born Latinos were middle class, earning more annually than the regional middle-class income of $35,000/year, and half of these U.S.-born Latinos also owned homes. The cultural background of North American Hispanics:

- Is patriarchal and male dominated;
- Maintains strong family ties, though women often marry outside the Latin American culture, facilitating both social mobility and assimilation; and
- Comes from peasant stock, but today is more economically sophisticated.

Despite prejudices and other problems met by their immigrant ancestors, the scenario is that these Hispanic-Americans will increasingly provide political, economical, and social leadership.

Next we will target the Mexican culture. If we can appreciate how much there is to learn about this one people, then readers may be ready to discover more about the myriad other cultures within Central and South America.

Cultural Test of Mexico: Self-Assessment

Simply check the appropriate column if you know or do not know of the following cultural tendencies.

AWARE   UNAWARE

1. Mexico has one of the highest birthrates and the youngest population in the Americas (total population approaching 90 million).   ( )   ( )
2. Since the coming of the Spanish in 1519, the landed oligarchy has had to share property and power with a large, rural bourgeoisie of small landowners, today's principal domestic providers of capital for industrial and financial development.   ( )   ( )
3. Mexico is a country in transition, struggling to broaden its social and democratic base, while attempting to balance the demands of an expanding middle class with those of the disadvantaged masses and radicalized militants.   ( )   ( )
4. Over 60 years ago, the Mexican revolution prompted the implementation of a single political party (PRI), which is now being severely challenged to reform and to be open to a multi-party system.   ( )   ( )

5. To effectively understand and communicate with Mexicans, one should learn to speak Spanish (it takes 25 percent more words in Spanish to express an idea than in English). ( ) ( )

6. In Spanish, Mexicans customize their language and speak metaphorically through anecdotes, sayings, and jokes. ( ) ( )

7. Mexicans value belief in the divine, the family, personal relations, and individual respect or dignity. ( ) ( )

8. Mexican managers tend to be individualistic—delegation and teamwork do not come naturally, but must be learned. ( ) ( )

9. Information must be *personalized* to be meaningful to Mexicans. ( ) ( )

10. Among Latin Americans, Mexicans are the most status conscious; status is related to family, school, wealth, position, and authority. ( ) ( )

11. Latin Americans observe lines of authority; those in high authority (*jefes*) are expected not to admit error, so the tendency is to place blame elsewhere (*echando la culpa*). ( ) ( )

12. To show respect for both authority and the individual, organizational communications tend to be indirect and circuitous. ( ) ( )

13. Since Mexican culture is orally oriented, documentation tends to be insufficient and communication tools are more visual and colorful. ( ) ( )

14. Mexican tradition is more humanistic and religious, rather than scientific or technical. ( ) ( )

15. In the Mexican legal tradition, the suspect is guilty until proven innocent; here Napoleonic Code is the opposite of English Common Law. This legal system also reflects Roman law as transmitted by the Spanish, and to a limited degree, the legal traditions of the indigenous peoples such as the Aztecs.   ( )   ( )

16. Like in Japan, the women's equality movement in Mexico progresses very slowly, sharply defining gender differences.   ( )   ( )

17. For outsiders to succeed with Mexicans, developing personal relationships is not only critical, but time-consuming.   ( )   ( )

18. Mexican writer Octavio Paz describes his own people as believers and lovers of fairy tales, fantasies, myths, and legends; as nihilists who are both sorrowful and suspicious; and as joyful quietists who can explode into emotion and celebration.   ( )   ( )

19. Geographical diversity has divided Mexico into four regional subcultures. The republic's main business, political, and population centers are Mexico City and Guadalajara. The northern region, with its major city of Monterrey, is dominated by rugged mountains, dry Sonoran desert, and people with fierce, aggressive behavioral styles. *La Frontiera* (border region) has nine cities with burgeoning populations, representing a multi-

cultural blend of the U.S. and
Mexico. The south and south-
eastern regions are impacted by
climate (hot, humid, tropical, low-
land terrain) and subsistent
agriculture.   ( )   ( )

20. Mexican culture is distinctly
different from Mexican-American
or *Chicano* culture; the former is
more traditional in terms of Spanish
and "Indian" orientation; the latter
is an acculturation, a bicultural mix
of the American culture, which is
highly organized, and the Mexican
culture, which is more casual and
comfortable.   ( )   ( )

21. In Mexico, if a foreigner invites a
Mexican business acquaintance out
for dinner or entertainment, you,
the host, are expected to pay. There
is no concept of "dutch treat," where
each pays his own way. On the other
hand, among Mexicans, the males
may show their manliness or
machismo by friendly arguing over
who pays the tab.   ( )   ( )

22. Mexican merchants, especially in
public markets, anticipate bargaining with the buyer and rarely post
fixed prices. They size up the customer, and quote a price that leaves
room for *regateando* or negotiation;
the naive and unwary are fair game
for a higher price.   ( )   ( )

23. Traditionally, *mordida* or "bite"
was a form of economic leveling to
facilitate getting business done or
to avoid punishment, but is less

acceptable in modern Mexico.
What North Americans would
consider a bribe or "pay off,"
Mexicans would rationalize
as a tip or supplement to low wages
of the worker, particularly public
officials. Matters of morality, such
as corruption or profiting from the
wealthy, have different cultural
perspectives.   ( )   ( )

24. Among the ordinary folk in Mexico,
the collective self-image suffers from
centuries of overlords. This is evident
in excessive regard for the wealthy
and powerful and tendency to be
overawed or intimidated by conde-
scending attitudes and diminutive
speech patterns. The poor favor
handcrafted miniatures, toys, and
animals. This is neither the case
with the upper or business class in
this culture, nor with typical Hispan-
ics in other countries.   ( )   ( )

25. Mexican males are given to a
curious courtesy toward women
called *piropos*—a compliment on
the female's attractiveness; a dis-
closure that her charms are valued
and appreciated. Although the
custom is diminishing, some
women are saddened not to receive
this traditional attention. This
characteristic is also found in other
Hispanic cultures.   ( )   ( )

*Answer Key: If you checked 20 or more "aware," congratulations
on your cultural sensitivity! If you were "unaware" on six or
more items, you may wish to read and research Latin American
culture in general, and Mexican culture in particular (see the
Bibliography for further reading).*

Keep in mind that within each national or macroculture, such as Mexico, there are many variations to be found in the sub or microculture. For example, Mexicans of Native American or "Indian" heritage, such as Aztec or Mayan, have a very distinctive language and customs and traditions. For 200 years, they have exerted strong influence on their country's social and political life, particularly by providing national leaders such as Juárez and Hidalgo. Mexican "Indians" constitute about 30 percent of the population, while another 60 percent have varying degrees of this racial mixture. In contrast, in the U.S. the Indian is less than one percent of that population.

The Case of Argentina

In our examination of culture specifics, we leave the most northern country of Latin America and travel to its most southern nation. Since we could not cover all the cultures of Central and South America, we chose Argentina because its culture is the least known due to its geographic location, and because it is a land of 21st century opportunity. It is the eighth largest country in the world—twice the size of Alaska. With a robust economy, its people dance both to the tango and the tune of capitalism [or so says Walter K. Wilson to whose review we are indebted for this synopsis (*The Lamp,* summer 1996, pp. 16-26)]. Argentina is bounded by three countries: Uruguay to the east; Paraguay to the north; and mountainous Chile, which separates Argentina from the Pacific Ocean. Argentina and the other founding nations of MERCOSUR (Brazil, Uruguay, and Paraguay) have a combined population of 200 million and a gross domestic product of $650 million. They trade freely and move toward greater free markets, deregulation, and privatization. Chile, which is already an associate member, and Bolivia eventually hope to join this economic agreement.

Although Spanish is the principal language, many Argentinians in the business community and the upper classes speak English because of historical British influences. With the shift from military to civilian political leadership, the Menem Administration has fostered free markets and deregulation, controlled inflation, and tied the peso to the dollar as freely convertible currency. Such reforms have restored foreign investor confidence in this huge country, promoting economic growth and stability. These are some of the reasons we chose Argentina, a pacesetter for Latin America, as the target culture to end our Latin American study.

Argentina: A Profile

Capital: Buenos Aires
Government: Federal Republic
President: Carlos S. Menem
Population: 34 million
Language: Spanish
Currency: Peso
Geography: 1.1 million square miles
Major industries: Food (dairy, baking, beverages, fishing), steel, metallurgy, textile, oil and natural gas, petrochemicals, cars
Natural resources: Oil, natural gas, hydroelectricity, prairies for cattle, grain, oilseeds, etc.
Gross domestic product: $280 billion
Inflation rate: 1.7 percent
Oil demand: 515,000 bpd; growth rate (1990–95): 4 percent a year
Motor fuels growth rate (1990–95): 7 percent a year
Oil production: 720,000 bpd
Natural gas production: 2.96 bcfd
Oil imports: 10,000 bpd
Oil exports: 280,000 bpd
National anthem: *Himno Nacional Argentino*
   (*Statistics based on 1995 data.*)

From "Argentina, Land of New Opportunity," by Walter K. Wilson, The Lamp, *Summer 1996, p. 21.*

Cultural Influences

- **Inhabitants.** About 20 percent of the population descend from the original "Indian" peoples who now live largely in remote areas. The other 80 percent have Spanish or Italian ancestry or are immigrants from Europe. Argentina's cosmopolitan and progressive citizens express intensive opinions about the government, military, police, politics, and taxes, but usually avoid personal criticism, except among very close friends. Gregarious by nature, Argentinians are noted for their respect to the individual, acceptance of failure, and lack of punctuality.

- **Geography.** Argentina is over a million square miles and has a large plain that rises from the Atlantic Ocean to the towering Andes Mountains in the west where it borders Chile. The northwest is home to the *Chaco* (swamp) and the great rivers of the *Plata* system. The rolling pampas, home to ranches and cowboys, are in the central part of the country, and are famous for wheat and cattle-raising. Sheep-raising occurs in the southern tableland of Patagonia. Although Argentina's climate is generally temperate, the Chaco region is subtropical, while in the sub-antarctic region of southern Patagonia, winters are cold.
- **History.** The Spanish entered the Rio de la Plata area in 1516. Their culture continues to dominate Argentina. By 1580, they had established Buenos Aires as a center of government, and today, the city continues to serve as the nation's capital. In 1810, the tradition of revolutionary revolts and *juntas* began as Argentina gained independence in 1816 under the leadership of Gen. Jose' de San Martín. After decades of instability, Col. Juan Perón became president in 1946. Under his dictatorial rule, and with the help of his wife Evita, the unions, and the military, the economy so declined that he was exiled in 1955. When provisional military government fared no better, he returned with assistance from the Perónists, and was elected president. His second wife, Maria, became vice president. When Perón died the next year, his widow became the first woman to head a national government in the Western Hemisphere. In 1976, her administration ended with a bloodless coup and establishment of martial law. The inept military juntas were responsible for a campaign supposedly against leftist terrorism, which itself resulted in thousands of kidnappings, arrests, assassinations, and executions, as well as the loss of a war against the British over the Falkland Islands. With the return of civilian rule and democracy to Argentina, the election of President Carlos Menem in 1989 brought on sweeping economic reforms and emerging prosperity, aided by numerous international agreements.
- **Religion.** Ninety percent of Argentinians are nominal Roman Catholics, practicing only on special occasions; only a fourth of these are regular practitioners.

Social Customs

- The *Señors* (men), *Señoritas* (unmarried, usually younger women), and *Señoras* (married, usually older women) typically shake hands while slightly nodding to show special respect. They use first names only when invited to do so by a close acquaintance.
- To show spontaneous affection when greeting friends, women kiss one another on the cheeks and shake with both hands; whereas, men give one another a full embrace.
- Argentinians do not yell at one another from a distance, but instead raise a hand and smile.
- Females do not usually talk to strangers without an introduction.
- Before you ask an Argentinian a question, you should open with a greeting.
- If you are invited to an Argentinian's home or office, wait for an invitation to be seated.
- Argentinians appreciate compliments about their children, the décor of their home or office, and the practice of reserved manners.
- They eat European style with the knife in the right hand and fork in the left. At a dinner table, they consider you to have bad manners if you place your hands in your lap, use a toothpick, blow your nose, or clear your throat (you should excuse yourself from the table). Waiters will respond if you raise your hand and extend your index finger.
- Dress is usually conservative. Hats are removed when in buildings, elevators, or in the presence of women.
- In families, the eldery are respected, the wife is the household manager, and deference is given to the father as the head.
- Traditionally, business hours are 8 A.M. to noon, and 3 P.M. to 9 P.M. Stores usually close on Sundays.
- Soccer is the most popular sport, followed by racing, boating, and basketball.

Summary Insights

In Appendix A, we have examined some of the general characteristics of culture throughout Latin America. This included the Hispanic communities of the U.S. where Dade County's Miami aspires to become the "capital" of Latin America because of the influx of immigrants and refugees from Cuba and other Central and South American nations. To conclude our Latin American profile, we have also reviewed in some detail two prototype countries for the whole diverse Latino culture. The first was Mexico, and we included a self-assessment, so you can evaluate your understanding of the lively, generous, and hard-working people of Mexico, known especially for their arts, music, and food. Then we offered an overview of the pacesetting country of Argentina, which may come into its own in the next century. Its capital, Buenos Aires, is the largest metropolitan area in Latin America, with the world's largest boulevard, elegant shops, and 150 parks!

Latin Culture Elsewhere

You can apply many of the culture general tips and insights provided throughout this book when analyzing Latino culture. Whether you are visiting the continent of South America, or doing business with Cuban-Americans or even Filipinos, there is a basic pattern of Latino culture to understand. In addition, there is much diversity within Latin American culture that requires special cultural sensitivity, such as when dealing with the "Indian" populations of Bolivia or Chile, the Japanese and African communities of Brazil, or other minority groups.

Russian/American Cultural Synergy in Space

National cultures and their representatives also alter behaviors as a result of major socio-political events. With the demise of Communism and the U.S.S.R. in 1992, the "Cold War" with the United States ended. A new era was begun favoring more free enterprise, more democracy, and more cooperation with the West. This dramatic transition is most evident in terms of both the Russian and U.S. space programs, which shifted from a competitive race to collaboration (refer to Brian Harvey's *The New Russian Space Programme,* (1996) and David Harland's *The Mir Space Station* (1997), both published by Wiley-Praxis, Chichester, UK).

Exchanging Personnel and Facilities

When the leaders of both countries opted to promote joint efforts in space developments, Russian Space Agency cosmonauts began to fly on NASA's shuttle Orbiter, while American astronauts began long-term missions on *Mir,* the Russian space station. Forever, the culture of these two agencies began to change and be impacted by their counterpart's personnel and practices. When Shannon Lucid returned in 1996 after almost six months aloft with two male cosmonauts, she observed how all three marveled at the shift from antagonists to cooperators. The process of learning from each other's culture and competencies goes on first as the American Orbiter docks with the Russian station, and continues as a consortia of both countries and some dozen other nations construct the International Space Station (ISS) for the next century.

A contractor from Rockwell International, Bruce Brandt, wrote a memoir on just one dimension of this new synergy (*Aerospace America,* Nov. 1995, pp. 4-7). In it, he described his multicultural experiences in designing a system for the Orbiter to dock with *Mir* a hundred miles up in microgravity. American and Russian engineers met many political, technical, and personal challenges. Brandt made 30 visits to Kalingrad for this purpose, and he described the American team when they first entered Russia as:

- initially naive and filled with anxiety about the unknown;
- in a rush to conclude business and get back home;
- facing unexpected language barriers requiring special translations (e.g., common words and technical terms have different meanings in each language);
- producing different understandings after long discussions that ended in apparent agreement; and
- trying to define mutual roles and responsibilities (for more than two years) before Rockwell and RSC-Energia were able to sign a contract allowing the latter to produce space hardware for the former.

Yet that contract became a prototype for more such aerospace agreements between businesses in both countries. Along the way, the Americans learned that they could not impose U.S. government specifications and standards upon their Russian contractors. So Rockwell incorporated the essence of applicable specifications into the Russian procurement spec, a document with no references! The technical specifications, along with hardware and documentation deliverables, became the contract—just one example of how the two corporate cultures were changed. Both had to form a close partnership to build high-fidelity engineering units and systems to replicate form, fit, and function. Testing throughout included math model simulations in the U.S. and on-site testing in Moscow, as the hardware and engineering systems of both countries were integrated.

Cultural Learning

By working together, the Americans learned Russian family and workplace values. They appreciated the need for group consensus at the design and production stage. Team leaders had to consider diverse opinions before decision-making. The "Yankees" discovered an attitude of equality exists for the majority in the Russian workplace, with only a few of higher rank at the top. Their counterpart's engineering skill, design elegance, and the quality of their docking mechanisms impressed them. They were humbled having to work through interpreters to communicate, and learned to share "worlds."

Professional contacts grew into personal friendships and mutual respect. Problems and anomalies were resolved on the ground in the same configuration as flight hardware. Thus, the *Atlantis* Orbiter was modified for successful docking with the *Mir* station after several years of intense work. On June 29, 1995, over eastern Russia, Cmdr. Robert Gibson flew a beautiful approach and brought the two vehicles together almost perfectly. The Russian/American system aligned and continued into an automatic mode of rigidizing, retracting, and structural latching. In the mating tunnel, Gibson shook hands with *Mir* Cmdr. Vladimir Dezhurov.

That picture went around the world and is symbolic of what international cooperation can accomplish over national conflict. Multiple NASA missions continue as each country blends technical expertise and assets for the benefit of humanity. The original partners are now joined with European, Japanese, and Canadian space agencies in building the ISS, and early in the 21st century, they should construct a lunar base. Having begun his Russian experience in 1975 as part of the historic *Apollo-Soyuz* mission link-up, Bruce Brandt concluded his memoir with this pithy conclusion about the advantages of working together on leading-edge technology and research:

> The alternatives to noncooperation are competition, duplication, and isolation. These lead to mistrust, greed, and wars, both literal and figurative. A far better path is to build an international asset that may be viewed with pride, one that should foster oneness of purpose for years to come.

Larger Implications

Space is the place for synergy, because off-world macroprojects are so complex, dangerous, and expensive. Not only were the two cultures of these space agencies and contractors transformed, but spacefarers are creating a whole new space culture aloft (see Philip Harris's *Living and Working in Space* (1996), Wiley-Praxis, Chichester, UK). But what about back on Spaceship Earth? Space agencies and global corporations are learning the value of joint enterprises. The West is undertaking projects and programs throughout the former Soviet Bloc and Eastern Europe, as well as with another former adversary, Vietnam. Use imagination to project ahead when North and South Korea give up their conflict, and the two cultures intermingle and collaborate. For further information on the cultures described in Appendix B, see *Managing Cultural Differences,* 4th ed., Chs. 10-12.

Bibliography

To supplement the material presented in *Multicultural Management 2000*, the authors have carefully chosen the following titles for the reader's consideration. Some of the following works were used in the preparation of this text.

Abramms, B., and Simons, G. F., eds., *Cultural Diversity Sourcebook.*

Atkinson, P. E. *Creating Culture Change—The Key to Successful Total Quality Management.* San Diego, CA: Pfeiffer & Company, 1992.

Axtell, R. *Gestures: The Do's and Taboos of Body Language Around the World.* New York: Wiley & Sons, 1991.

Bartlett, C. A., and Ghoshal, S. *Managing Across Borders—The Transnational Solution.* Cambridge, MA: Harvard University Press, 1989.

Bedi, H. *Understanding the Asian Manager.* North Sydney, Australia: Allen & Unwin, 1991.

Biech, E., and Jones, J. E., eds. *The HR Handbook.* Amherst, MA: HRD Press, 1996.

Black, J. S. et al. *Global Assignments—Successfully Expatriating and Repatriating International Managers.* San Francisco, CA: Jossey-Bass, 1992.

Brake, T., Walker, D., and Walker, T. *Doing Business Internationally: The Guide to Cross-Cultural Success.* Chicago, IL: Irwin Professional Books, 1995. (Accompanying 1994 worldbook available.)

Brannen, C. *Going to Japan on Business.* Berkeley, CA: Stone Bridge Press, 1991.

Business Week, *Preparing Your Business for the Global Economy.* New York, NY: McGraw-Hill, 1996.

Coates, J. F., Jarratt, J., and Mahaffie, J. B. *Seven Critical Forces Reshaping the World.* Bethesda, MD: World Future Society Bookstore, 1991.

Condon, J. C. *Good Neigbors—Communicating with Mexicans.* Yarmouth, ME: Intercultural Press, 1985 (in Spanish, 1994.)

Cooper, R. *Thais Mean Business: The Foreign Businessman's Guide to Doing Business in Thailand.* Singapore: Times Books International, 1992.

Cooper, R., and Cooper, N. *Culture Shock Thailand.* Singapore: Times Books International, 1986.

Davidson, W. H. and de la Torre, J. *Managing the Global Corporation.* New York: McGraw-Hill, 1989.

De Mente, B. *Etiquette Guide to Japan.* Tokyo: Yenbooks, 1990.

_____. *Business Guide to Japan.* Tokyo: Yenbooks, 1990.

Donohue, W. A., and Kolt, R. *Managing Interpersonal Conflict.* Newbury Park, CA: Sage, 1992.

Drucker, P. *Drucker on Asia.* Oxford, UK: Butterworth-Heinemann, 1996.

Duning, S. P. *Doing Business in Asia.* Lexington, MA: Lexington Books, 1995.

Eddy, R. *Reflections on Multiculturalism.* Yarmouth, ME: Intercultural Press, 1995.

Elashmawi, F. "Japanese Culture Clash in Multicultural Management." *Tokyo Business Today,* Feb. 1990: 36-39.

_____. "Multicultural Business Meetings and Presentations: Tips and Taboos." *Tokyo Business Today,* Nov. 1991: 66-68.

_____. "Testing Your Intercultural Communication Skills—Interacting with the Japanese." *International Business Communication,* 1(2) (1989): 23-26.

Elashmawi, F., and Maruyama, M. "Testing Your Intercultural Communication Skills—Interacting with Americans." *International Business Communication,* 1(3) (1989): 16-19.

Featherstone, F. (ed.) *Global Culture—Nationalism, Globalism, and Modernity.* Newbury Park, CA: Sage, 1990.

Ferguson, H. *Tomorrow's Global Executives.* Homewood, IL: Dow Jones-Irwin, 1988.

Fernandez, J. P. *Managing A Diverse Workforce.* Lexington, MA: Lexington Books, 1991.

Fieg, J. P. *A Common Core: Thais and Americans.* Yarmouth, ME: Intercultural Press, 1989.

Fisher, G. *Mindsets—The Role of Culture and Perception in International Relations.* Yarmouth, ME: Intercultural Press, 1991.

Furnham, A., and Bochner, S. *Culture Shock: Psychological Reactions to Unfamiliar Environments.* New York: Methuen & Co., Ltd., 1986.

Gerstein, M. S. *The Technology Connection: Strategy and Change in the Information Age.* Reading, MA: Addison-Wesley, 1987.

Gibson, D. V. (ed.) *Technology Companies and Global Markets.* Rowman & Littlefield, 1991.

Gibson, D. V., and Smilor, R. W. (eds.) *Technology Transfer in Consortia and Strategic Alliances.* Lanham, MD: Rowman & Littlefield, 1992.

Gibson, D. V., Kozmetsky, G., and Smilor, R. W., (eds.) *The Technopolis Phenomenon—Smart Cities, Fast Systems, Global Networks.* Lanham, MD: Rowman & Littlefield, 1992.

Giffi, C. et al. *Competing in World-Class Manufacturing—America's 21st Century Challenge.* Homewood, IL: Business One Irwin, 1990.

Glover, W. G., and Shames, G. W. *World-Class Service—International Hospitality, Travel and Tourism Industries.* Yarmouth, ME: Intercultural Press, 1991.

Gochenour, T. *Considering Filipinos.* Yarmouth, ME: Intercultural Press, 1990.

Gudykunst, W. B. *Bridging Differences—Effective Intergroup Communication.* Newbury Park, CA: Sage, 1991.

Gump, D. P. *Space Enterprise Beyond NASA.* New York, NY: Praeger, 1990.

Hall, E. T. *The Basic Works of Edward T. Hall.* New York, NY: Bantam/Doubleday, 1989.

Hall, E. T., and Hall, M.R. *Hidden Differences—Doing Business with the Japanese.* Garden City, NY: Anchor/Doubleday, 1987.

Hamzah-Sendut, T., Madsen, J., and Thong, G. *Managing in a Plural Society.* Singapore: Longman, 1990.

_____, and _____. *Understanding Cultural Differences—Germans, French, and Americans.* Yarmouth, ME: Intercultural Press, 1989.

Harris, P. R. *High Performance Leadership: HRD Strategies for the New Work Culture.* 2nd ed. Amherst, MA: HRD Press, 1994.

_____. *Living and Working in Space: Behavior, Culture, and Organization.* 2nd ed. Chichester, UK: Wiley/Praxis, 1996 (in USA, John Wiley & Sons.)

_____. *New Work Culture—HRD Strategies for Transformational Management.* Amherst, MA: HRD Press, 1998.

Harris, P. R., and Moran, R. T. *Managing Cultural Differences: Leadership Strategies for the New World of Business.* 4th ed. Houston, TX: Gulf Publishing, 1996. (Accompanying *Instructor's Guide,* 1996.)

Hendon, D. W., Hendon, R. A., and Herbig, P. *Cross-Cultural Business Negotiations.* Westport,CT: Quorum/Greenwood Publishing, 1996.

Hess, J. D. *The Whole World Guide to Culture Learning.* Yarmouth, ME: Intercultural Press, 1994.

Hill, R. *EuroManagers & Martians; We Europeans.* 3rd ed. Yarmouth, ME: Intercultural Press/ Europublic SA. 1994, 1997.

Hofestede, G. *Cultures and Organizations—Intercultural Cooperation and Its Importance for Survival.* New York, NY: McGraw-Hill, 1991.

Honda, H. et al. *Working in Japan—A Guide to Foreign-Born Engineers.* Fairfield, NY: American Society of Mechanical Engineers, 1991.

Hopkins, L. A. et al. (eds.) *Cultural Diversity Supplement.* Amherst, MA: ODT Inc., 1996.

James, D. L. *Doing Business in Asia—A Small Business Guide in the World's Most Dynamic Market.* Cincinnati, OH: Betterway Books, 1993.

Jamieson, N. *Understanding Vietnam.* Berkeley, CA: University of California Press, 1993.

Jamieson, D., and O'Meara, J. *Managing Workforce 2000—Gaining the Diverse Advantage.* San Francisco, CA: Jossey-Bass, 1991.

Johansen, R. *Leading Business Teams.* Reading, MA: Addison-Wesley, 1990.

Johnson, M. J., and Moran, R. T. *Robert T. Moran's Cultural Guide to Europe.* Oxford, UK: Butterworth-Heinemann, 1992.

Kalb, R., and Welch, P. *Moving Your Family Overseas.* Yarmouth, ME: Intercultural Press, 1992.

Kelly, R. M. *The Gendered Economy: Work, Careers, and Success.* Newbury Park, CA: Sage, 1991.

Kelly, C., and Meyers, J. *The Cross-Cultural Adaptability Inventory.* Yarmouth, ME: Intercultural Press/NCS Assessment Inc., 1997. (Available with Manual, Action-Planning Guide, and Cultural Passport Participant Workshop.)

Kilmann, R. H., Saxton, M. J., and Serpa, R. *Gaining Control of the Corporate Culture.* San Francisco, CA: Jossey-Bass, 1985.

Knouse, S. B., Rosenfeld, P., and Culbertson, A. (eds.) *Hispanics in the Workplace.* Newbury Park, CA: Sage, 1985.

Kohls, L. R. *Survival Kit for Overseas Living.* 3rd ed. Yarmouth, ME: Intercultural Press, 1996.

Kohls, L. R., and Brussow, H. I. *Training Know-How for Cross-cultural and Diversity Trainers.* Yarmouth, ME: Intercultural Press/Adult Learning Systems, 1995.

Kohls, L. R., and Knight, J. M. *Developing Intercultural Awareness.* Yarmouth, ME: Intercultural Press, 1994.

Koslow, L. E. *Business Abroad—A Quick Guide to International Business Transactions.* Houston, TX: Gulf Publishing, 1996.

Kras, E. *Management in Two Cultures—Bridging the Gap Between U.S. and Mexican Managers.* 2nd ed. Yarmouth, ME: Intercultural Press.

Landis, D., and Bhagat, R. (eds.) *Handbook of Intercultural Training.* Newbury Park, CA: Sage Publications, 1996.

Lanier, A., and Gay, C. W. *Living in the U.S.A.* 5th ed. Yarmouth, ME: Intercultural Press, 1996.

Leppert, P. *Doing Business with the Chinese: A Taiwan Handbook for Executives.* Sebastopol, CA: Patton Pacific, 1990.

_____. *Doing Business in Singapore: A Handbook for Executives.* Sebastopol, CA: Patton Pacific, 1990.

Locke, D. C. *Multicultural Understanding—A Comprehensive Model.* Newbury Park, CA: Sage, 1990.

Makridakis, S. G. & Assoc. *Single Market Europe: Opportunities and Challenges for Business.* San Francisco, CA, 1991.

Mann, R. *Expats in Malaysia: A Guide to Business, Working, and Living Conditions.* Toronto, Canada: Gateway Books, 1989.

Matsushita, K. *Velvet Glove, Iron Fist.* Tokyo, Japan: PHP Institute, 1991.

McGregor, D. *Human Side of Enterprise.* 25th anniversary printing. New York, NY: McGraw-Hill Books, 1985.

McKay, D. and M. F., and Duke, M., (eds.) *Space Resources.* Washington, D.C.: U.S. Government Printing Office, 1992 (SP-509, 5 vols.).

McLucas, J. L. *Space Commerce.* Cambridge, MA: Harvard University Press, 1991.

McManus, M. L., and Hergert, M. L. *Surviving Mergers and Acquisitions.* Glenview, IL: Scott Foreman/Harper Collins, 1988.

Meyers, S., and Lambert, J. *Managing Cultural Diversity—A Trainer's Guide.* Solana Beach, CA: Intercultural Development Inc., 1991.

Morales, R., and Bonilla, F. "Latinos in a Changing U.S. Economy." *Race and Ethnic Studies.* Thousand Oaks, CA: Sage Publications.

Moran, R. T. *Getting Your Yen's Worth—How to Negotiate with Japan, Inc.* Houston, TX: Gulf Publishing Co., 1990.

Moran, R. T., and Riesenberger, J. R. *The Global Challenge—Building the New Worldwide Enterprise.* New York, NY: McGraw-Hill, 1994.

Moran, R. T., and Stripp, W. G. *Dynamics of Successful International Business Negotiations.* Houston, TX: Gulf Publishing Co., 1985.

Moran, R. T., Braaten, D. O., and Walsh, J. E. (eds.) *International Business Case Studies for the Multicultural Marketplace.* Houston, TX: Gulf Publishing, 1994 (with *Instructor's Guide*).

Moran, R. T., Harris, P. R., and Stripp, W.G. *Developing Global Organizations: Strategies for Human Resource Professionals.* Houston, TX: Gulf Publishing Co., 1993.

Moran, R. T. (ed.) *Global Business Management in the 1990s.* Washington D.C.: Beachman Publishing, 1990.

Morrison, A. M. et al. *Leadership Diversity.* San Francisco, CA: Jossey-Bass, 1992.

Morrison, T., Conway, W. A., and Douress, J. I. *Dun & Bradstreet's Guide to Doing Business Around the World.* Englewood, NJ: Prentice Hall PTR, 1997.

Nanus, B. *The Leader's Edge: Seven Key Ways to Leadership in a Turbulent World.* Chicago, IL: Contemporary Books Inc., 1990.

Nydell, M. K. *Understanding Arabs—A Guide for Westerners.* Yarmouth, ME: Intercultural Press, 1987.

O'Hara-Devereaux, M., and Johansen, R. *Globalwork—Bridging Distance, Culture, and Time.* San Francisco, CA: Jossey-Bass, 1994.

Ohmae, K. *Fact and Friction.* Tokyo, Japan: The Japan Times, Ltd., 1990.

Organization for Economic Co-operation and Development, *Future Trends: An Information for Scanning the Future.* Paris, FR: OECD, 1997 (3rd Ed., CD-ROM or full text).

Osland, J. S. *The Adventure of Working Abroad—Hero Tales from the Global Frontier.* San Francisco, CA, 1995.

Parker, G. M. *Team Players and Teamwork—The New Competitive Business Strategy.* San Francisco, CA: Jossey-Bass, 1990.

Peters, T. *Thriving on Chaos: Handbook for a Management Revolution.* New York, NY: Knopf, 1987.

Piet-Pelon, N. J., and Horby, B. *Women's Guide to Overseas Living.* 2nd ed. Yarmouth, ME: Intercultural Press, 1996.

Putti, J. M., and Chia-Chan, A. *Culture and Management: A Casebook.* Singapore: McGraw-Hill, 1990.

Rearwin, D. *The Asia Business Book.* Yarmouth, ME: Intercultural Press, 1991.

Reich, R. B. *The Work of Nations—Preparing Ourselves for 21st Century Capitalism.* New York, NY: Knopf, 1991.

Renesch, J. (ed.) *New Traditions in Business—Spirit and Leadership in the 21st Century.* San Francisco, CA: Berrett-Koehler Publishers, 1992.

Renwick, G. W. et al. *A Fair Go For All—Australian and American Interactions.* Yarmouth, ME: Intercultural Press, 1991.

Rheingold, H. *Virtual Reality.* New York, NY: Summit Books, 1991.

Rhinesmith, S. H. *Manager's Guide to Globalization—Six Skills to Success in a Changing World.* 2nd ed. Homewood, IL: Dow-Irwin, 1996.

Richmond, Y. *From Da to Yes—Understanding East Europeans.* Yarmouth, ME: Intercultural Press, 1996.

Richmond, Y. *From Nyet to Da—Understanding the Russians.* Yarmouth, ME: Intercultural Press, 1992.

Rowland, D. *Japanese Business Etiquette.* 2nd ed. New York, NY: Warner Communications, 1993.

Sackman, S. A. *Cultural Knowledge in Organizations—Exploring the Collective Mind.* Newbury Park, CA: Sage, 1991.

Schein, E. *Organizational Culture and Leadership.* San Francisco, CA: Jossey-Bass, 1991.

Schneider, B. (ed.) *Organizational Climate and Culture.* San Francisco, CA: Jossey-Bass, 1990.

Sears, W. H. *Back in Working Order—How American Institutions Can Win the Productivity Battle.* Glenview, IL: Scott Foresman/Harper Collins, 1984.

Seelye, H. N., and Seelye-James, A. *Culture Clash—Managing in a Multicultural World.* Yarmouth, ME: Intercultural Press, NTC, 1995.

Segall, M. H. *Human Behavior in Global Perspective.* New York, NY: Pergamon, 1990.

Sekaran, U., and Leong, F. T. (eds.) *Womanpower.* Newbury Park, CA: Sage, 1991.

Senge, P. M. *The Fifth Discipline: The Art and Practice of Learning Organizations.* New York, NY: Doubleday, 1990.

Shea, G. F. *Mentoring—A Practical Guide.* Los Altos, CA: Crisp Publications, 1992.

Simons, G. F. et al. *Cultural Diversity—Fresh Visions & Breakthroughs for Revitalizing the Workplace.* Princeton, NJ: Peterson's/Pacesetter Books, 1996. (Distributed by ODT Inc., Box 134, Amherst, MA 01004 USA.)

Simons, G. F., and Weissman, G. D. *Men and Women: Partners at Work.* Los Altos, CA: Crisp Publications, 1991.

Stewart, E. C., and Bennett, M. E. *American Cultural Patterns—A Cross-Cultural Perspective.* Yarmouth, ME: Intercultural Press, 1991.

Storti, C. *The Art of Coming Home.* Yarmouth, ME: Intercultural Press, 1997.

Tan, R. *Chinese Etiquette: A Matter of Course.* Singapore: Landmark Books, 1992.

_____. *Indian and Malay Etiquette: A Matter of Course.* Singapore: Landmark Books, 1992.

Tatsuona, S. M. *Created in Japan: From Initiators to World-Class Innovators.* New York, NY: Harper & Row, 1990.

Terpstra, V., and David, K. *The Cultural Environment of International Business.* Cincinatti, OH: South-Western Pub., 1985.

Thiederman, S. *Profiting in America's Multicultural Marketplace.* Lexington, MA: Lexington Books, 1991.

_____. *Bridging Cultural Barriers to Corporate Success.* Lexington, MA: Lexington Books, 1990.

Thurow, L. *The Management Challenge: Japanese View.* Cambridge, MA: MIT Press, 1985.

Training Management Corporation. *Doing Business Internationally: The Resource Book to Business and Social Etiquette.* Princeton, NJ: Princeton Training Press, 1997.

Trompenaars, F. *Riding the Waves of Culture—Understanding Cultural Diversity in Business.* 2nd ed. London, UK: The Economist Books, 1997. (Includes CD-ROM disk.)

Wallach, J., and Metcalf, G. *Working with Americans—A Practical Guide for Asians on How to Succeed with U.S. Managers.* New York, NY: McGraw-Hill, 1995.

Zambrana, R. "Understanding Latino Families." *Race and Ethnic Studies.* Thousand Oaks, CA: Sage Publications.

Zodl, J. A. *Export-Import: Everything You and Your Company Need to Know to Compete in World Markets.* Cincinnati, OH: Betterway Books, 1995.

A principal source of cross-cultural learning materials is the Intercultural Press, P.O. Box 700, Yarmouth, Maine 04096, USA. Request to be placed on a complimentary mailing list for their quarterly newsletter of offerings. In addition to books and instruments (e.g., The Cross-Cultural Adaptability Instrument by Kelly and Meyers), they also offer mulation games (e.g. Ecotonos and Barnga), as well as training videos, such as:

Cold Water (foreign student experience in USA)

Cultural Diversity (in business)

Doing Business in the Americas (Argentina, Brazil, and Mexico)

Working Together—Managing Cultural Diversity

West Meets East: in Japan

Index